IMAGES
of America

ASTORIA

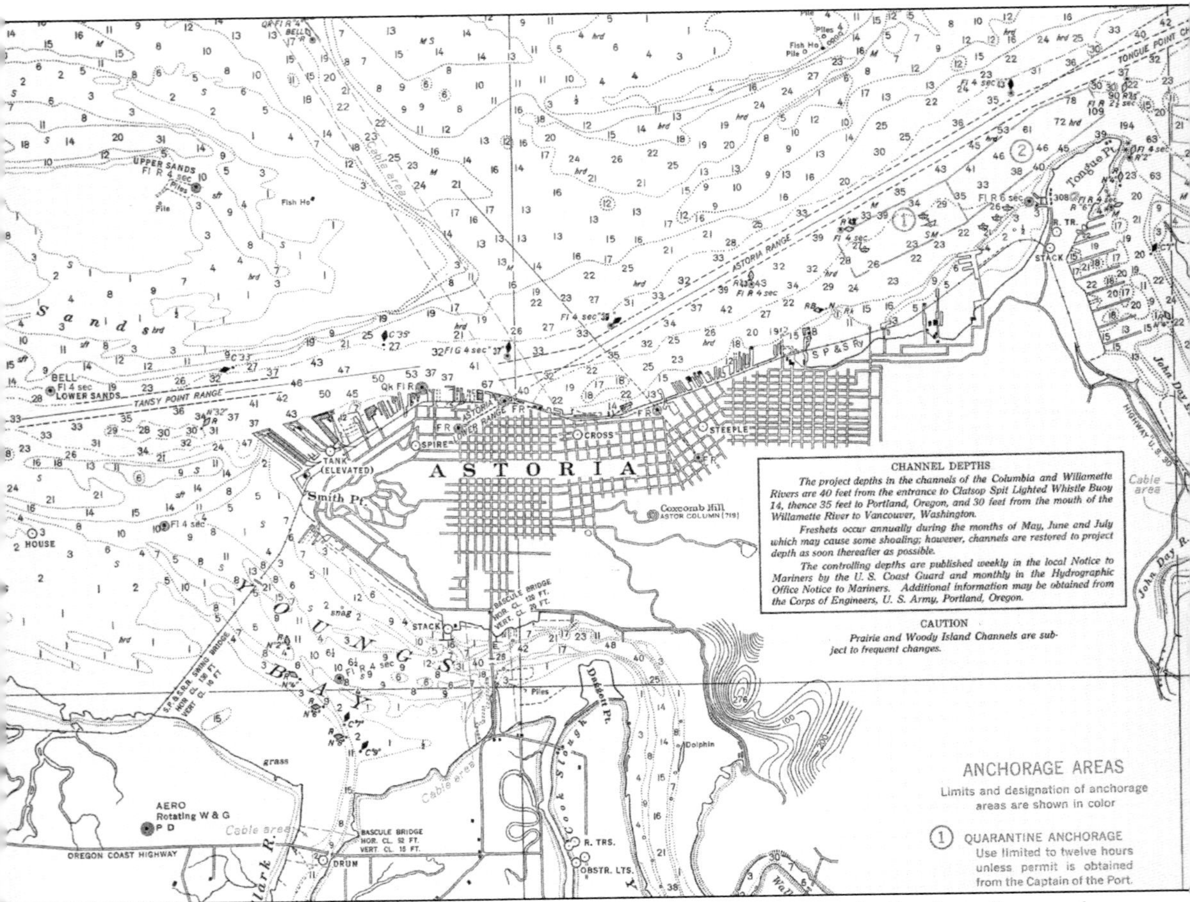

Astoria Peninsula. This map of Astoria was taken from US Coast & Geodetic Survey chart No. 6151, printed in 1949. It shows the development of the town along the waterfront and reveals the peninsular nature of the land. The Spokane, Portland & Seattle Railway skirted along the north and western edges of town and fed the development of the port at Smith Point, the naval station at Tongue Point, and the many canneries along the Columbia River. Travel from Astoria to Washington state was by ferryboat until 1966, when the longest continuous truss bridge in North America was completed, spanning 4.2 miles of river. (CRMM archives.)

On the Cover: Astoria photographer Frank Woodfield took a series of photographs of horse-seining crews. Pictured in 1912, members of a seining crew pose on a tree stump on Sand Island in the Columbia River. Hired by the Columbia River Packers Association, some members of the crews came from as far away as the Midwest to work the season on the river. (CRMM No. 175-3445.)

IMAGES
of America

ASTORIA

Jeffrey H. Smith
of the Columbia River Maritime Museum

ARCADIA
PUBLISHING

ISBN 978-0-7385-7527-8

Published by Arcadia Publishing
Charleston, South Carolina

Printed in the United States of America

Library of Congress Control Number: 2010942497

For all general information, please contact Arcadia Publishing:
Telephone 843-853-2070
Fax 843-853-0044
E-mail sales@arcadiapublishing.com
For customer service and orders:
Toll-Free 1-888-313-2665

Visit us on the Internet at www.arcadiapublishing.com

To the volunteers and staff of the museum and, in particular, Bill Williams, who has invested more time than anyone in organizing the photograph collection

Contents

ACKNOWLEDGMENTS

The archive of photographs held at the Columbia River Maritime Museum, numbering over 23,000, were the sole source for the images in this book. For almost 50 years, this collection has been growing through the generosity of donations from the community. It is a wealth of visual information about the Columbia River and, in particular, Astoria and its environs. We are grateful to all the donors, volunteers, scholars, and staff who have contributed over the years to make this resource available to future generations.

The credit for the idea and impetus for this book belongs to Blue Anderson, the store manager of the Columbia River Maritime Museum. She felt strongly that a book about Astoria's maritime past would make for an interesting read. Her initiative, willing assistance, and encouragement were greatly appreciated.

Also deserving of credit are the members of the staff and volunteers who gave the manuscript a read for content and accuracy and helped with the identification of images. In particular, thanks go to David Pearson and Betsey Ellerbroek for their support and timely assistance. We also wish to thank local historian Liisa Penner and historic preservationist John Goodenberger for their help in crafting the text. Any errors that persist are the sole responsibility of the author. Special acknowledgment goes to Lynette Thiel-Smith, whose research skills and knowledge of local history filled in many blanks in the narrative and aided in the selection of images.

Thanks also go to Arcadia editorial staff members who shepherded the book through all its phases, keeping things on schedule. Your ready answers to our questions made the whole process a pleasure.

INTRODUCTION

This book is a selection of images used to illustrate the fascinating past that is Astoria's, not intended as a complete history but rather a visually interesting and hopefully entertaining look back over the past. Our wish is that you will find it a convenient way to learn, remember, and share with others.

Astoria's story is one of advancement and recession, one that has tested its residents with cycles of boom and bust. The first European and American transplants here found a culture and society thousands of years old, one well adapted to nature's cycles. The indigenous Chinook and Clatsop had a thriving trade network with other groups extending along the coast as well as inland and were living a relatively comfortable life surrounded by abundant food and resources. That began to change with the arrival of trade ships from Europe and the United States at the mouth of the Columbia River in the latter half of the 18th century. In a published account of his third voyage around the globe in 1776 to 1779, Capt. James Cook made note of the vast fur resources in the area. As word spread, many came seeking their fortune in the Pacific Northwest fur trade. In 1792, Capt. Robert Gray, from Boston, was the first nonnative to sail into the river, and having done so, named it Columbia's River. Contact with outsiders introduced diseases that decimated native populations. By the time Lewis and Clark journeyed to this area between 1805 and 1806, the society that had thrived was beginning to struggle with the resulting loss of life from those illnesses.

In 1811, New York entrepreneur John Jacob Astor sought to expand his fur trade empire in the West. He sent two groups, one overland and another by ship, to establish a post on the Columbia River near its mouth. Representing the Pacific Fur Company, they were to construct a fortification and establish a fur trade enterprise in the Pacific Northwest to compete with the rival Northwest Company and Hudson's Bay Company. Astor had garnered the cooperation of the Russian-American Company and sought to exclude the British from trading on the West Coast. When the United States declared war with the British in 1812, Astor's enterprise was in a precarious state. British blockades of merchant shipping on the East Coast inhibited Astor's ability to support the Pacific Fur Company at the mouth of the Columbia River. In 1813, his partners at what was now referred to as "Astoria" sold their interests to their competitors and the post transferred to British control and became known as "Fort George" in honor of King George III of England. The Treaty of 1818 established joint US–British occupancy of territory west of the Continental Divide to the Pacific Ocean. In 1846, the Oregon Treaty resolved the boundary dispute. What had started out as Astoria and then became Fort George was now again Astoria under American control as part of the Oregon Territory.

By the mid-19th century, immigrants were arriving by way of the Oregon Trail and settling in and around Astoria, which, as described by Lt. Neil Howison of the US schooner *Shark* in 1846, consisted mainly of 10 houses, a copper and blacksmith's shop, and a warehouse. Many of these early arrivals, including missionaries, intermarried with the Clatsop and Chinook, assimilating and supplanting much of their remaining culture. Descendants of the Clatsop and Chinook continue to maintain their unique identity and heritage against ongoing economic and political pressures.

The immense forests and abundant salmon attracted loggers and fishermen from Scandinavian countries, Finland, and southern Europe, as well as laborers from Asia. Combined with the resident population, they contributed to Astoria's booming growth and rise as a significant coastal town by the late 1800s. The county government was established in 1844, which was 15 years ahead of Oregon statehood. The first post office west of the Rockies was established in Astoria in 1847, and the US Custom House was monitoring the commerce in and out of the river at Astoria beginning in 1849. In 1861, the outbreak of the Civil War focused attention on the strategic importance of the Columbia River as a route of commerce. Defensive fortifications were constructed at its mouth just downstream from Astoria. The town itself was incorporated in 1876 by the Oregon Legislature.

As the town grew, available buildable land became scarce. Dense forests up steep hillsides were cleared, and streets and structures were built out on pilings over the water. The area toward the west end of town was settled mainly by people of Finnish origin and became known as Finn Town. Along Bond Street, close to the river and next to the Finnish neighborhood, were the bunkhouses and businesses occupied by the Chinese, known as Chinatown. At one time, over 2,000 Chinese lived and worked in Astoria. The east side of town, Upper Astoria or Uppertown, was settled by immigrants who were mostly German and Scandinavian (Norwegians, Danes, and Swedes). The main commercial district was located in between. Until streets and streetcars connected the two, each end of town was isolated and accessible most conveniently by boat. Because of this isolation, each developed in ways that differentiates them socially even today. In Finn Town, saunas were distinguishing centers of social exchange, and both communities adopted a vernacular style of residence.

Being built over the river, Astoria was ideally situated for maritime activities and commerce. Moving logs by water was more efficient than hauling them by land, so a lumber mill was established on the waterfront. Fishing, fish processing, and packing became lucrative endeavors, with Astoria boasting as many as 22 canneries at the zenith in the 1880s. Businesses and industries supporting these activities flourished as well. The challenge of bringing ships safely over the Columbia River bar was being met by capable ships' masters known as the Bar Pilots. This elite group established their headquarters in Astoria in 1846. As a result, maritime commerce became more dependable and profitable. Boatbuilding and shipbuilding thrived in Astoria because there was ready access to raw materials and a high demand for vessels.

The population of Astoria was recorded at 499 in 1860 and, by 1900, had grown to over 8,000. Due to its rapid growth, influx of immigrants, and large seasonal workforce, the community developed a frontier-town reputation, one notorious for its bawdy waterfront district. The town was rife with the hazards of shanghaiing—a practice of conscripting men as sailors by coercive techniques such as kidnapping. A reporter for the *Sunday Oregonian* newspaper on Jan. 1, 1882, said, "Astoria affords every opportunity and allurement of vice in its lowest forms, and on Saturday night the town fairly howls. During the fishing season it is perhaps the most wicked place on earth for its population."

Going into the 20th century, residents of Astoria were looking to a bright future. The community had survived its troublesome growing pains to become a city with a well-defined central commercial district, an active port and waterfront, and a community with well-established schools, churches, hospitals, and civic institutions. In 1911, Astoria celebrated its centennial in high style. Electrification of Commercial Street by the fledgling Pacific Power and Light Company brought an air of progress to the occasion. Consolidation of many canning operations into the Columbia River Packers Association (CRPA) and the Union Fishermen's Cooperative Packing Company perpetuated Astoria's reputation as the salmon-canning capital of the world despite declining catches. Plans for a major passenger and freight terminus west of town were brought to fruition in 1914, only to have the two vessels in service, the *Great Northern* and the *Northern Pacific*, taken over by the government to help in the transport of troops and materiel elsewhere during the Great War, from 1914 to 1918. Automobiles were replacing the horse, and roads connecting Astoria to other parts of the state were improved.

Much of Astoria's downtown was built on wooden pilings over the water, a practice that was continued despite a serious fire that had burned a significant section of the waterfront in 1883. Unfortunately, this practice had a calamitous consequence on the night of December 8, 1922. Flames broke out in the heart of the commercial district and quickly spread under the boardwalks and streets, taking with them the water pipes needed to fight the blaze. The fire consumed over 32 city blocks. Astorians awoke to find the horrible blackened remnants of their town smoldering in the snow, just 17 days before Christmas. Despite the devastation, Astoria's citizens and business community rallied and immediately began rebuilding. The city initiated the effort by replacing the streets and utilities, making it possible for the business and property owners to start again. Within three years, much of the downtown was rebuilt, this time using masonry and concrete to replace the wood. The result is that, today, Astoria has one of the most complete historic downtown districts in the state, boasting an inventory with the highest percentage of buildings dating from the mid-1920s.

Astoria struggled through the 1930s along with the rest of the country, but much of its workforce remained gainfully employed in the canneries, fisheries, and logging activities. When the United States declared war against the Axis powers in 1941, Astoria experienced another surge of growth. The 1940 census showed 10,389 people living in Astoria. After the war ended, the number nearly doubled, and by 1950 had settled back down to 12,331. The area at the east end of town called Tongue Point saw significant development as a naval base. Just south of town, a new Navy hospital was constructed to aid in the recuperation of returning wounded combatants. A USO center was established in the old 1904 city hall building. It was later expanded with the construction of a new armory facility to the east. During the war years, both Tongue Point and the Port of Astoria were engaged in outfitting vessels for the Navy and Merchant Marine. Fifty escort carriers built in shipyards upriver in Portland and Vancouver during World War II were sent to Astoria to be commissioned and receive their crews and equipment.

In the mid-1930s, schools of tuna were showing up off the Oregon coast in significant numbers, and by 1940 the processing of tuna surpassed salmon at Astoria's Columbia River Packers Association canneries. Packed under the Bumble Bee label, this product became a brand recognized worldwide. Postwar, Astoria continued to see growth in the fish-processing industry and wood-products enterprises. Indeed, with the canneries in full operation and the plywood mill pumping out fumes, Astoria had developed a distinctive aroma, playfully referred to as "the smell of money" by local residents.

By the 1960s, the postwar boom had faded and global factors were asserting an influence on local industry. The CRPA sold their majority interest to Castle & Cooke, a prominent Hawaii-based seafood company, and became the newly named Bumble Bee Seafoods Incorporated. Given National Historic Landmark status in 1966 as the oldest continuously operating cannery in the country, the operation closed in 1980, ending a most lucrative era. The next blow to the local economy came when the city's largest employer, the Astoria Plywood Mill, closed its doors in 1989, succumbing to pressure from newer and more efficient plants better able to handle the smaller logs being supplied to mills. This closure ended milling activities that had been on that site continuously since 1870. What had been a strong economic engine in the community now was considered an eyesore and a blight, right in the heart of town. Burlington Northern Santa Fe Railway's announcement that they were ceasing service in 1996 brought an end to 98 years of rail service to the city and the port. The city was left with no canneries, no railroad service, no mill, and many run-down commercial and residential properties. The older generation remembered wistfully the better days of the past, and the new generation of Astorians was forced to leave to pursue gainful employment elsewhere. The city was in decline.

Once again with their backs up against the wall, citizens of Astoria responded. The leadership of the city, mindful of the community's heritage and determination, sought ways to capitalize on what resources the city still possessed. Concerned residents with an eye to the past recognized the abundant historic structures within the city limits and began the process of inventorying those assets. The Historic Landmarks Commission was established by the city to assist property owners in rehabilitating and restoring their investments. With many of the Victorian and Craftsman homes restored and the Historic Downtown District established, others from outside began to take notice of Astoria's charms. Many came to visit and later returned to make Astoria their home. The visual appeal of Astoria did not escape the eyes of Hollywood filmmakers, who used the city as the backdrop for several feature films, including *The Goonies*, *Kindergarten Cop*, and *Free Willy*. Gradually, the economy shifted from resource extraction to tourism. The long and storied past of Astoria became a resource in itself, collected and shared by several museums and historical organizations. The Port of Astoria and the local chamber of commerce have teamed up to entice deepwater cruise ships to visit, bringing many ships and thousands of visitors to the area each season. The city boasts a thriving art and theater community, many fine restaurants and hostelries, vibrant gathering places, and boutique and antique shops. Where once the railroad ran, now a beautiful river walk extends along the waterfront and a colorful vintage trolley clatters over the tracks, its conductors regaling passengers with tales and trivia about the town. The site of the mill is now a revitalized mixed-residential neighborhood. The US Coast Guard is the city's largest employer. Two cutters, the *Alert* and *Steadfast*, and their crews are stationed here. Tongue Point continues to serve as a buoy depot and is the home for the buoy tender *Fir* that services the aids to navigation on the lower river and along the Northwest Coast. What had been the Naval Air Station Astoria during World War II is now Astoria Regional Airport and the Coast Guard's Sector Columbia River.

The Finns have a word that is unique to their understanding of themselves but that also best describes the character of Astoria and its residents: *Sisu*. It stands for the philosophy that what must be done will be done, regardless of what it takes. Sisu is a special strength and persistent determination and resolve to continue and overcome in the moment of adversity, a combination of stamina, perseverance, courage, and determination held in reserve for hard times. Astoria has had its share of hard times and proven that this concept is one that has deep roots in the community. Today, Astoria is poised to take full advantage of its unique heritage and share it with the rest of the world.

One

Humble Beginnings

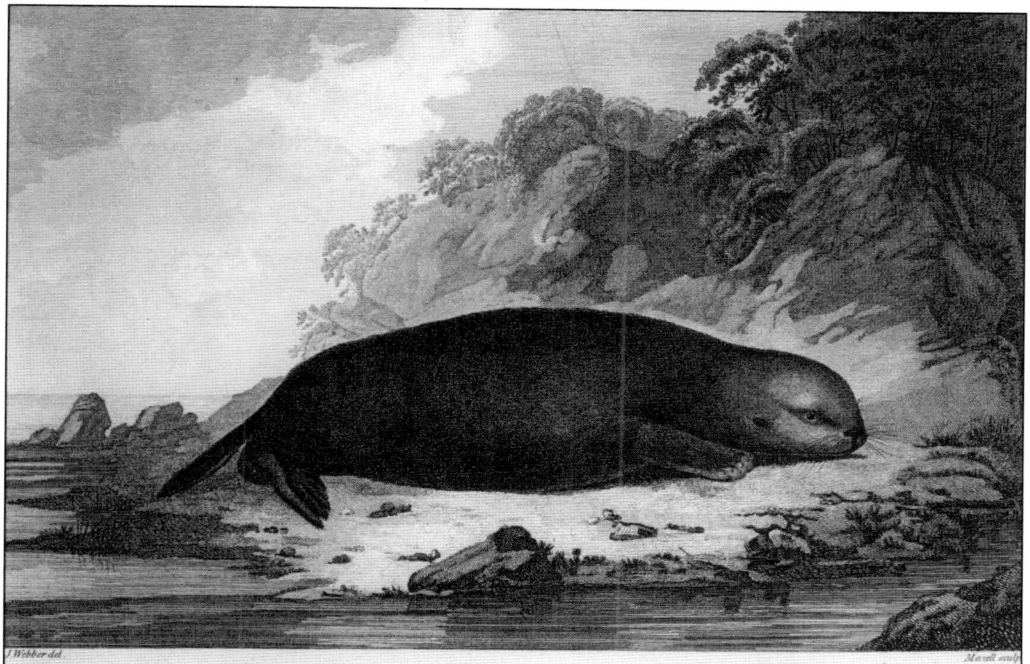

Soft Gold. Capt. James Cook, in the account of his third voyage around the world, reported that fur-bearing animals, such as this sea otter, were to be found in abundance in Northwest waters. When it was learned that the luxurious fur was highly prized in China, where it could be sold for a huge profit, many sought their fortunes in the Pacific Fur Trade. (Illustration from *Cook's Atlas of His Third Voyage*, CRMM No. 280-5676.)

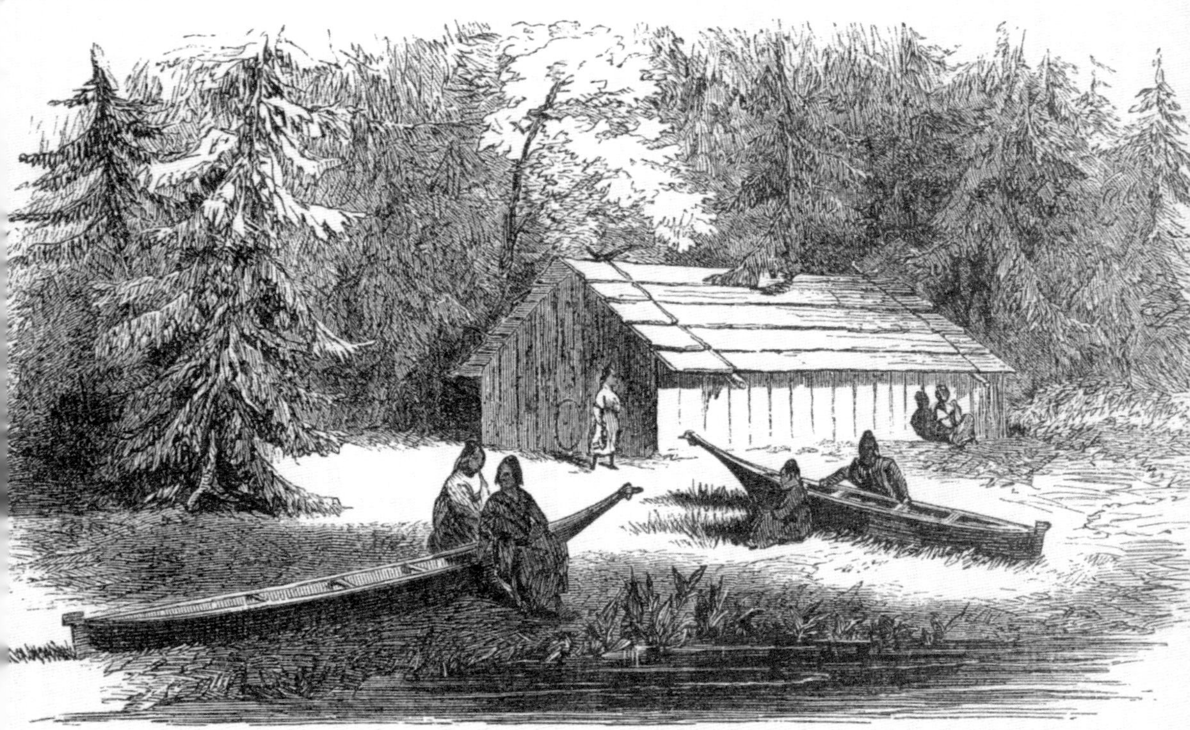

OUTSIDE OF AN INDIAN LODGE.

Contact. When European and American explorers and traders arrived at the mouth of the Columbia River, they encountered the Chinook on the north shore and the Clatsop on the south. They found a rich material culture and a highly developed economic system based on trade. Cedar was a vital natural resource used for clothing, baskets, canoes, and the construction of longhouses. (CRMM collection, 80.67.84; illustration from *The Northwest Coast* by James G. Swan.)

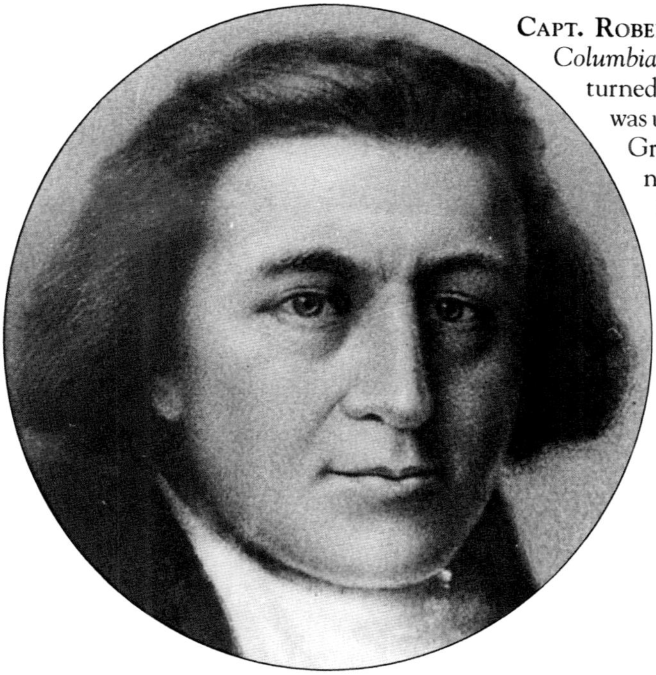

Capt. Robert Gray. On May 11, 1792, the *Columbia Rediviva* crossed the bar of what turned out to be a large river. The vessel was under the command of Capt. Robert Gray, an American. It was Gray who named the waterway Columbia's River. Fifth-mate John Boit made this journal entry on May 18, saying, "The river in my opinion would be a fine place for to set up a factory." The Astor party would do exactly that in 1811. (CRMM No. 520-10762.)

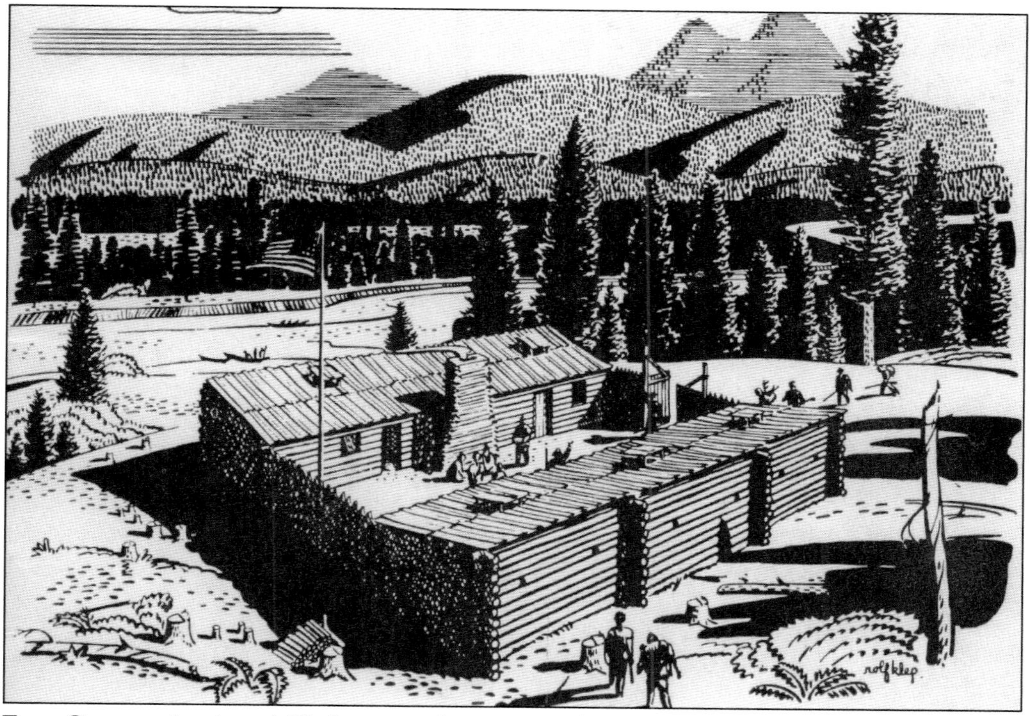

Fort Clatsop. Lewis and Clark wintered over in 1805–1806 at a fort they built and named Fort Clatsop, which was just south of where Astoria would be established five years later in 1811. This rendition of Fort Clatsop was done in preparation of the Lewis and Clark sesquicentennial in 1955. Illustrator Rolf Klep based his drawing on the information in the expedition journals, and it was used to design the replica fort constructed for the celebration. (CRMM collection; illustration by Rolf Klep.)

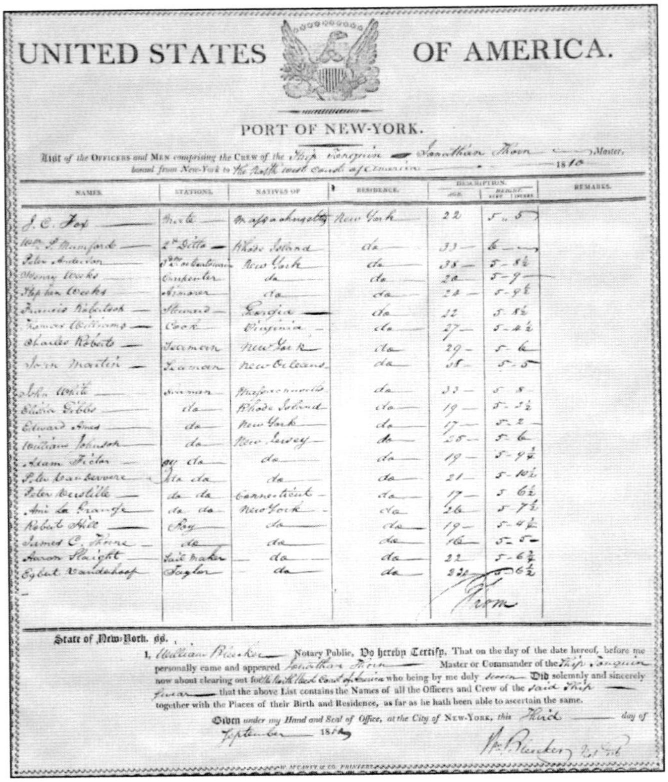
UNITED STATES OF AMERICA.

PORT OF NEW-YORK.

List of the Officers and Men comprising the Crew of the Ship Tonquin — Jonathan Thorn, Master, bound from New-York to the North west Coast of America — 1810

NAMES.	STATIONS.	NATIVES OF	RESIDENCE.	AGE.	HEIGHT.	REMARKS.
J. C. Fox	Mate	Massachusetts	New York	22	5 " 5	
Wm. P. Mumford	2d Ditto	Rhode Island	do	33	6	
Peter Anderson	[illegible]	New York	do	38	5 - 8½	
Henry Weeks	Carpenter	do	do	20	5 - 9	
Stephen Weeks	Armorer	do	do	24	5 - 9½	
Francis Robertson	Steward	Georgia	do	22	5 - 8½	
Thomas Williams	Cook	Virginia	do	27	5 - 4½	
Charles Roberts	Seaman	New York	do	29	5 - 6	
John Martin	Seaman	New Orleans	do	38	5 - 5	
John White	Seaman	Massachusetts	do	33	5 - 8	
Elisha Gibbs	do	Rhode Island	do	19	5 - 3½	
Edward Ames	do	New York	do	17	5 - 2	
William Johnson	do	New Jersey	do	25	5 - 6	
Adam Fisher	do	do	do	19	5 - 9¼	
Peter Vanderveere	do do	do	do	21	5 - 10½	
Peter Verstille	do do	Connecticut	do	17	5 6½	
Ami La Grange	do do	New York	do	26	5 - 7½	
Robert Hill	Boy	do	do	19	5 - 4½	
James C. Thorne	do	do	do	16	5 - 5	
Aaron Slaight	Sail maker	do	do	22	5 - 6¾	
Egbert Vandehoof	Taylor	do	do	22	5 - 6½	

Thorn

State of New-York, ss.

I, William Bleecker, Notary Public, Do hereby Certify, That on the day of the date hereof, before me personally came and appeared Jonathan Thorn Master or Commander of the Ship Tonquin now about clearing out for the North West Coast of America who being by me duly sworn Did solemnly and sincerely swear that the above List contains the Names of all the Officers and Crew of the said Ship together with the Places of their Birth and Residence, as far as he hath been able to ascertain the same.

Given under my Hand and Seal of Office, at the City of New-York, this Third day of September 1810

Wm. Bleecker, Not. Pub.

Crew of the Ship *Tonquin*. This register lists the men who set sail aboard the Pacific Fur Company's ship *Tonquin*, bound for what would become Astoria. The fur-trading venture was organized by New York entrepreneur John Jacob Astor. The vessel, under the command of Capt. Jonathan Thorn, carried the supplies and cargo needed to establish a trading post. A second party under Wilson Price Hunt was sent overland. (CRMM collection, 69.187.)

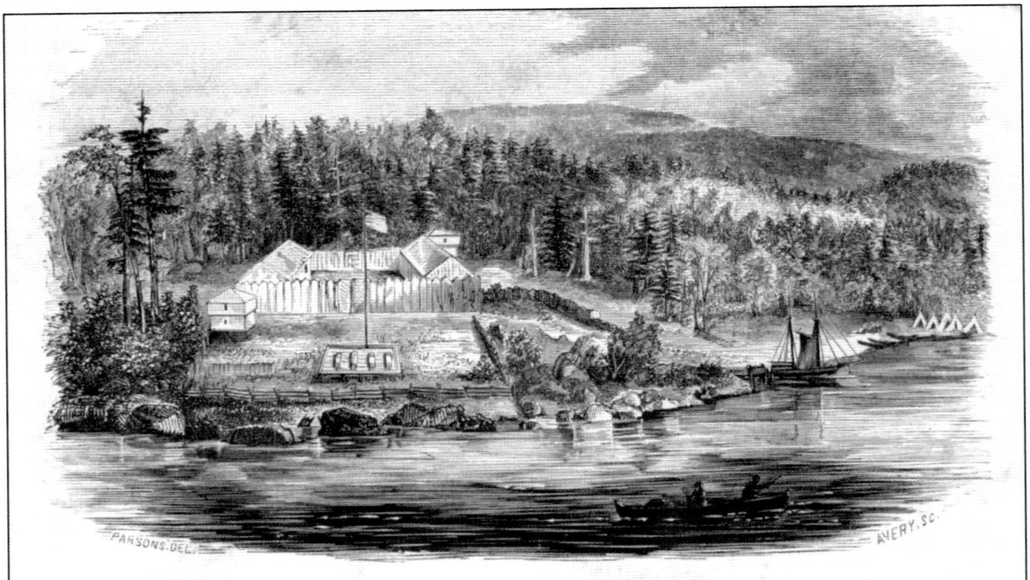

ASTORIA, AS IT WAS IN 1813.

Empire of Astoria. The beleaguered overland party sent by Astor arrived at Astoria in the spring of 1812. With the resupply ships delayed or lost, and war with Britain looming, certain members of the venture capitulated to the realities of their bleak situation and sold their interests to representatives of the Northwest Company. When the British war sloop *Racoon* arrived in 1813 to take the fort, they found it already in British hands. (CRMM collection, 80.67.77, original; illustration from *Narrative of a Voyage to the Northwest Coast of America* by Gabriel Franchere.)

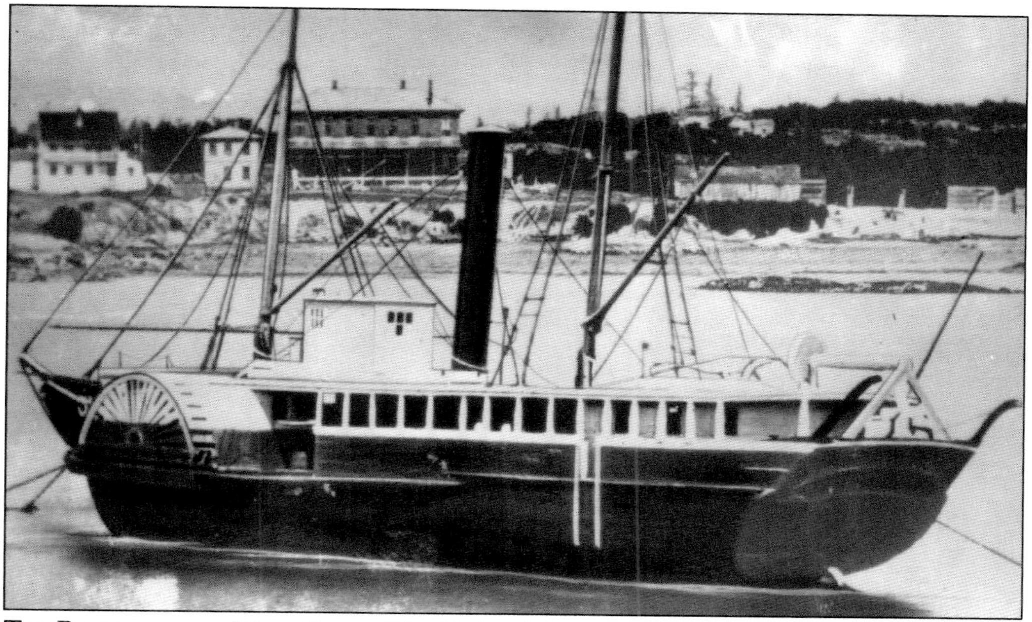

The *Beaver* on the West Coast. The Hudson's Bay Company steamer *Beaver* arrived on the West Coast in 1836 and is shown here in Victoria, British Columbia, still bearing her masts that were used in the voyage over from England. She was the first steamboat to ply the Columbia River and was a regular visitor to Astoria and the Hudson's Bay Company Fort Vancouver. Eventually, over 500 steamboats would be built and operated on the river, establishing the Columbia as the vital commercial route it is today. (CRMM No. 570-12963.)

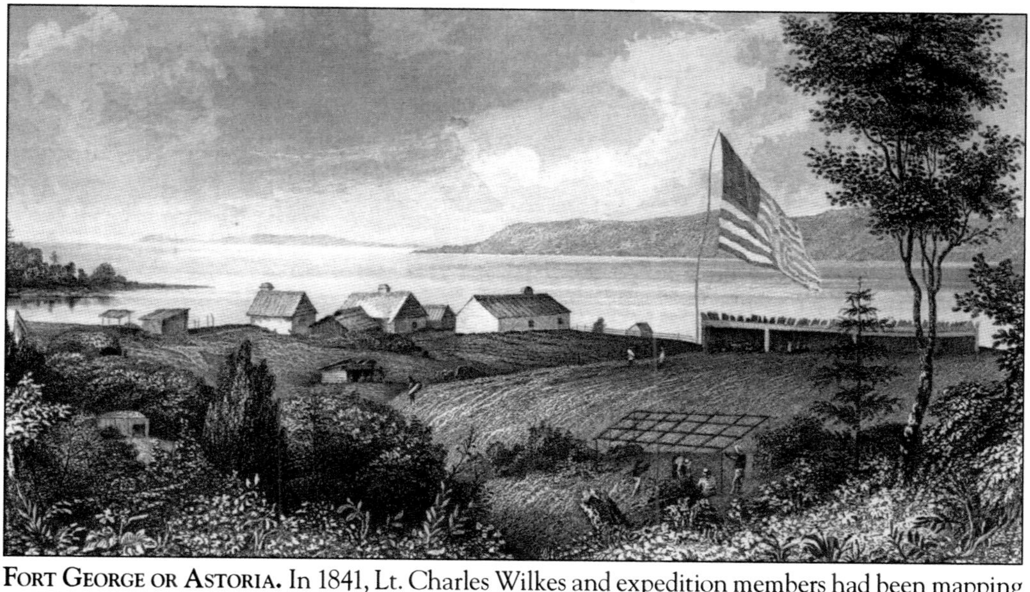

Fort George or Astoria. In 1841, Lt. Charles Wilkes and expedition members had been mapping and doing scientific research in the region. On July 18 of that year, the navy sloop *Peacock*, with expedition members aboard, ran afoul of the Columbia River's bar. The ship was lost on the sand spit that now bears its name, but her crew made it safely ashore. Officers and scientists were given temporary quarters at Fort George, which was still under Hudson's Bay Company control, while the crew built a long lean-to for their quarters, naming it "Camp Peacock" and flying a large American flag. This engraving was done after a drawing by artist T. Agate. (CRMM No. 030-267.)

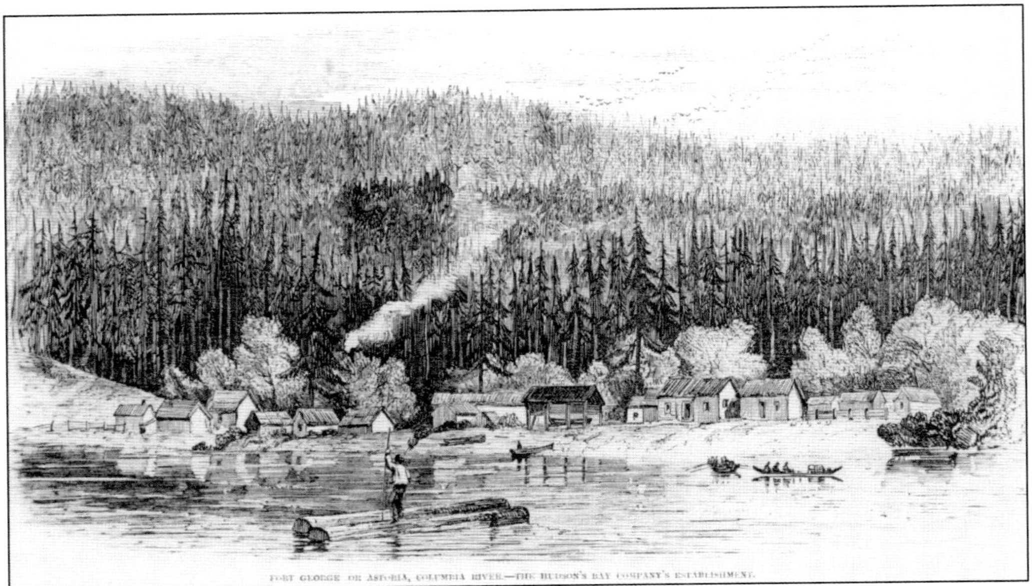

US TERRITORY AGAIN. Since 1818, Astoria had been jointly occupied by both the British and Americans. Fort George had become a minor concern when interests were shifted to Fort Vancouver upriver when HBC absorbed the Northwest Company. Americans continued to settle in the area, and the town was growing. By the time this illustration ran in the *London News* in 1849, the region had been firmly placed into American hands. (CRMM No. 030-139.)

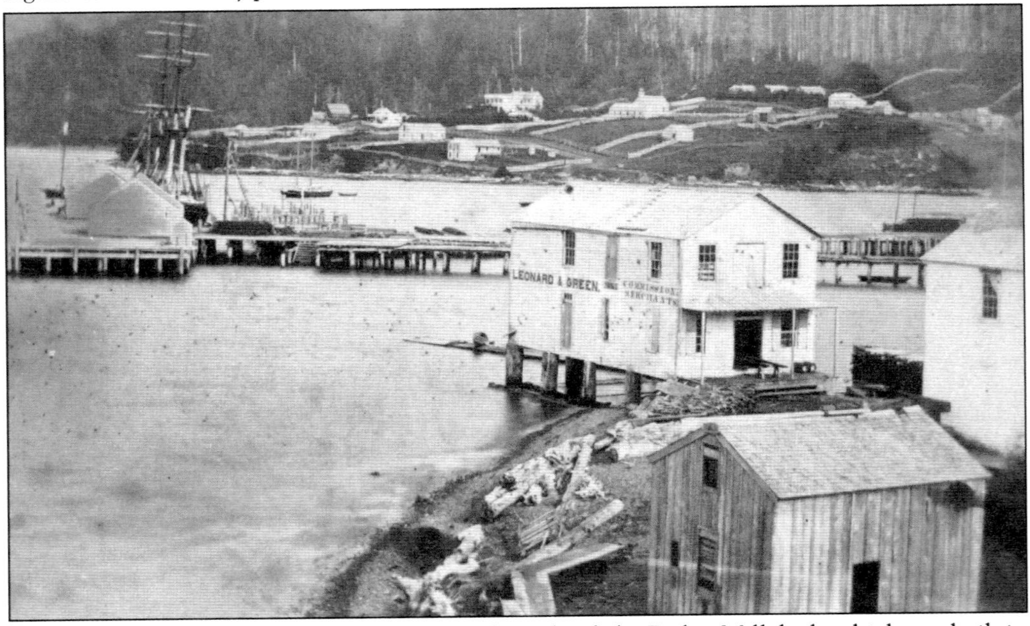

ASTORIA IN THE 1850S. This shows Astoria's first wharf, the Parker Mill dock, which was built in 1851 and managed by Captain Hustler until 1860. Prior to its existence, ships would lay at anchor in the river and transfer cargo and passengers to the Leonard and Green building, formerly a Hudson's Bay Company warehouse. The rustic building (foreground) was one of the Shark Cabins, built by survivors of the USS *Shark*, shipwrecked on the bar in 1846. It was used by a succession of new arrivals while their own homes were built. In the distance of this image lie Shively's post office and the Methodist church. (CRMM No. 035-731.)

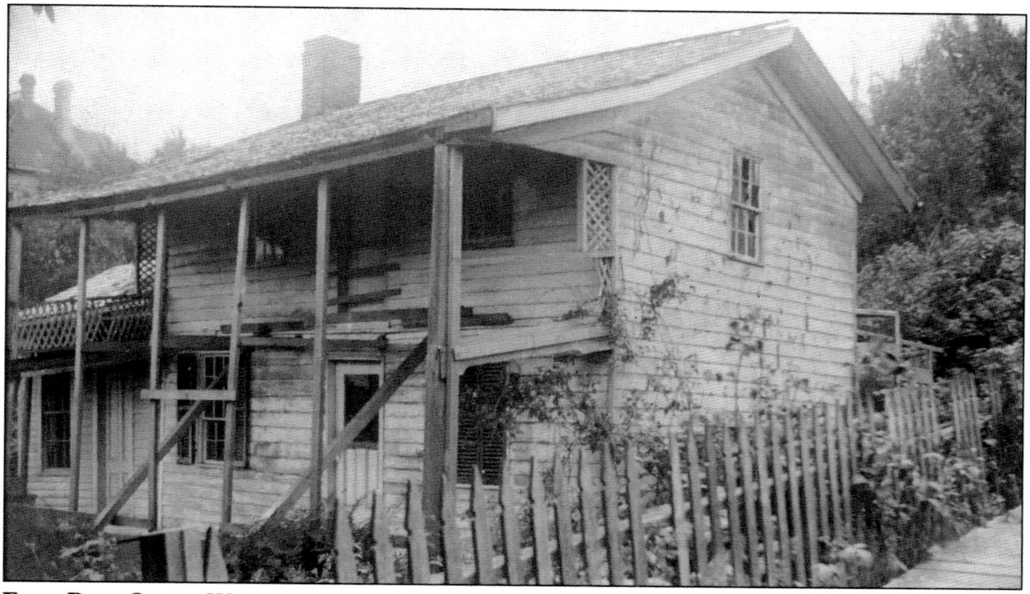

First Post Office West of the Rockies. In 1847, John Shively, the newly appointed postmaster, purchased this residence and established the first US post office west of the Rockies—in his home. The house served as the post office until 1849, when Shively left for the California gold fields. The building fell into disrepair, as seen in this photograph, and was burned by the fire department in 1906. In 1955, a marble obelisk was placed on the original site, and it is still standing there today on Fifteenth Street between Exchange and Franklin. (CRMM No. 030-176.)

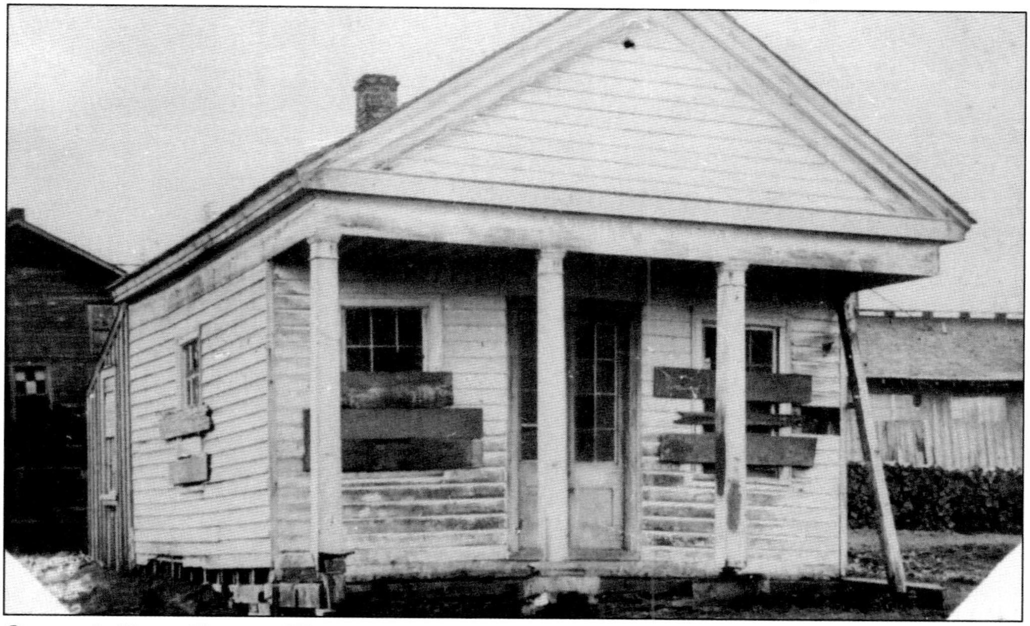

Oregon's First Custom House. In response to increased shipping activity on the Columbia River, a US custom house was established to collect revenues in Astoria. It was the first custom house west of the Rockies. John Adair, appointed by President Polk, was the first commissioned custom agent on the Pacific coast. In 1852, Adair had this custom house built in Upper Astoria, near present-day Thirty-Fourth Street and Marine Drive. A replica of the building stands near the original site. (CRMM No. 030-179.)

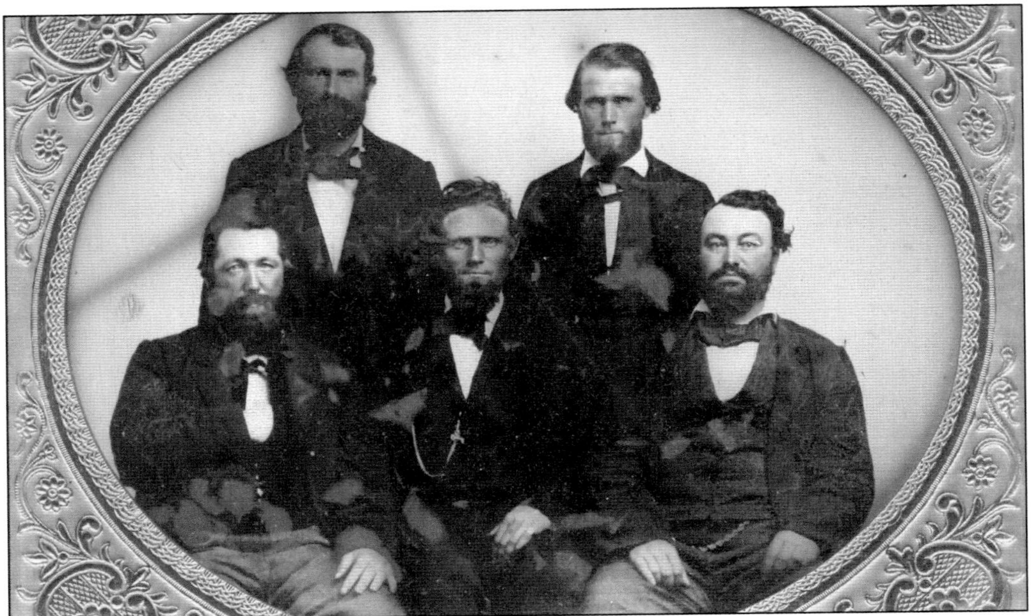

Enterprising Pilots on the Columbia. These men were some of the first to offer safe piloting of vessels across the treacherous Columbia River Bar. Pictured here from left to right are (first row) A.C. Farnsworth, Charles Edwards, and J.G. Hustler; (second row) Moses Rogers and Alfred Crosby. Hustler came here in 1849 and received his first branch pilotage from the newly formed Board of Pilot Commissioners in 1852. Competing with Captain Flavel initially, he later worked for him, even on occasion taking command of Flavel's favorite vessel, the *Jane A. Falkenberg*, on trips to California and back. (Bernier collection.)

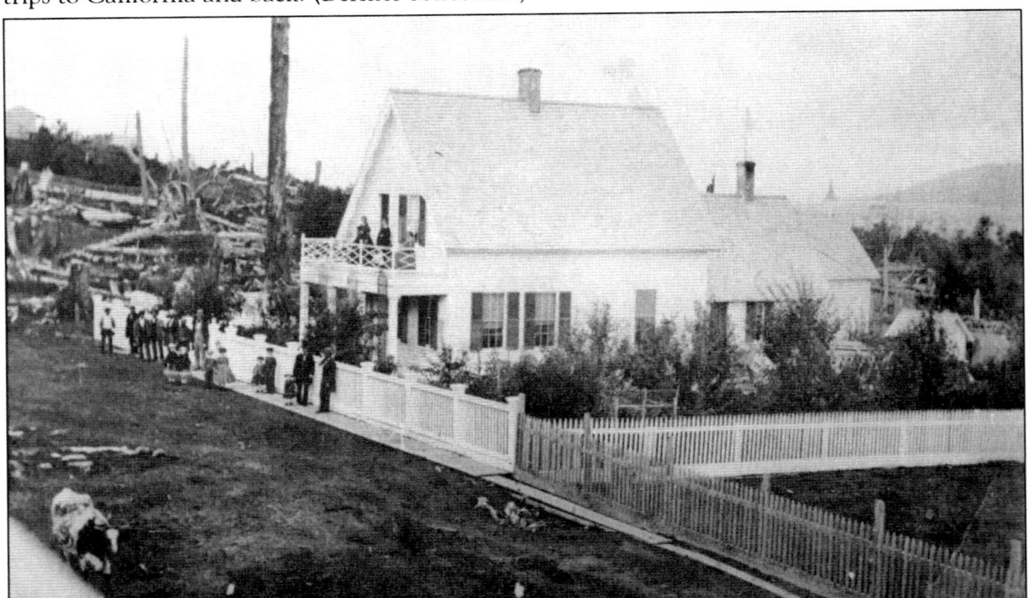

Captain Crosby's Home in 1860. The residence of bar pilot Capt. Alfred Crosby was located on the corner of Squemoqua (Commercial) and Washington (Sixth) Streets and was built in 1858. The eight-room structure, framed in Massachusetts and shipped around Cape Horn, was demolished in 1929 to make way for a service station. Today, the site is a playground. (Bernier collection.)

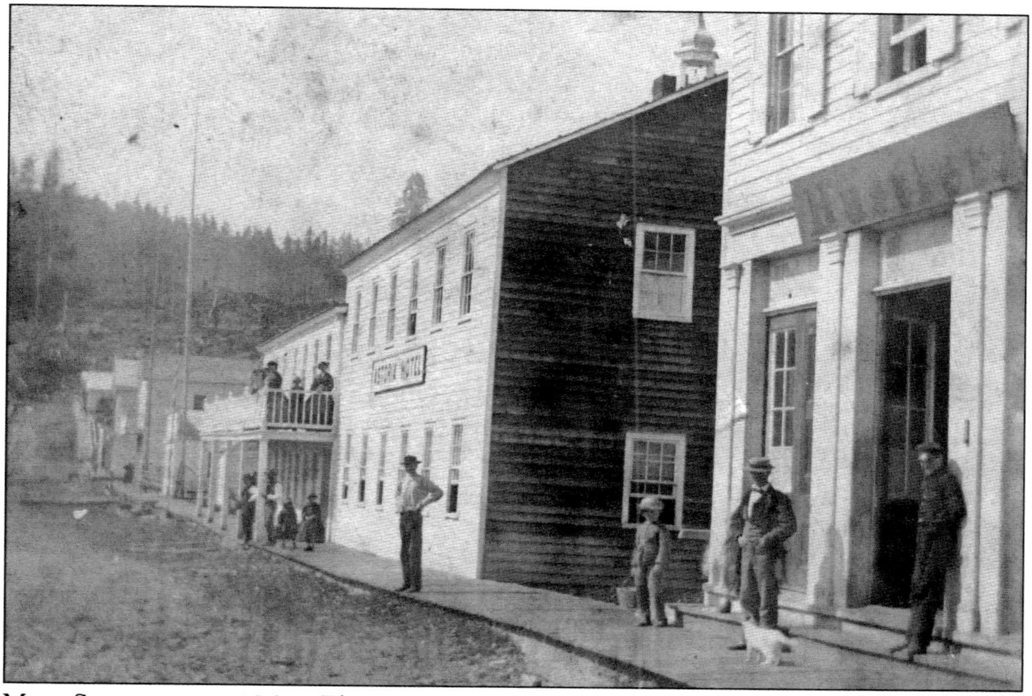

Main Street in the 1860s. This photograph shows Main Street (Ninth) as it looked around 1862. J.G. Hustler's store at No. 1 Main Street is the first building in the foreground. Hustler, retired as an active bar pilot, shows up as a merchant in the 1860 census. His store merchandise included dry goods and clothing. The Astoria Hotel next door was the first hotel in town. Conrad Boelling, an early resident of Astoria and Captain Flavel's father-in-law, owned the business. (CRMM No. 030-241.)

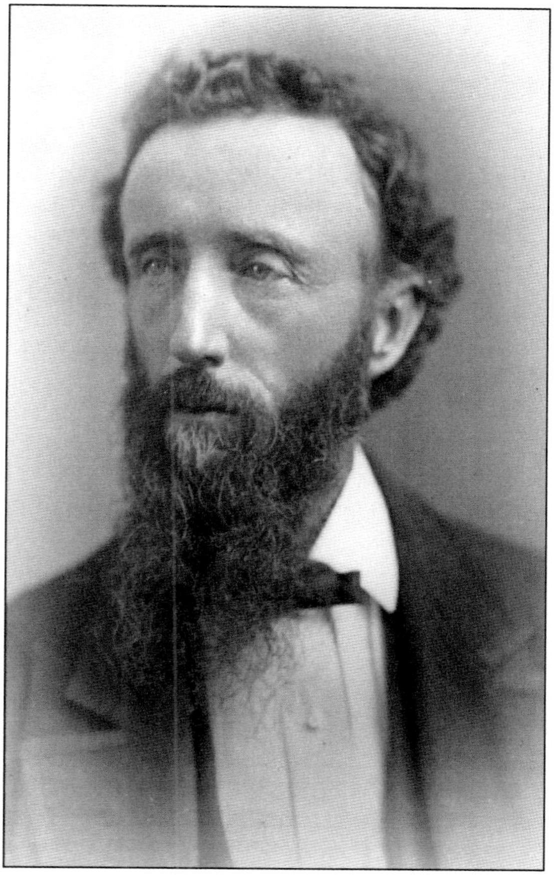

Capt. George Flavel. Captain Flavel first came to Oregon as captain of the steamship *Petty*. After receiving his branch license from the state of Oregon to operate as a pilot on the Columbia River Bar, he bought the schooner *California* and ran her in direct competition with the *Mary Taylor*, Hustler's boat. He acquired steam tugs to tow vessels and eventually drove off the competition. He ran the bar pilotage as a virtual monopoly for nearly 20 years. He invested in business and real estate and retired a very wealthy man. (CRMM No. 431-12100.)

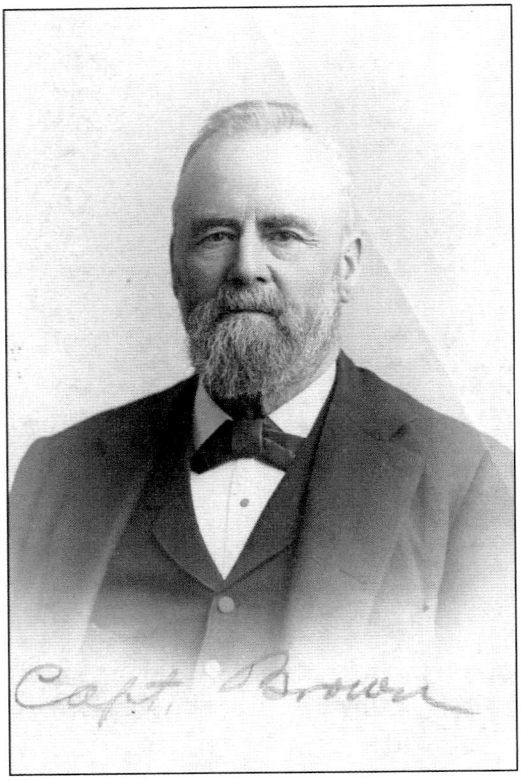

EARLY RIVER PILOT CAPT. HIRAM BROWN. Brown was possibly the longest continuously serving steamship pilot on the Pacific coast. In 1851, he served as a deckhand on the sidewheel steamer *Lot Whitcomb* that launched in 1850 in Oregon City. It ran twice per week between Portland and Astoria. He began piloting ocean steamships between Portland and Astoria in 1857 and continued for 33 years without missing a day. He was a business partner with Adam Van Dusen, a general merchandiser, and helped promote and enhance the town. (Bernier collection.)

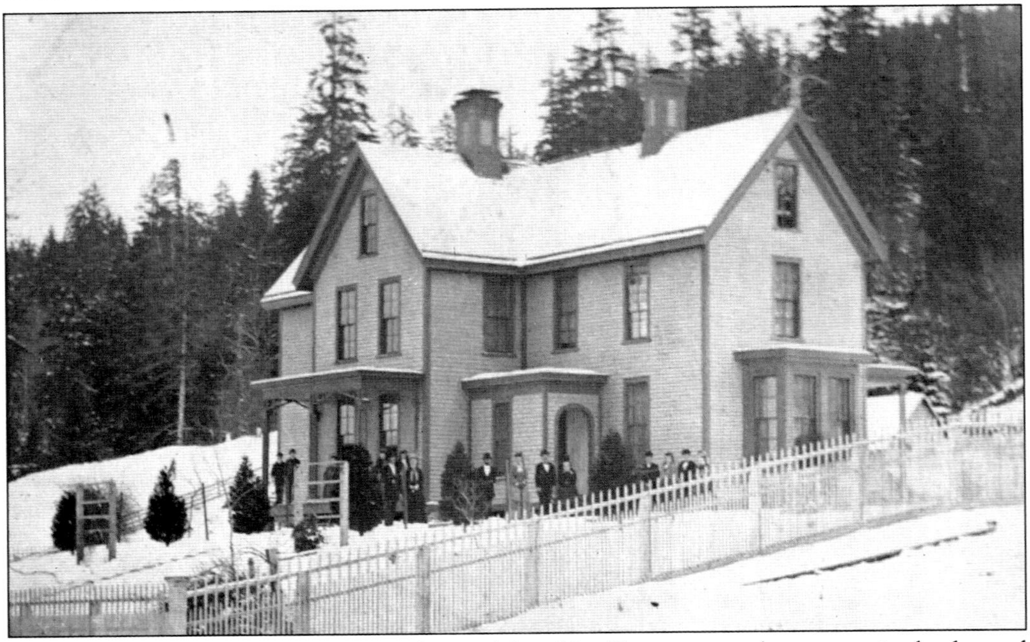

ADAM AND CAROLINE VAN DUSEN'S HOME. Adam Van Dusen, an early community leader and businessman, had this home built in 1864. The photograph was taken on January 21, 1874, upon the occasion of his daughter Florence's wedding to Washington Irving Wadleigh. The house, located on present-day Franklin Street between Sixteenth and Seventeenth Streets, was razed to make way for Columbia Hospital (now the Clatsop Care Center). (Woodfield collection.)

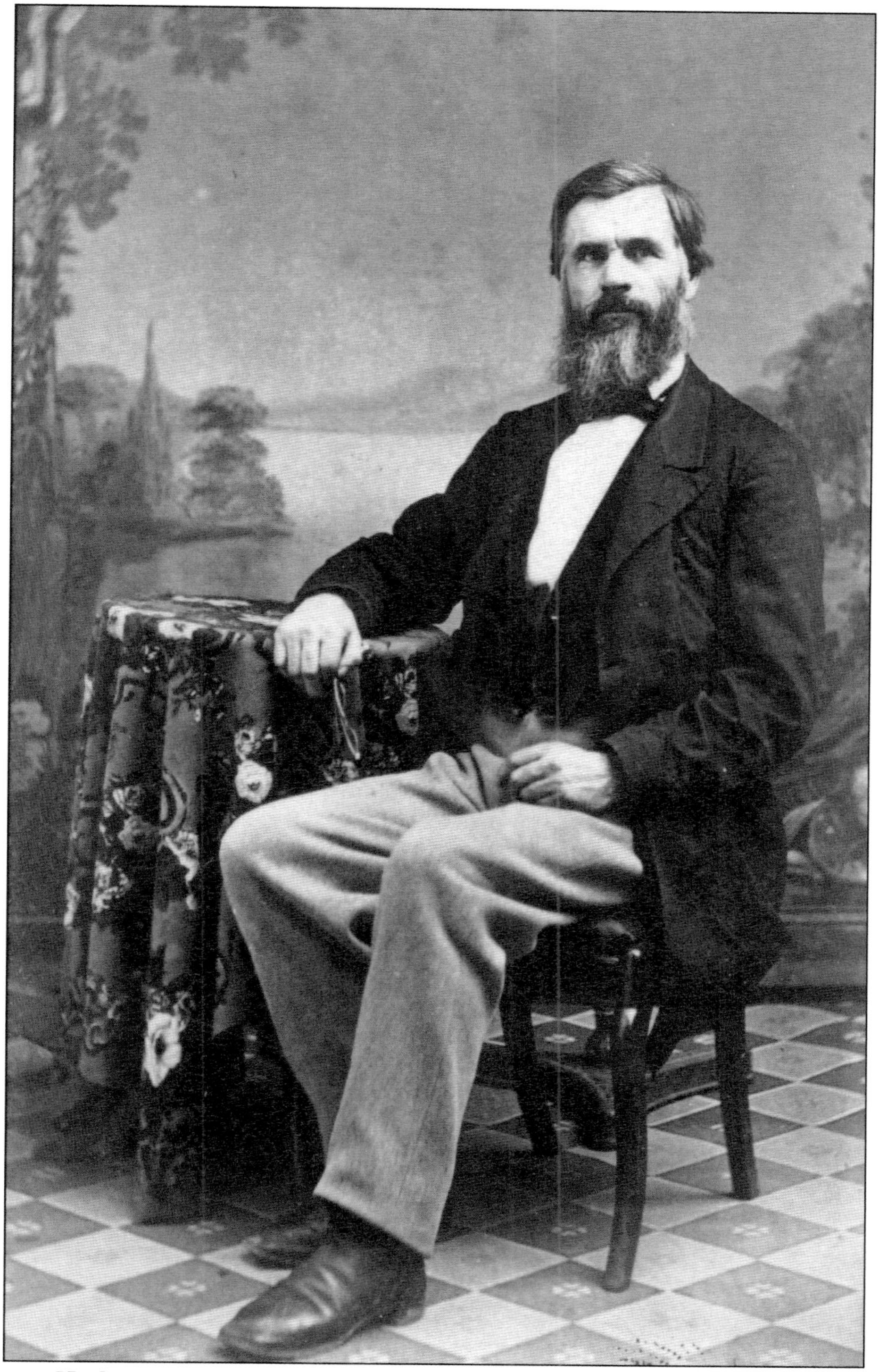

WILLIAM H. GRAY. Gray helped establish the First Presbyterian Church in Oregon at Gray House on Clatsop Plains in 1846. Gray was a prominent citizen of Astoria and served in civic capacities as judge, councilman, and bandleader. He is perhaps best known for writing his history of Oregon. (Bernier collection.)

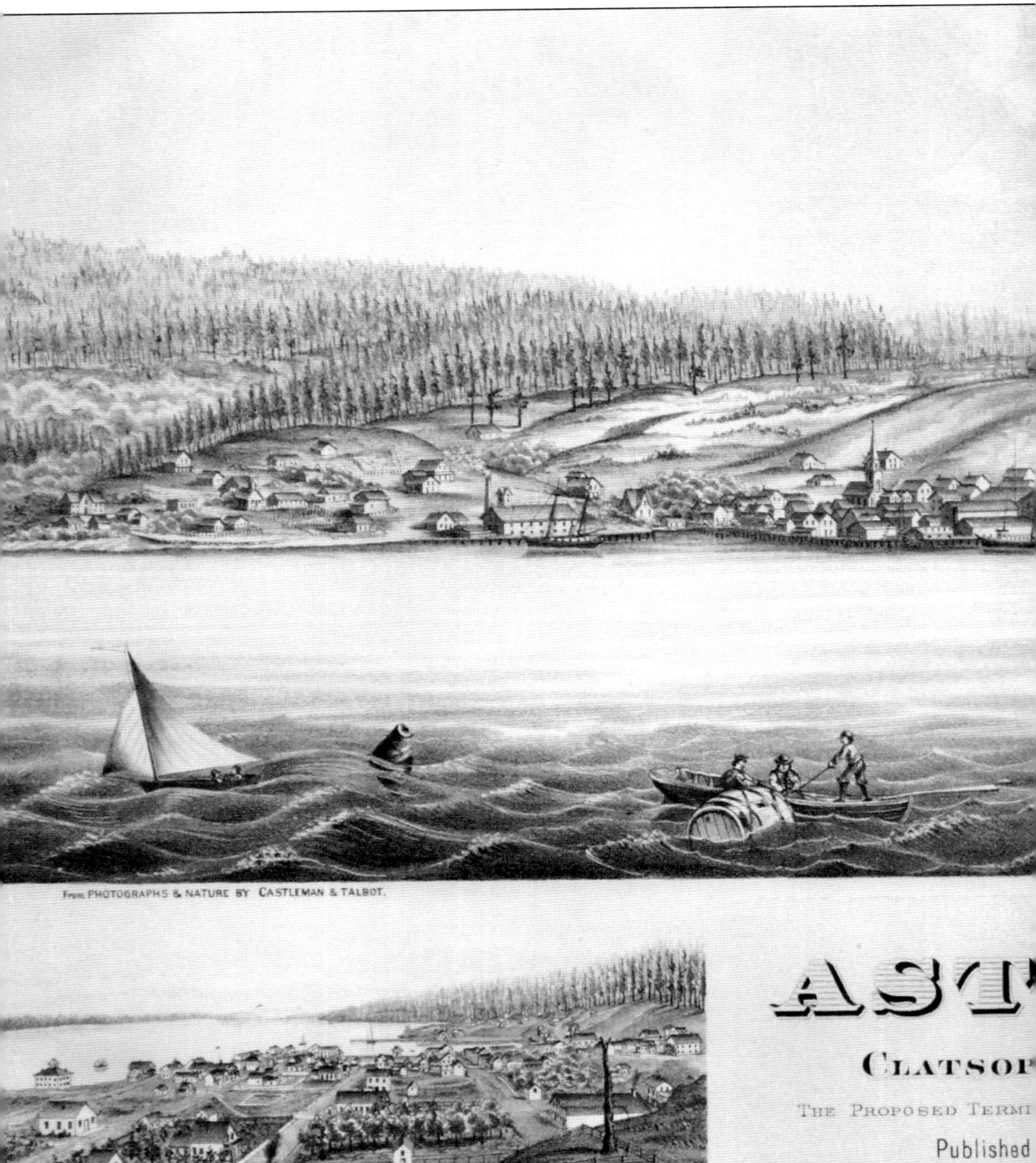

ASTORIA IN THE 1860s. By 1860, Astoria had grown to a population of 499 people. This print was published in 1870 by Capt. J.G. Hustler in order to promote further development and to encourage the extension of the North Pacific Railroad to Astoria. He had come here in 1849 as one of the first regular bar pilots and eventually worked for Captain Flavel. He later engaged in business and built and managed one of the town's first wharves. Astoria did not have a transcontinental

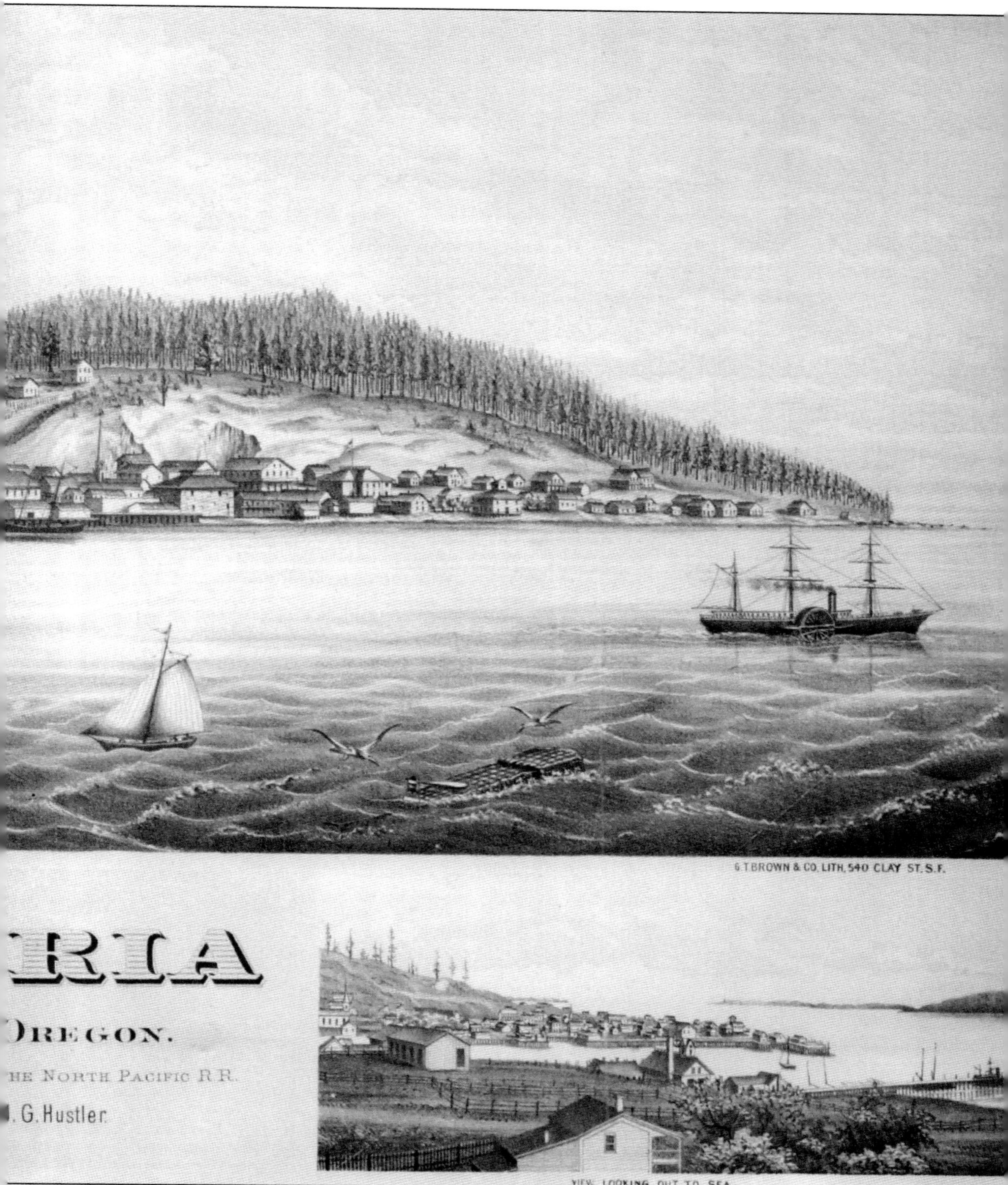

rail connection until 1898, to the great detriment of its growth as a port, despite surveys for that purpose having been done as early as the 1850s. The artwork was done by Castleman and Talbot based on photographs of the time and then engraved and printed. It represents a fairly accurate depiction of Astoria. (CRMM collection.)

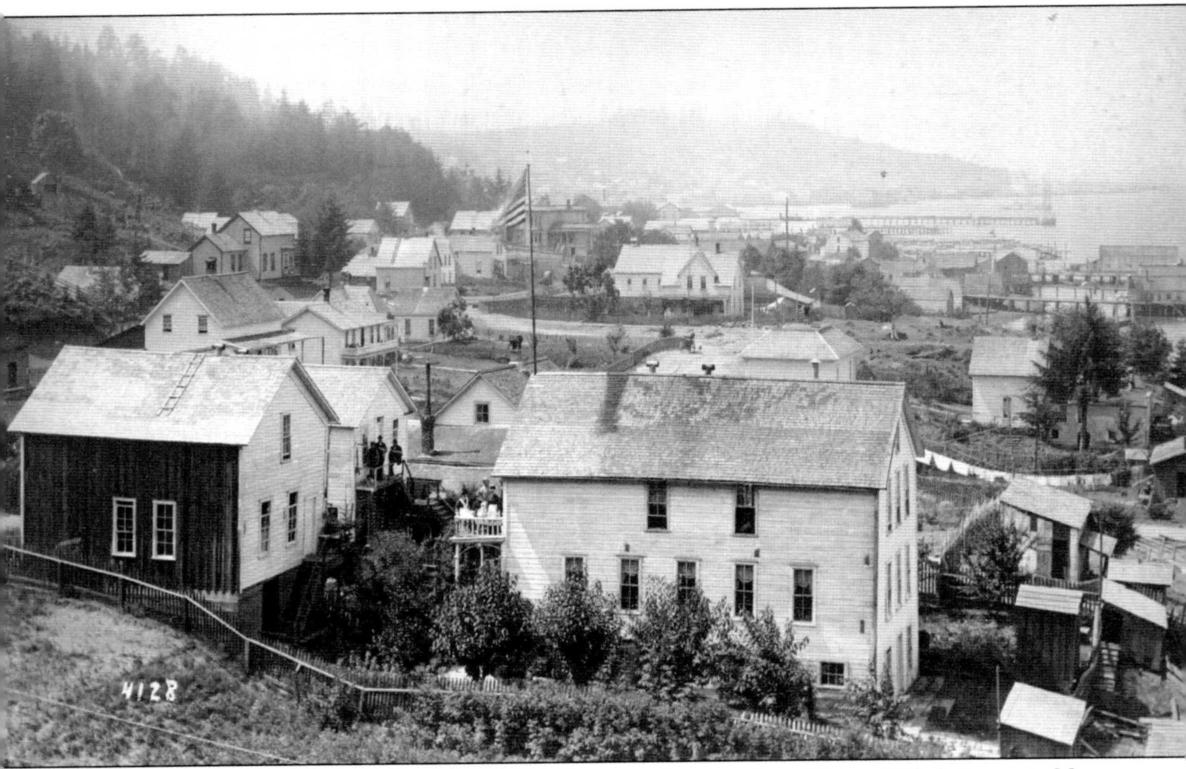

From Uppertown toward Astoria. This photograph taken from Thirty-Eighth Street in Upper Astoria looks westward across Scow Bay toward "Lower" Astoria. The image was taken sometime between 1877 and 1887. This area was predominately settled by Norwegians and Swedes arriving in the 1880s to work in the Upper Astoria canneries. The two earliest canneries in town can be seen on pilings in the water to the right in the middle foreground. (CRMM No. 030-187.)

Two

GRAND PLANS

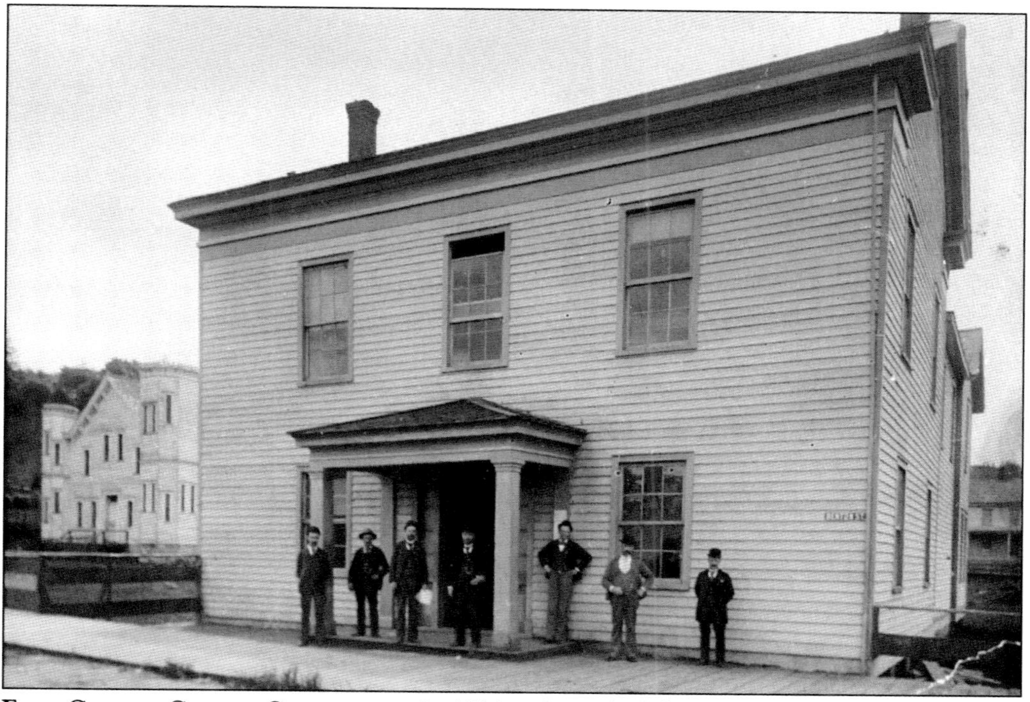

FIRST CLATSOP COUNTY COURTHOUSE. In 1854, early settler John McClure gave Clatsop County an Astoria block for the new county seat. The property, bordered by Benton Street (Eighth Street), Jefferson Street (Duane Street), Lafayette Street (Seventh Street), and Squemoqua Street (Commercial), was part of McClure's original land claim. The first courthouse, built in 1855, is pictured here in 1890 with county officials. The unique building with the towers on the left of the photograph is the second county jail. Constructed in 1882, it replaced the earlier 1865 structure deemed unsafe and a health hazard. (Woodfield collection.)

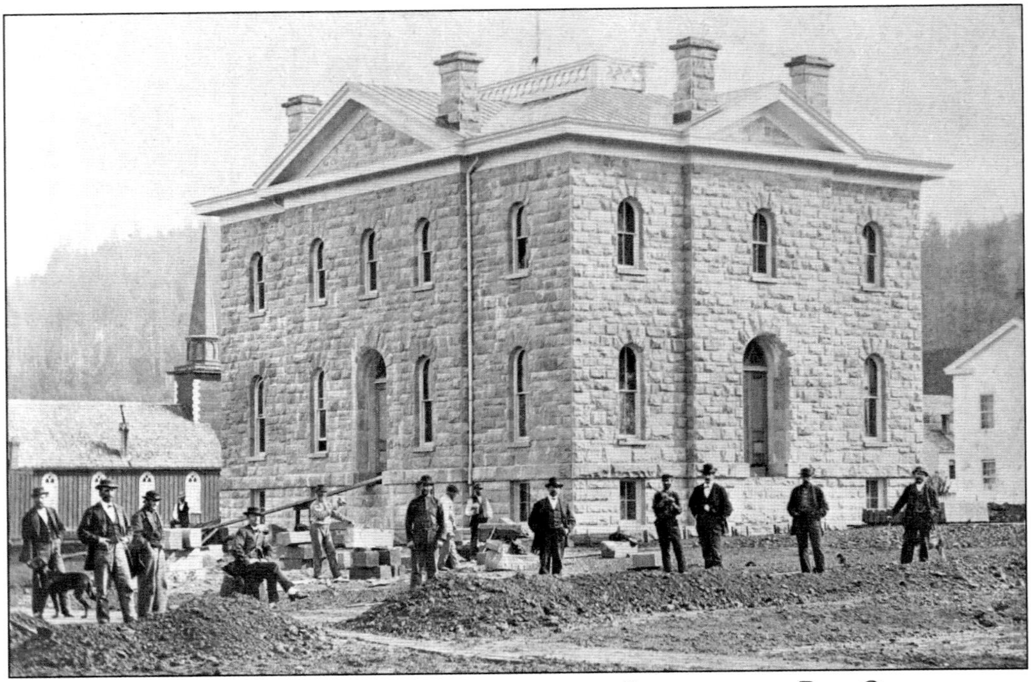

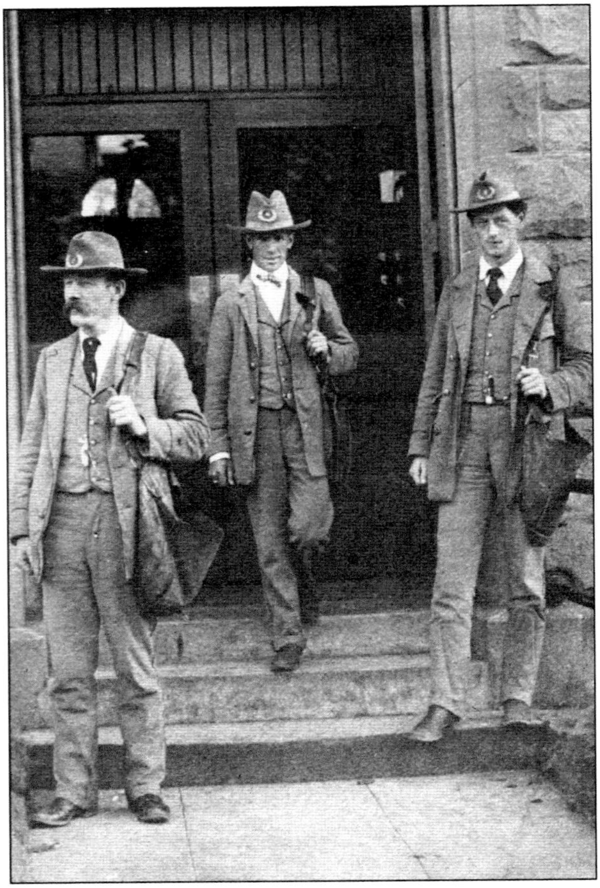

Combining the Post Office and Custom House. Construction on the post office and custom house began in 1869 and is pictured nearing completion in 1873. The stone structure stood in the middle of a block of property deeded by Captain Crosby to the US government. Inadequate heating contributed to the building's rapid deterioration, and in 1919 it was declared unsanitary. The fire department labeled it a firetrap in 1926. It would be another seven years before it was replaced. The Episcopal Church near the corner of Eighth and Commercial Streets (the site of the present Spexarth Building) is to the left. (Woodfield collection.)

Couriers on Their Rounds. Pictured from left to right are postal carriers August "Gus" Fricke, Andrew Dalgity, and Ted Sutton heading out to deliver the mail. After passing his civil service examination, Fricke served the downtown Astoria business district. This photograph was taken around 1906. (Woodfield collection.)

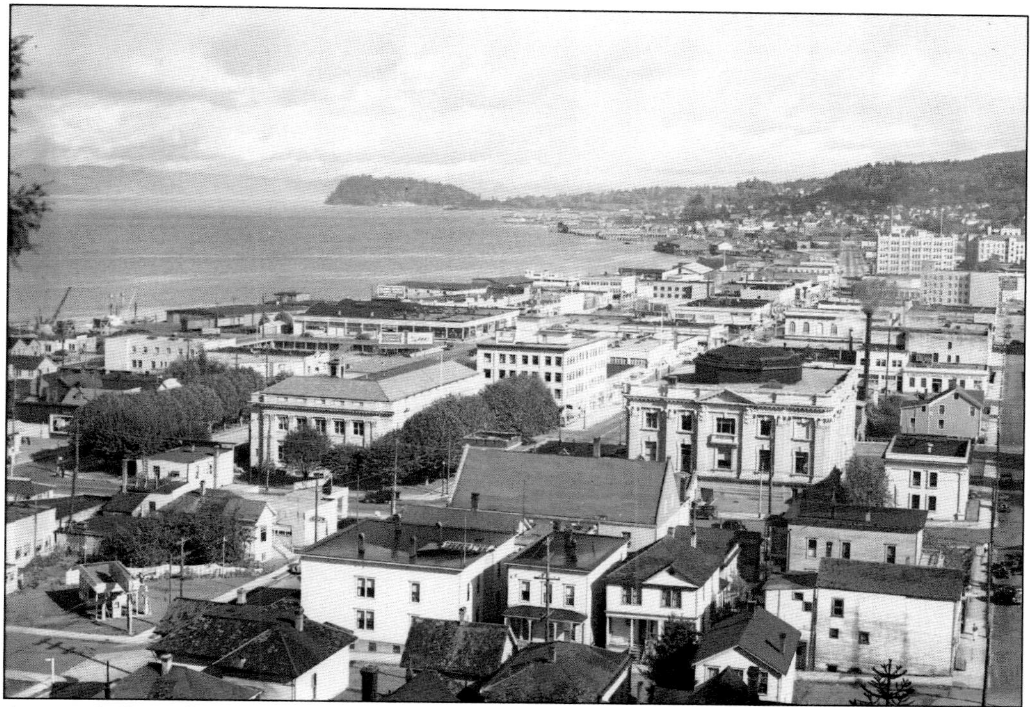

ASTORIA'S POST OFFICE. The large building in the center left of the image, surrounded by trees, is the most recent postal building, completed in 1933 on the site of the previous post office. It too incorporates the custom house and other federal agency offices. To the right is the Clatsop County Courthouse, and to the far right is the county jail that was built in 1914 and in use until 1976. (Woodfield collection.)

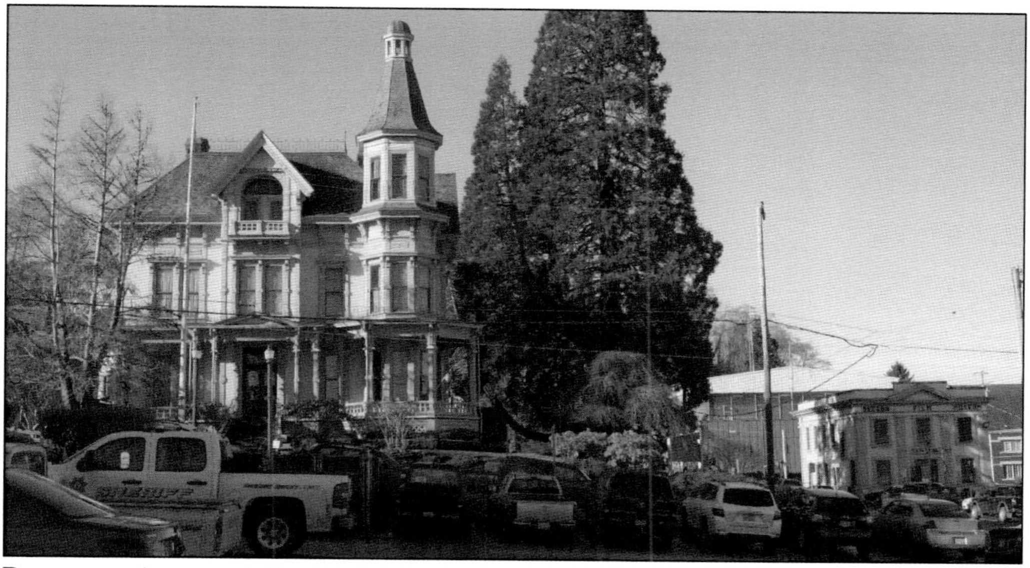

PROMINENT ASTORIAN'S RESIDENCE. Built in 1885, this grand Victorian home belonged to ship's pilot, entrepreneur, and businessman Capt. George Flavel. His first home once stood in the foreground of the photograph, where the parking lot is shown. To the right is the old county jail that was featured in *The Goonies*. This building is now the home of the Oregon Film Museum. Directly behind the building is the current county jail. (Author's collection.)

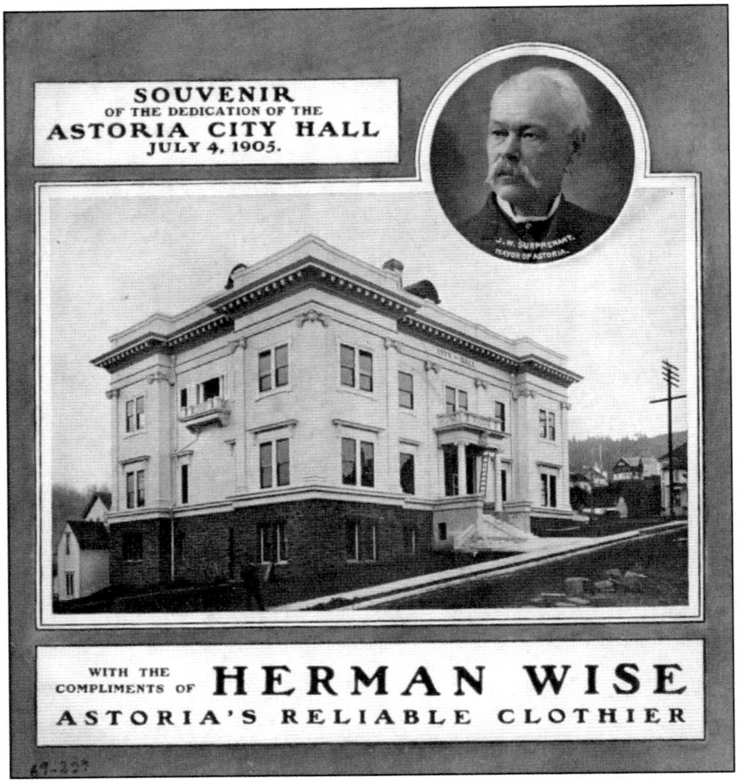

New Civic Center. As the city grew, a need for consolidating services prompted the building of a new centralized city hall. Designed by Portland architect Emil Schacht, the building provided space for a city jail, a municipal court, administrative offices, the assessor's offices, the assessor's office, and a library. Abandoned by the city after 1939, it became the USO center during World War II. Together with the attached Armory, the building provided recreational entertainment for military personnel during and after the war. (CRMM No. 030-228.)

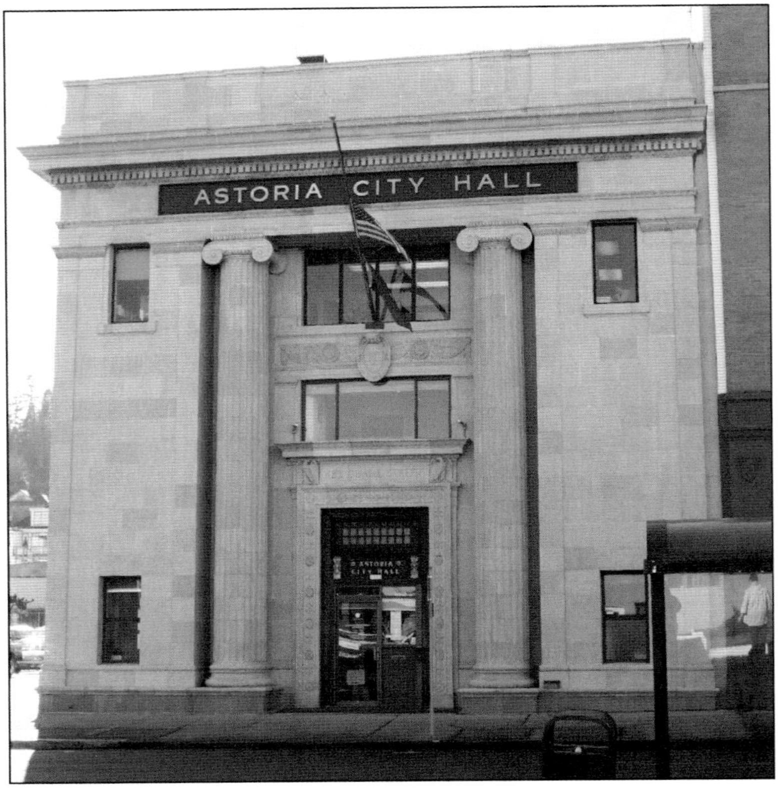

New Use for an Old Building. The Astoria Savings Bank was destroyed by fire in 1922 and rebuilt on the same site. The bank failed in 1929, and in 1939 the city moved its offices into the building. It continues to serve in that capacity, and plans are underway for its renovation. (Author's collection.)

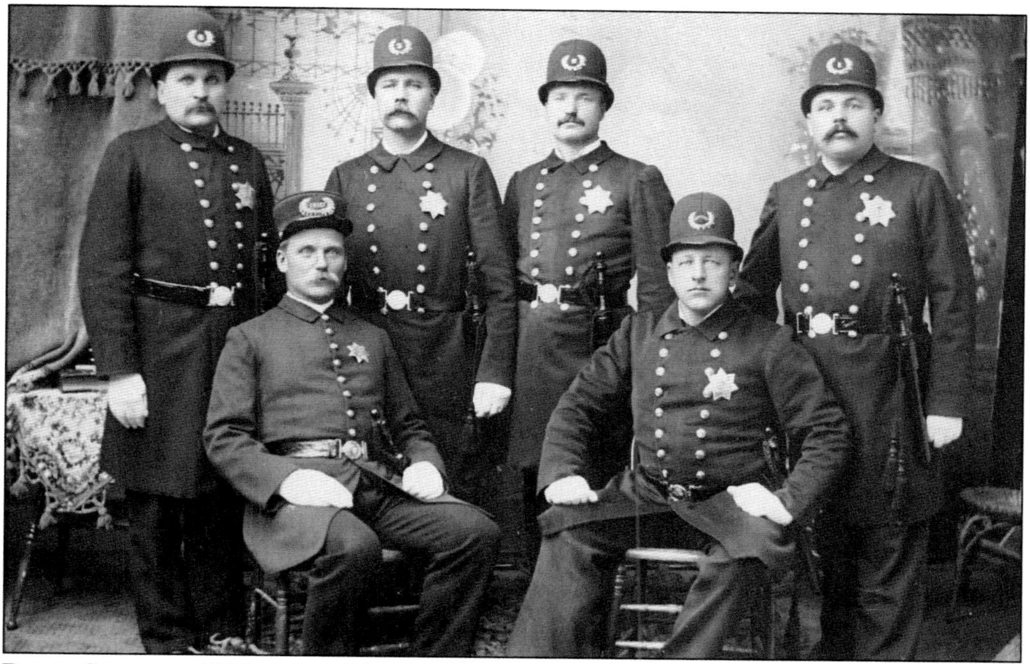

Police Squad of 1897. Astoria's boys in blue pose for the photographer in 1897. Pictured from left to right are (seated) Chief Clark Loughrey and Capt. Ed Hallock; (standing) patrolmen A.C. Thompson, O. Settem, J. Sinnott, and Al Seafeldt. Hallock became the police chief that same year. (Woodfield collection.)

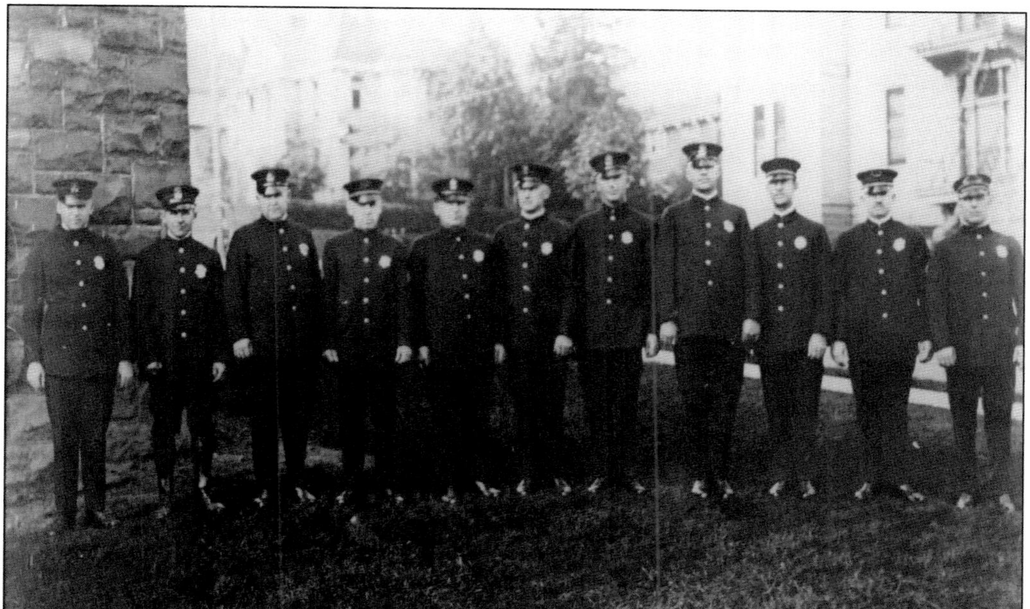

Police in Front of City Hall, c. 1918. Members of the Astoria Police Department stand outside the city jail that was located in the city hall. The building was on Sixteenth Street between Duane and Exchange Streets. The photograph, taken sometime around 1918, includes future chief Edward "Leb" Carlson (on the far right), who would later vigorously deny charges of graft. (CRMM No. 420-17318.)

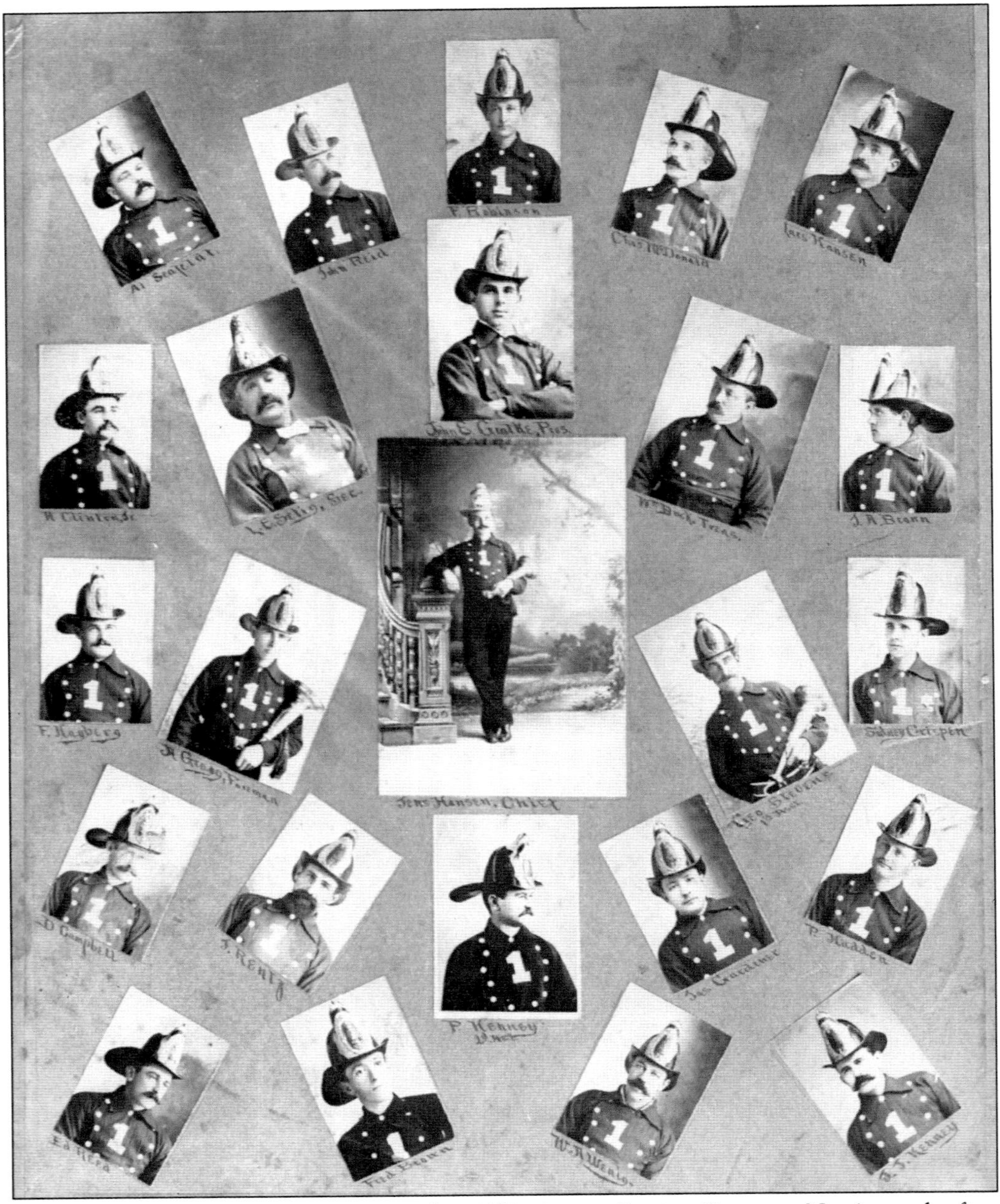

FIREFIGHTERS OF AEC NO. 1. Organized in 1870, Astoria Engine Company No. 1 was the first of Astoria's volunteer fire companies. This photograph was taken in 1897, the year it disbanded due to the formation of a paid fire department. Astoria's second company, Rescue No. 2, was incorporated in 1877. (Woodfield collection.)

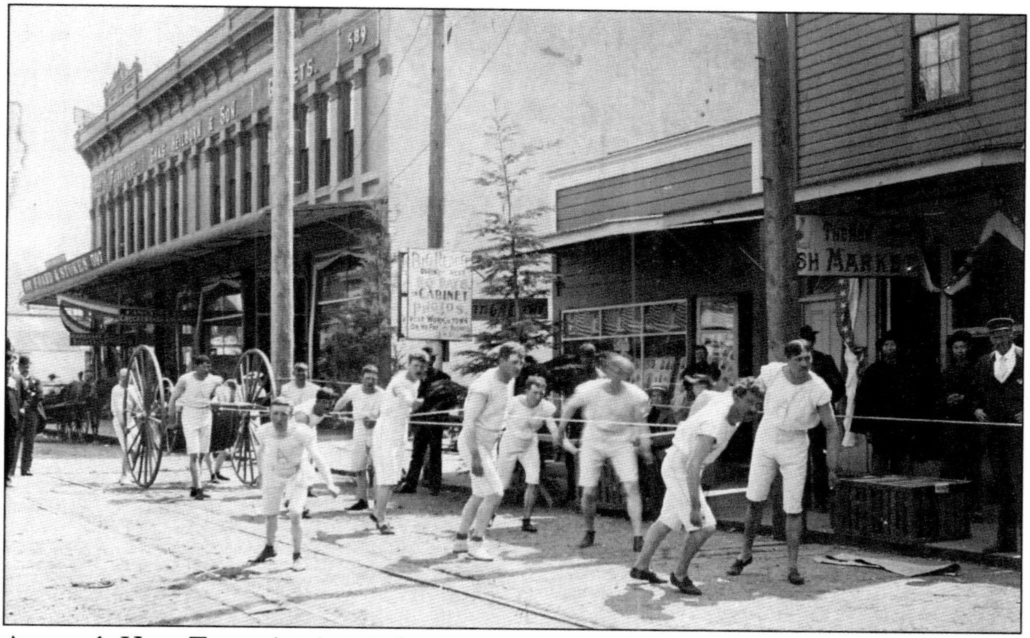

Astoria's Hose Team. An Astoria hose-cart team prepares to race down Commercial Street in this photograph taken around 1896. Hose-cart teams from all over Oregon and Washington raced against each other at musters for prize money and bragging rights. The businesses, pictured from left to right, are Foard and Stokes, the photography shop of J.H. Bratt, and the New Fish Market. (Woodfield collection.)

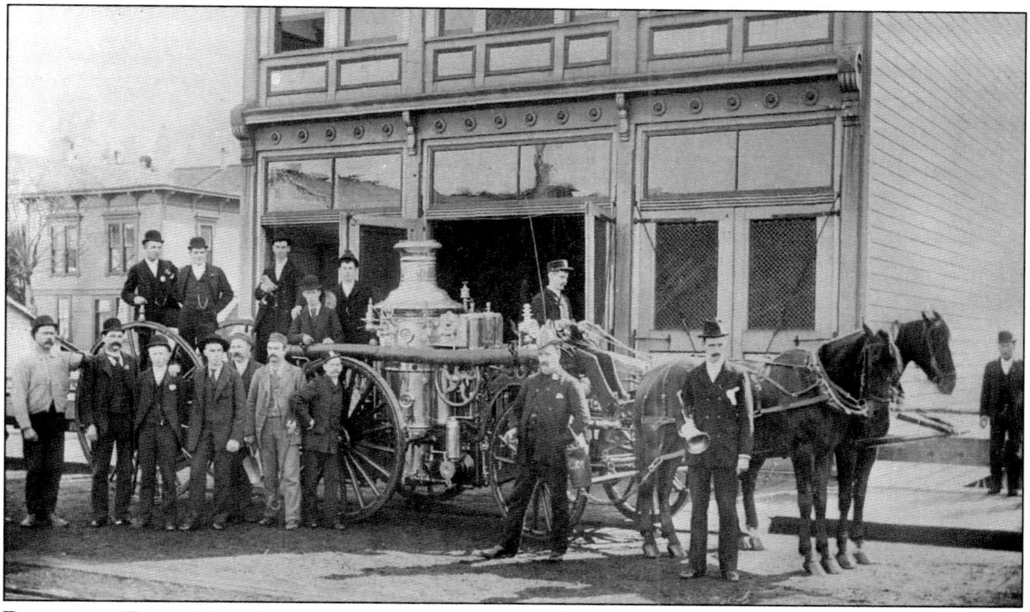

Proud of Their New Equipment. In 1890, Columbia Engine Company No. 3, the last of the volunteer departments, was organized. Members of the company are seen here in front of their station (on Marine Drive between Twenty-eighth and Twenty-ninth Streets) with the new Clapp and Jones Steam Engine. The pumper, which cost $4,400, was placed in their keeping by the city. The station was retired in 1928, and the building was sold to the Home Bakery. The structure was destroyed by fire in 1943. (Woodfield collection.)

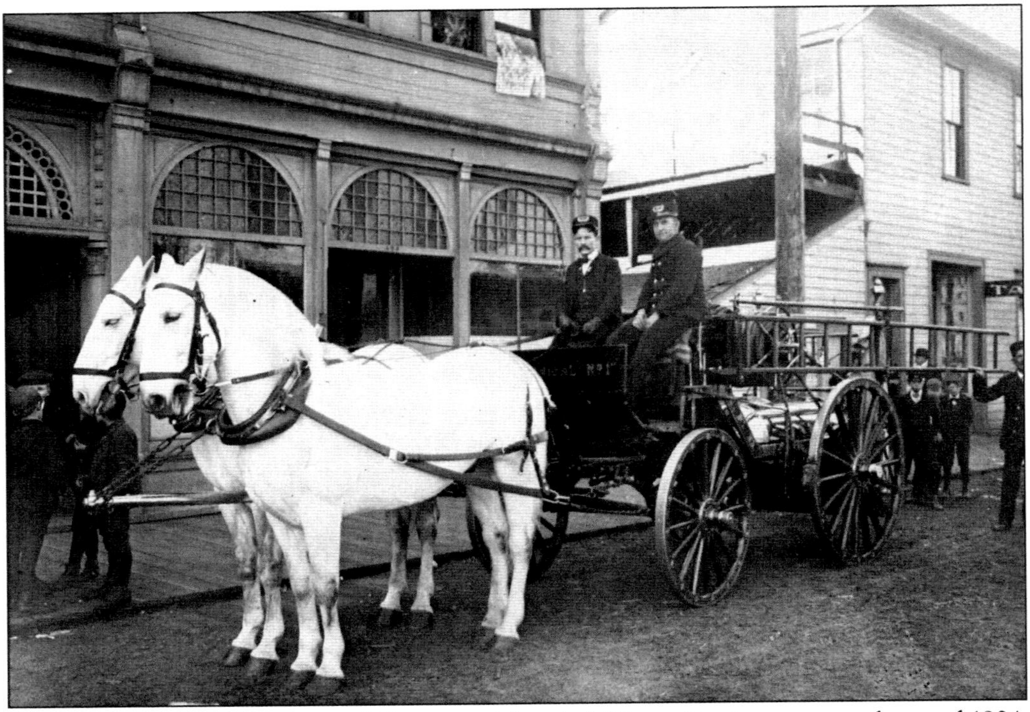

Chemical Engine. This image of Champion Chemical Wagon No. 1 was snapped around 1904. The chemical fire engine arrived in 1894 and was housed in a building at Tenth and Bond Streets. The firefighters are, from left to right, driver Daniel McDonald, who was considered one of the best horse handlers in the city; unidentified; and S.I. "Tiny" Arrigoni, who was at the back of the wagon. (Woodfield collection.)

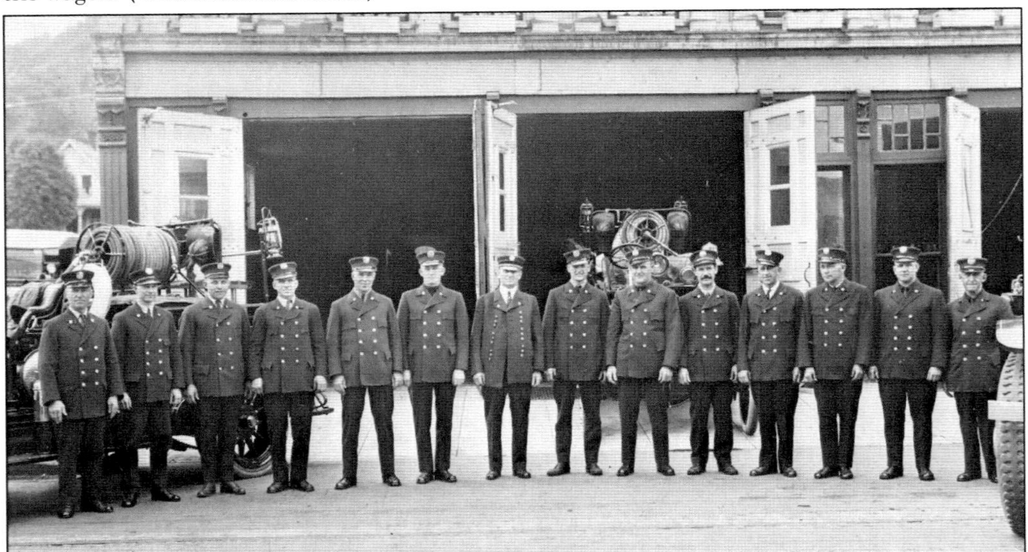

Professional Firefighters. Members of Astoria's professional fire department pose in front of Central Station on Fourth and Astor Streets in the mid-1920s. The paid department was first established in 1897. S.I. "Tiny" Arrigoni, first on the right, began his firefighting career as a volunteer with Astoria Fire Company No. 1 in 1877 and was later honored for 45 years of service. (Woodfield collection.)

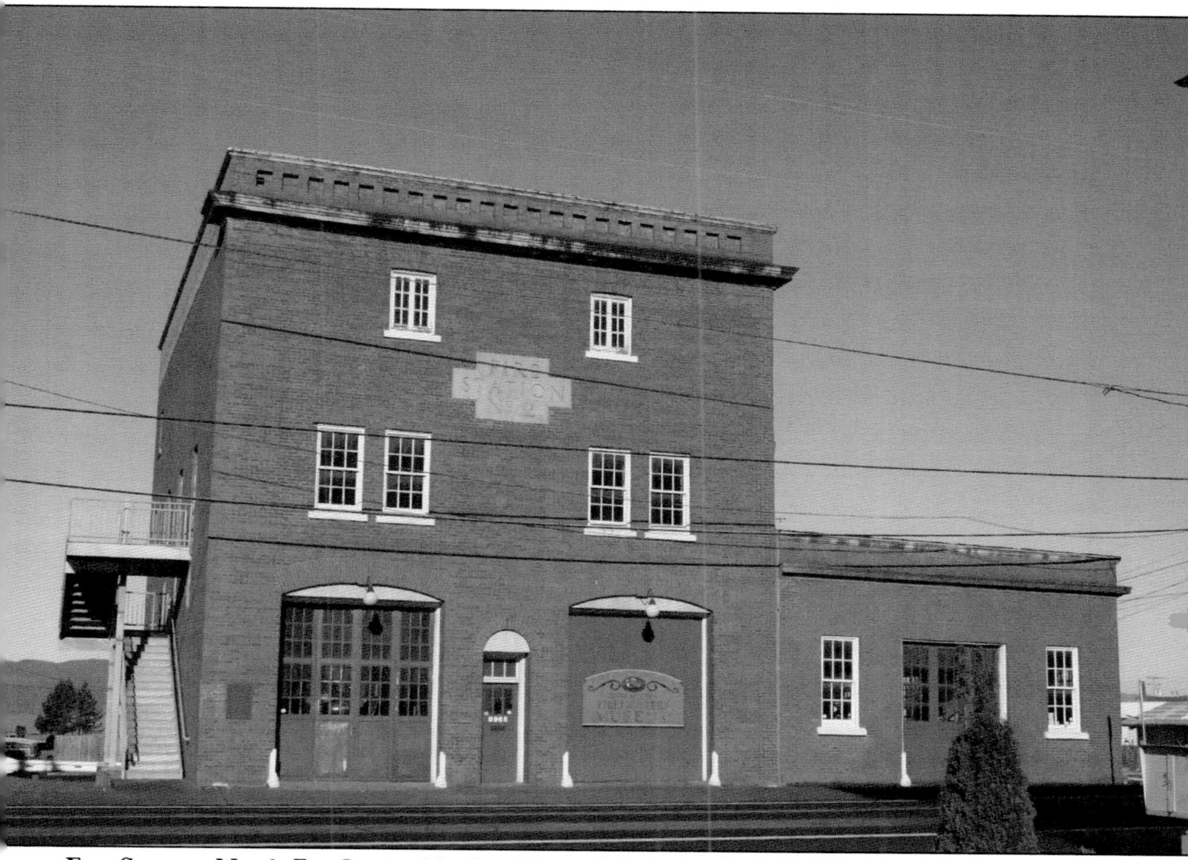

Fire Station No. 2. Fire Station No. 2 at Thirtieth Street and Marine Drive began as a brewery. In 1896, John Kopp's new North Pacific Brewery was built. The facility consisted of a five-story, wood-framed structure. The brick beer-storage building was remodeled in 1928 into the "new" fire station. The station was active until the combined Fire and Police Department Headquarters was constructed directly behind the building in the 1960s. Today, it houses a collection of unique firefighting apparatus. (Author's collection.)

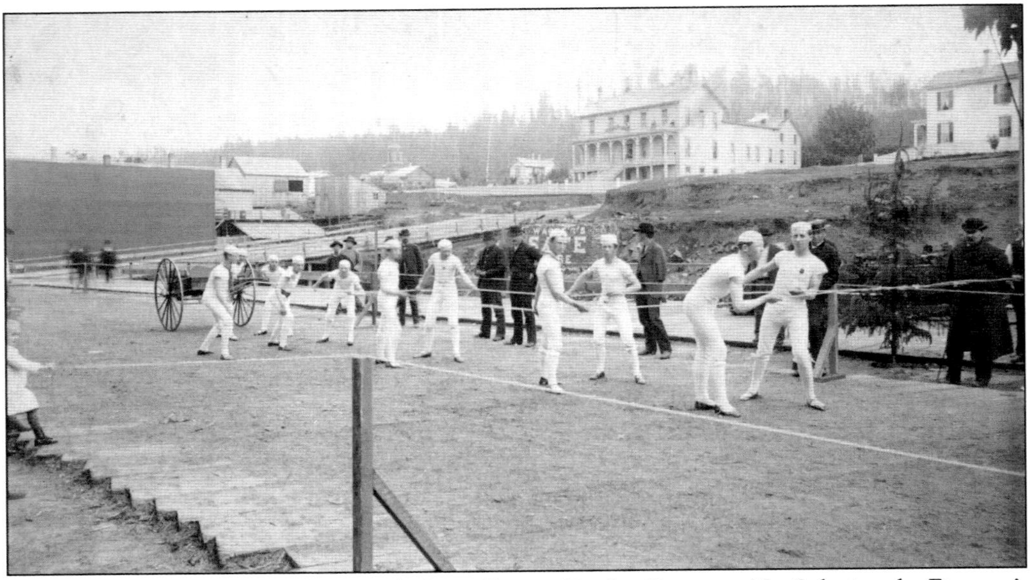

Hotel to Hospital. This photograph shows Rescue Tender Company No. 2 during the Firemen's Tournament in June 1885 and also captures the first hospital in the city. In 1880, the Catholic Sisters of Providence were asked to take charge of establishing a hospital in Astoria. The large three-story building (to right of center) known as the Arrigoni Hotel was purchased for that purpose. An additional wing built in 1895 added 40 beds to the existing 30, as well as service rooms and a chapel. (Bernier collection.)

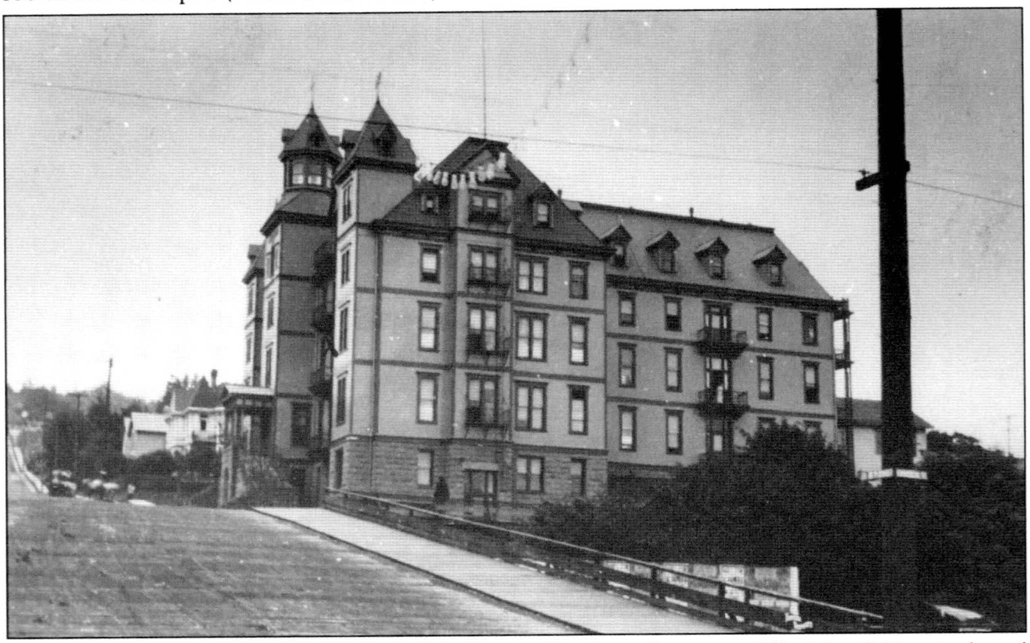

St. Mary's Hospital. Astoria's population was outgrowing the original St. Mary's Hospital, and in 1905 a new four-story frame building was constructed on the same block between Duane and Exchange Streets. The new St. Mary's, seen in this 1911 photograph (note the lighting done for the centennial celebration), fronted Sixteenth Street and faced the recently built city hall. The hospital would have been lost in the 1922 blaze, save for the tireless efforts of volunteers stationed on the roof with hoses to douse any sparks. (CRMM No. 030-234.)

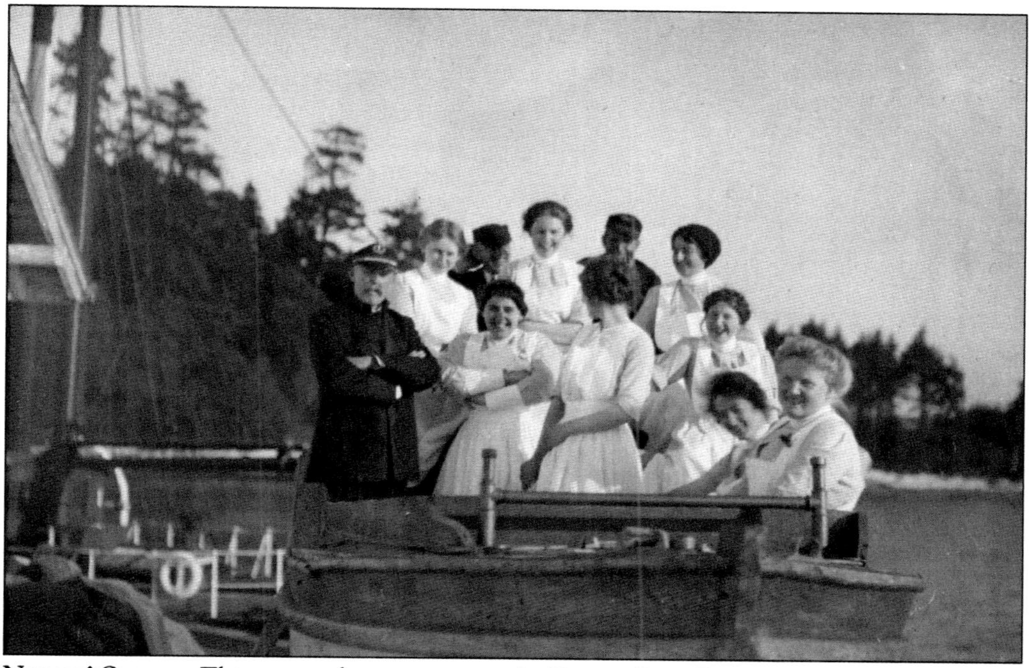

NURSES' OUTING. This group of nurses poses at the Tongue Point Buoy Station on a pleasant day in 1908. St. Mary's Hospital did not have its own school of nursing until 1909. Up to that point, they had nurses who were sent from St. Vincent's Hospital in Portland for their three months of probation. (Woodfield collection.)

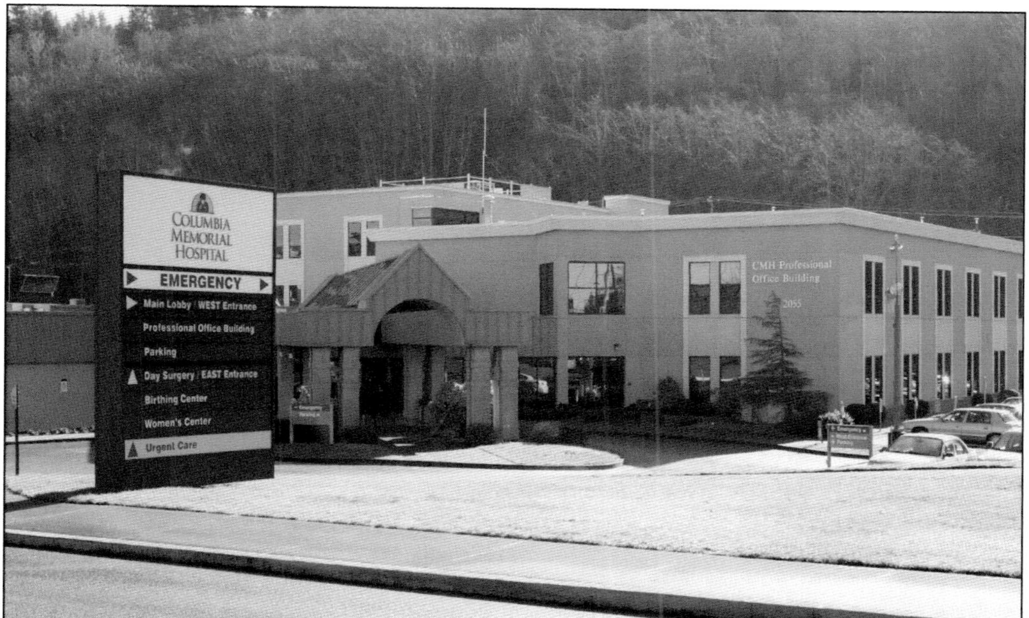

CURRENT HOSPITAL. Columbia Memorial Hospital, which opened in 1977, carries on the fine tradition of professional health care in Astoria. It was constructed on land reclaimed from the open water of Scow Bay, between Uppertown and the central business section of town. The original Columbia Hospital, now Clatsop Care Center, was built on the site of the 1864 Adam Van Dusen residence at Sixteenth and Franklin Streets. It opened its doors in 1927. (Author's collection.)

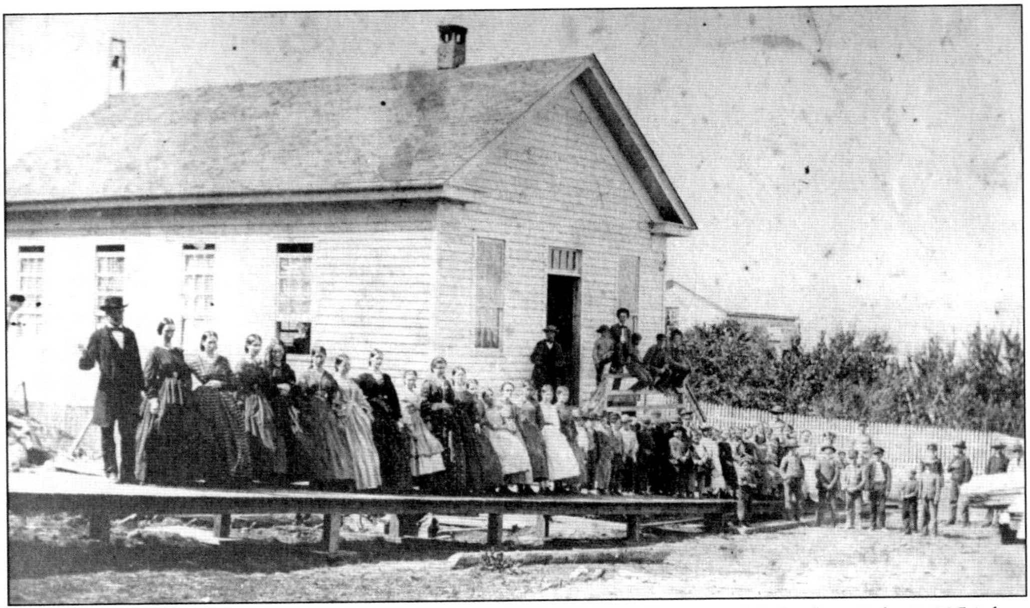

Astoria's First Schoolhouse. The Astoria School District was established on July 4, 1854, but it was not until 1859 that a building was erected specifically for use as a school. The class seen in this c. 1861 photograph was taught by Mr. Deardorff and included Bethenia Owens Adair and her son as well as George Conrad Flavel, son of Captain Flavel. Bethenia Owens-Adair would become one of the earliest women to practice medicine on the Pacific Coast and a proponent of social reform. (Woodfield collection.)

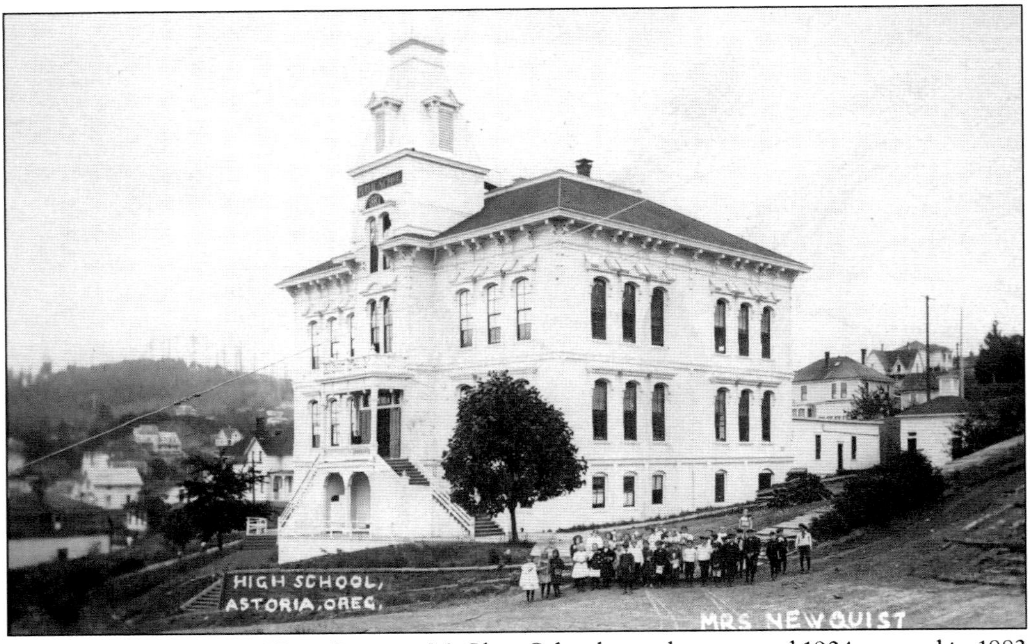

McClure School and High School. McClure School, seen here around 1904, opened in 1883 on Exchange Street between Seventh and Eighth Streets. The school served grades one through eight, the high school program having been dropped by the district in 1864. In 1890, high school students began attending classes at McClure, utilizing the second floor for their studies. In 1911, a high school was built at Sixteenth and Jerome Streets. (CRMM No. 030-250.)

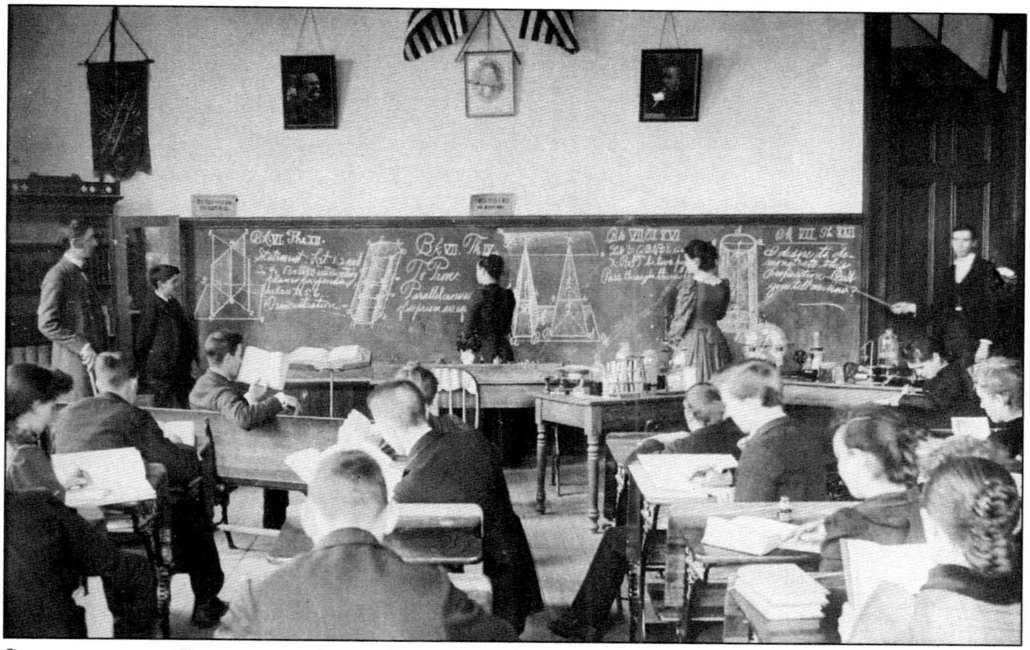

SOLUTIONS TO PROBLEMS. A mathematics class is pictured at McClure School in 1892. (Woodfield collection.)

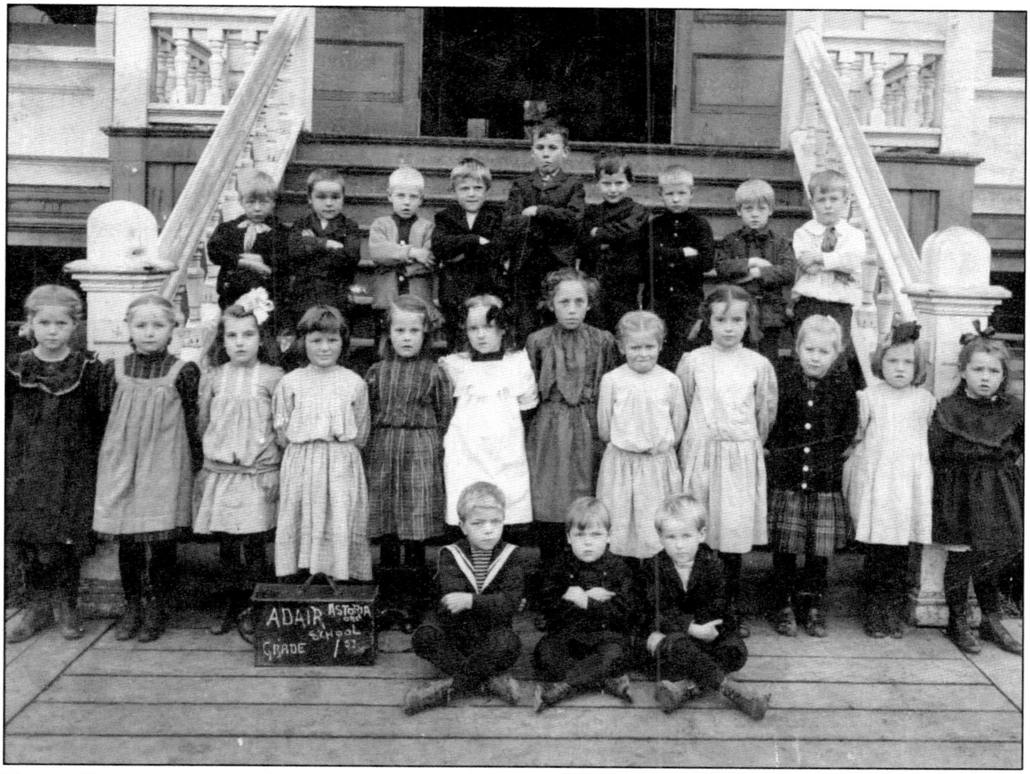

FIRST GRADE AT ADAIR SCHOOL. First graders at Adair School pose for their class photograph in 1911. In 1893, Adair School was built on Duane Street between Thirty-fifth and Thirty-sixth Streets in Astoria's Uppertown. (CRMM No. 420-9750.)

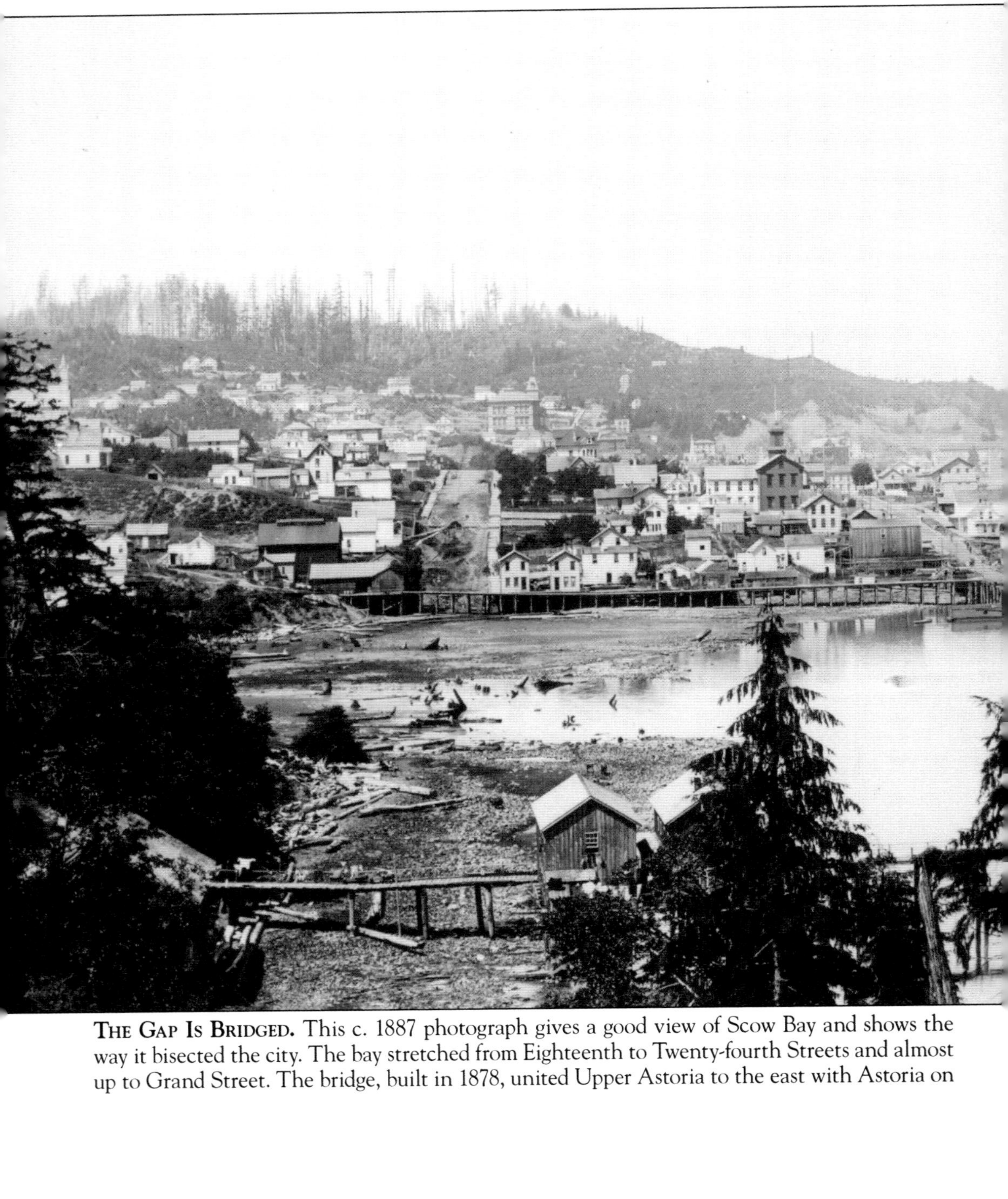

THE GAP IS BRIDGED. This c. 1887 photograph gives a good view of Scow Bay and shows the way it bisected the city. The bay stretched from Eighteenth to Twenty-fourth Streets and almost up to Grand Street. The bridge, built in 1878, united Upper Astoria to the east with Astoria on

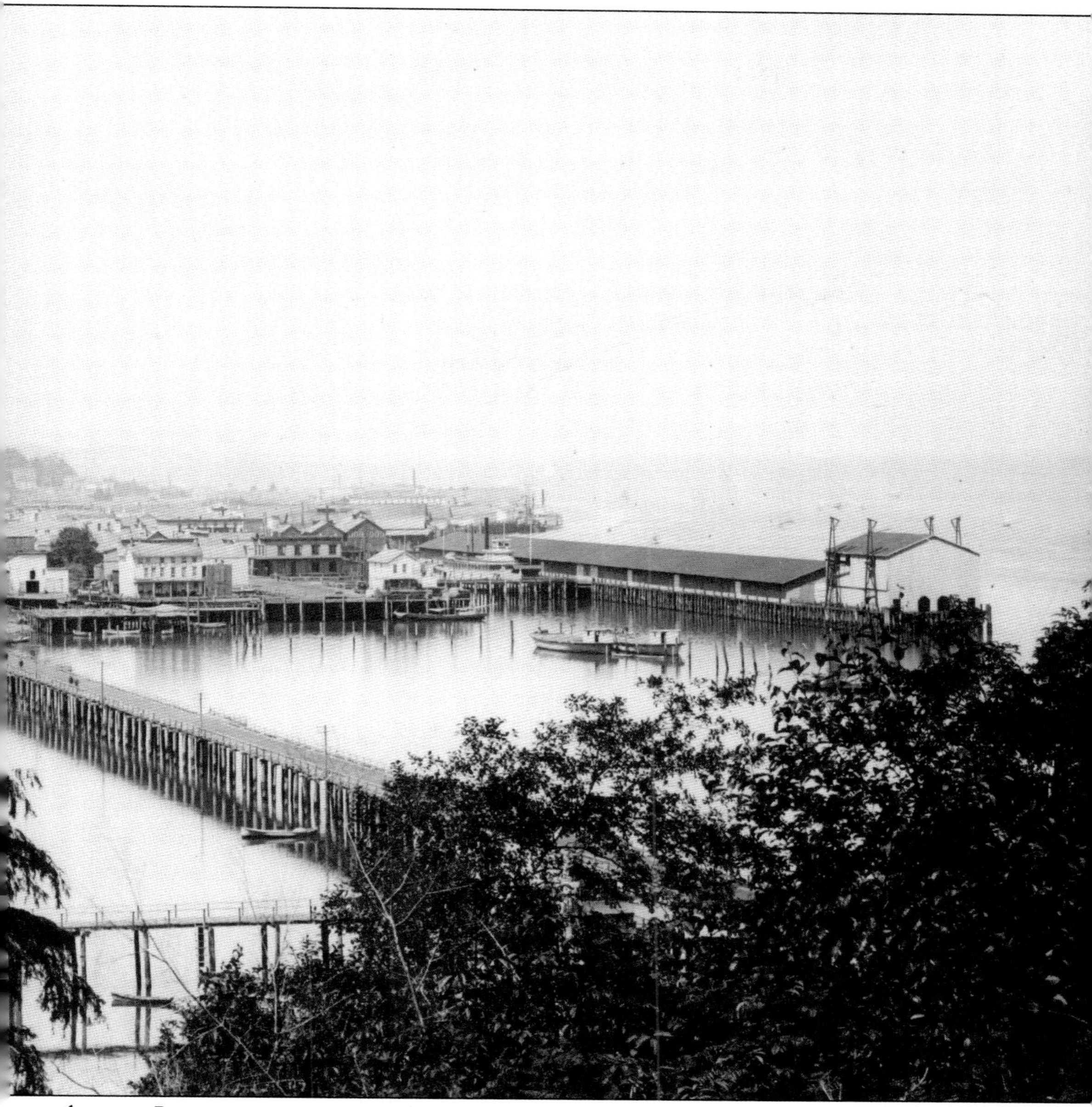

the west. Prior to its construction, there were only two ways to cross—by boat or by traversing a challenging path dug out from the rocky shoreline skirting the bay. The bridge became part of Exchange Street. (CRMM No. 167-2975.)

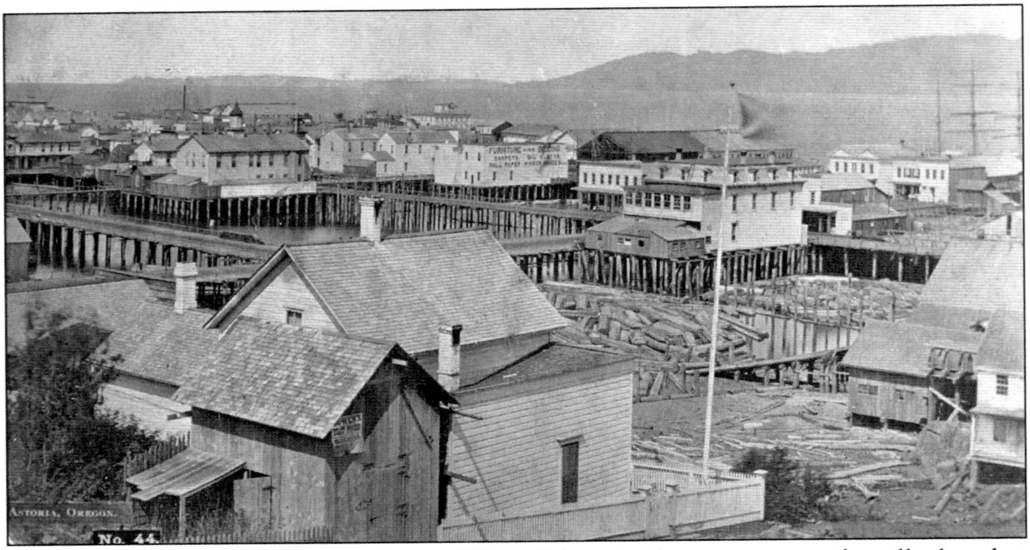

Built on Piles. Within the boundaries of "lower" Astoria, there was a second smaller bay that ran from Tenth to Fourteenth Streets and back to Exchange Street. Businesses in this area were built-out over the river on pilings. This photograph, taken approximately from Fourteenth and Exchange around 1879, illustrates this perfectly. The long building with the pointed tower on the left of the photograph housed city hall and a fire station. It was constructed at the corner of Commercial and Eleventh Streets sometime in the 1870s. (Woodfield collection.)

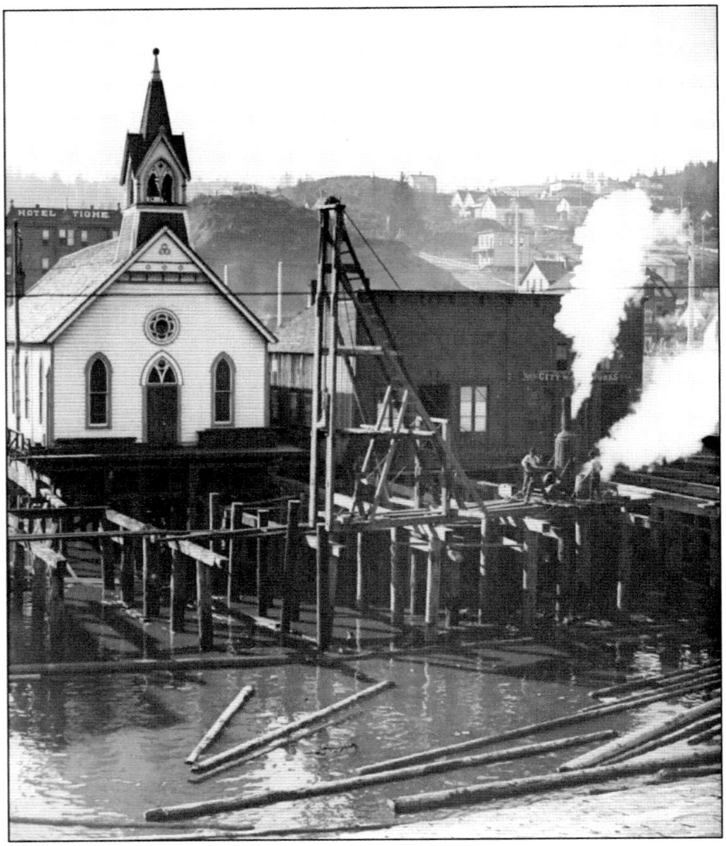

Road Work. The second Methodist Church and the City Waterworks on Duane Street wait for their fronting streets to be repaired in this c. 1896 photograph. The fact that the streets were made of wood and were built over tidal areas meant constant repair and replacement was necessary. Here, a steam-powered pile driver is getting into position to drive new pile to support the street. (CRMM No. 035-686.)

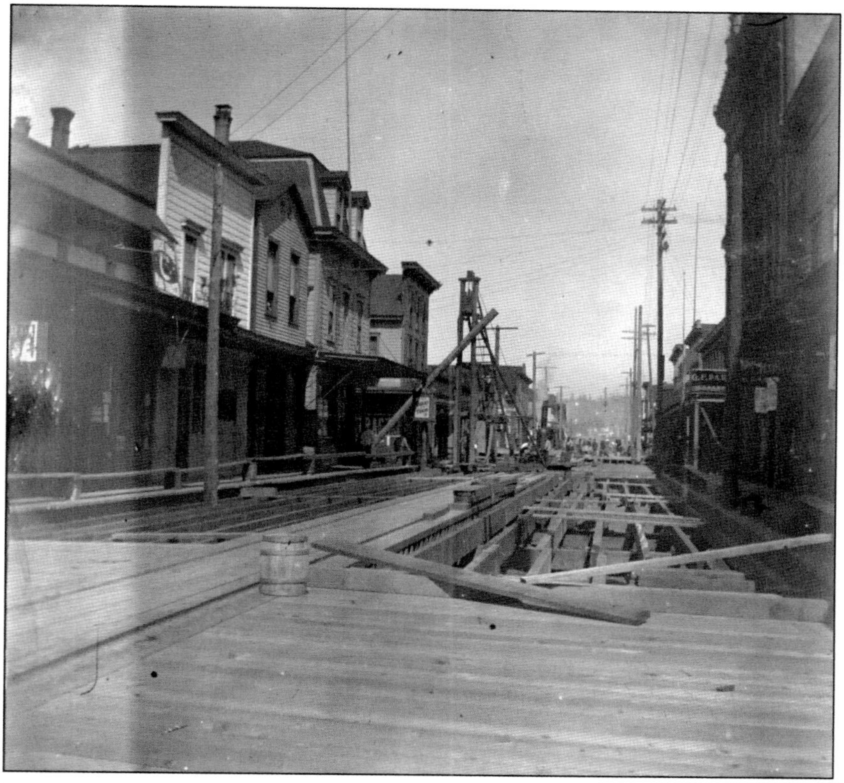

Replacing the Planks. This c. 1896 photograph looks down Bond Street and shows the steam-powered pile driver repairing the planking deck of the avenue. The viaduct under the street deck is clearly visible and helps explain why the city was so vulnerable to damage from fire. (CRMM No. 030-259.)

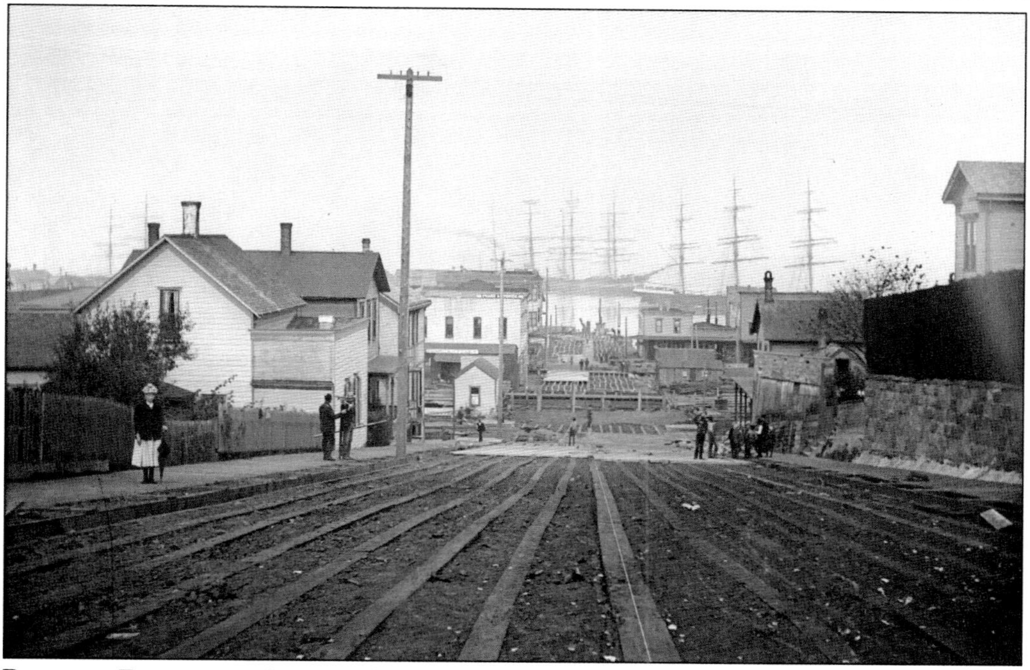

Planking Fourteenth Street. This c. 1900 photograph shows the length of Fourteenth Street from Exchange Street down to the Columbia River. Stringers run along the street, and the surface is being paved with planks. The young lady standing to the left of the photograph holds an umbrella and wears a Tam o' Shanter hat. Surveyors stand just below her. (CRMM No. 030-260.)

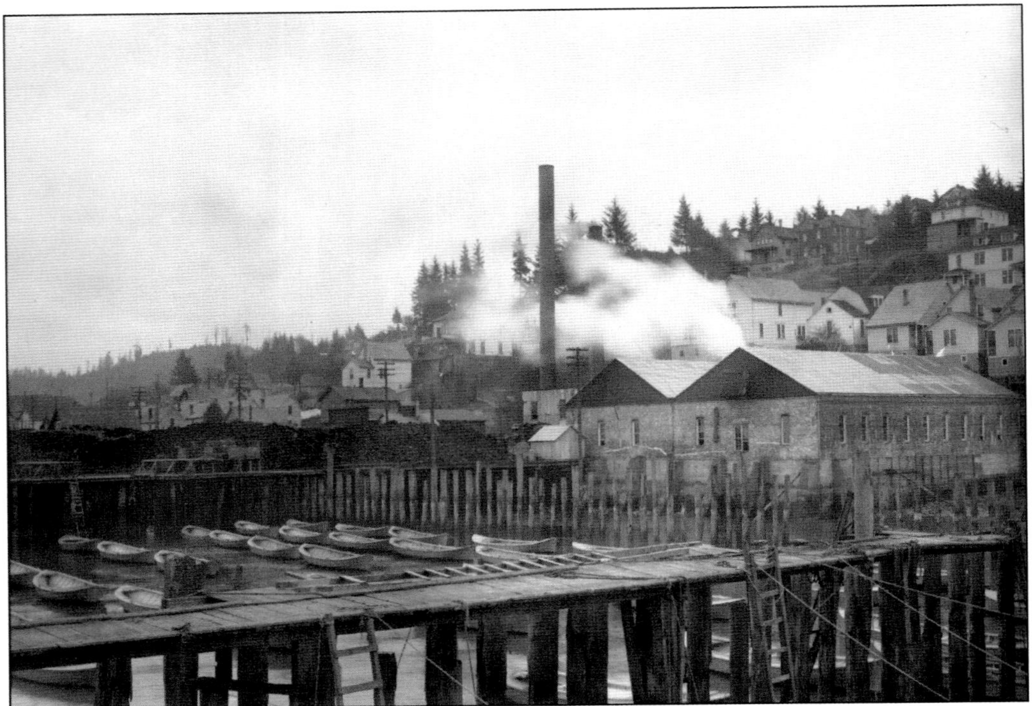

Astoria Generates Its Own Electricity. Trullinger's West Shore Mills was the site of the first electricity-generating plant in Astoria. By burning the waste wood from the mill and using the steam to turn newly purchased dynamos, enough power was generated to illuminate the arc lights installed throughout the city in 1885. In 1893, it became the powerhouse and storage barn for the Astoria Street Railway Company trolleys. (CRMM No. 035-692.)

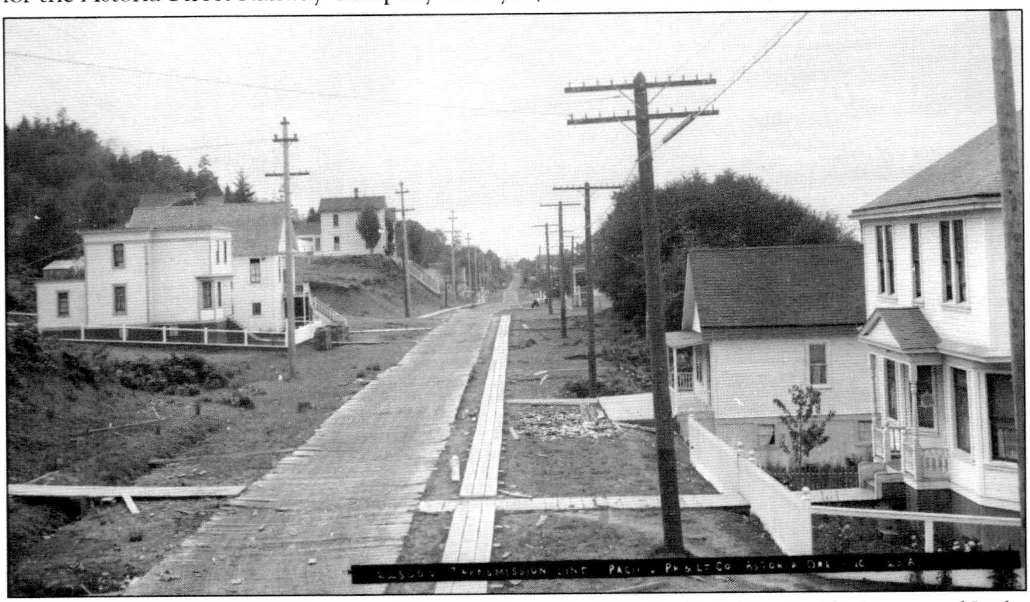

Pacific Power and Light Company New to Town. In 1910 the fledgling Pacific Power and Light Company brought in a high voltage transmission line through the Alderbrook area, connecting Astoria with other communities in the Northwest. This view is down Cedar Street looking west, clearly showing it as a plank road and boardwalk. (Woodfield collection.)

Three

Enterprise and Commerce

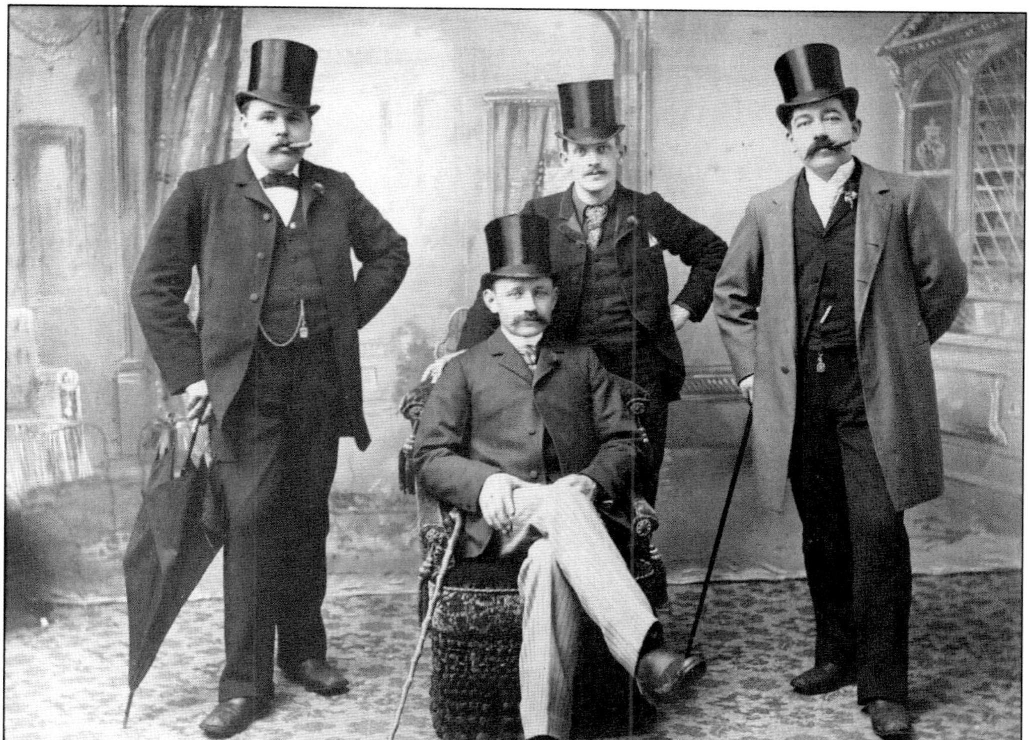

Flaunting Success. Pictured from left to right are Al Seafeldt (saloon operator and Johnson's backer), Albert Johnson (superintendent of Astoria's waterworks), Charles Berner (Johnson's trainer), and Henry A. Smith (Astoria's sheriff). In 1893, Johnson was challenged to a fight by Larry Sullivan, a notorious crimp (shanghaier). The April 1 fight took place in the powerhouse of the West Shore Mills, and betting was frenzied. Johnson, a diminutive man, was not favored to win over the much larger Sullivan; however, he carried the day. In 1895, Sheriff Smith absconded to Belgium with the county's tax receipts. (Woodfield collection.)

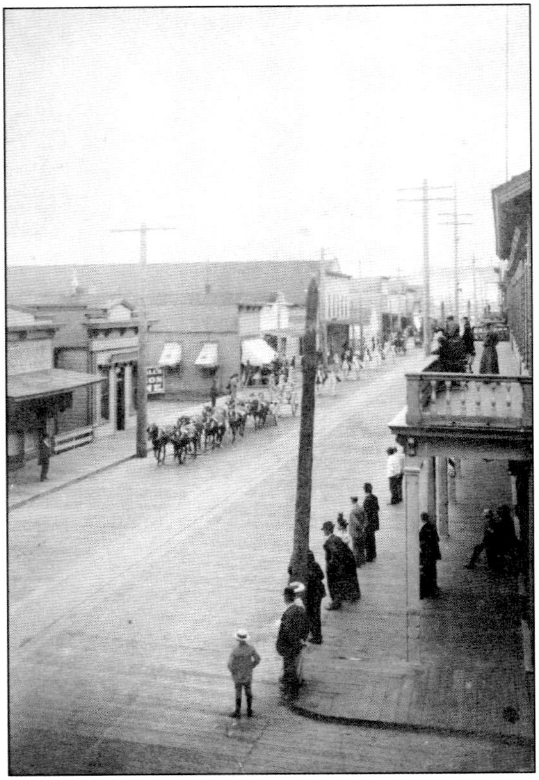

CIRCUS COMES TO TOWN. Standing on the balcony and in front of the Occident Hotel at the corner of what is now Tenth and Bond Streets, people watch the circus parade pass by in 1896. The Occident was built by Captain Flavel in 1869 and was owned by the family until 1913. Pres. Rutherford B. Hayes and Gen. W.T. Sherman stayed there while visiting Astoria. Flavel's office stands across the street at the center—the building with the awnings. (Bernier collection.)

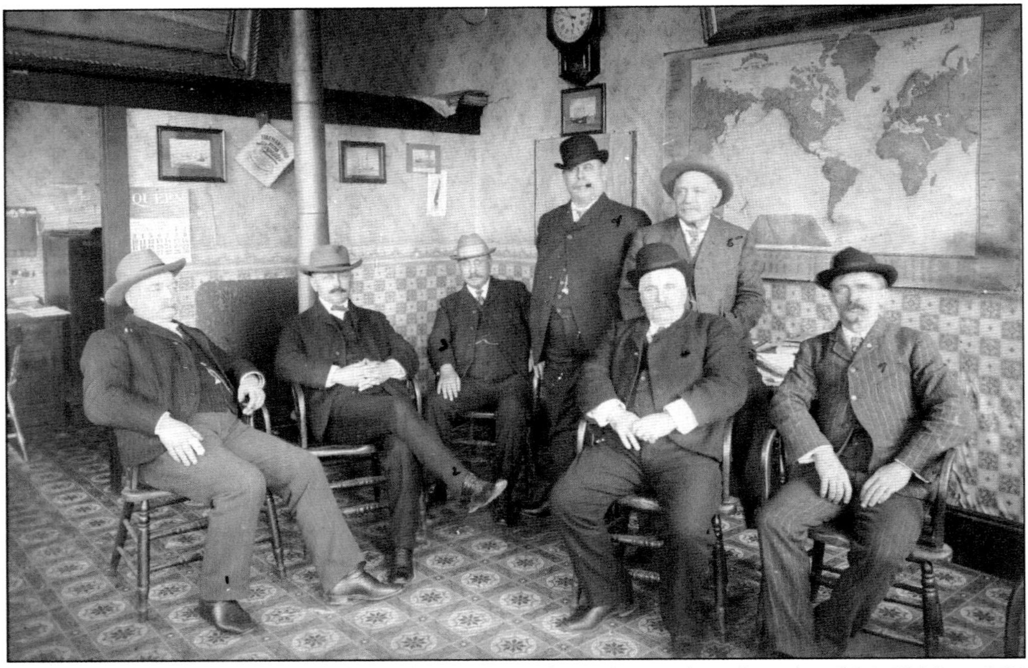

CAPTAINS OF INDUSTRY AND SHIPS. These Oregon bar pilots gathered on April 26, 1904, at 5:54 p.m. in an office that stood at the corner of Eleventh and Bond Streets. Pictured from left to right are Captain Howes, Voelmaton Boelling (Flavel's brother-in-law), Al Betts, Al Johnson, Captain Woods, Harry Mathews, and Captain Dunbar. (CRMM No. 420-9830.)

“Best Hotel in the City.” In an 1888 advertisement that ran in the *Oregon State Gazetteer and Business Directory*, J.G. Ross claimed that Astor House was the “Best Hotel in the City. House New and Newly Furnished Throughout.” The hotel’s rates started at $1 per day and a meal could be had for a quarter. If that was not enough to entice the traveler, there was a free coach to and from the house. (CRMM No. 030-17599.)

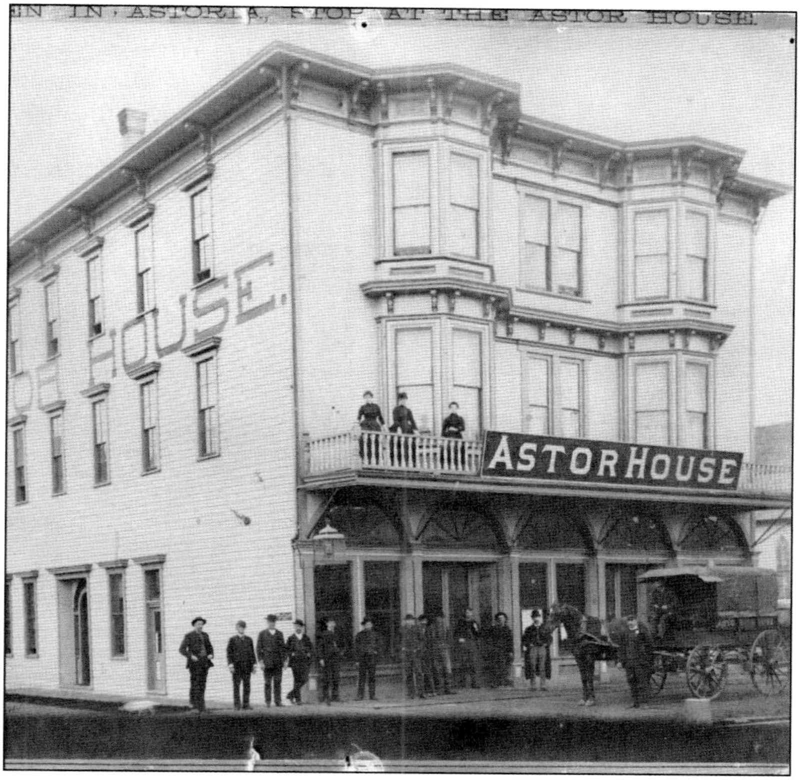

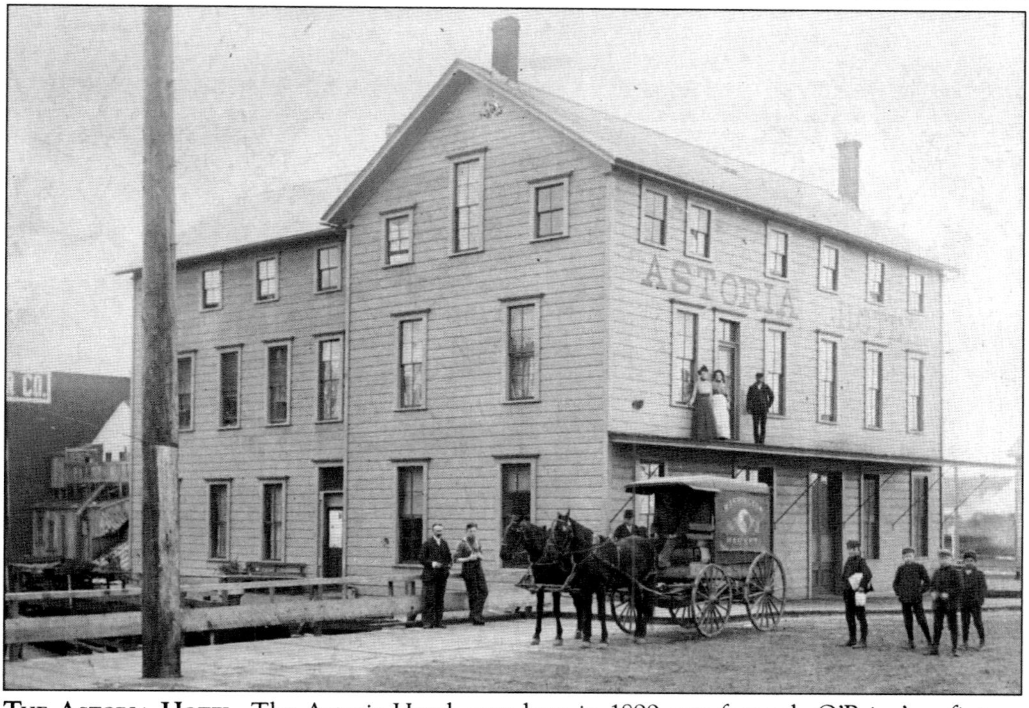

The Astoria Hotel. The Astoria Hotel, seen here in 1899, was formerly O’Brien’s, a fixture on Seventeenth Street since the 1870s. The wagon out front is from the Washington Market, a purveyor of meats on Ninth Street. (Woodfield collection.)

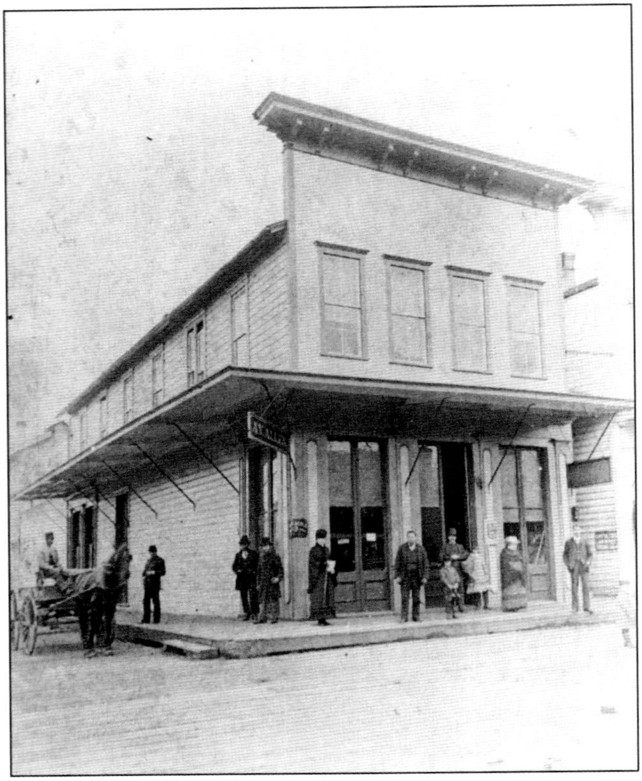

A.V. Allen. This 1880s photograph shows Albert Vine Allen's grocery store on Squemoqua (Commercial) Street at the corner of Cass (Tenth) Street. Allen, a well-respected citizen of the town, began his business with partner C.H. Page in 1880. He bought out Page in 1881 and continued to manage his interests until 1909. (CRMM No. 420-17328.)

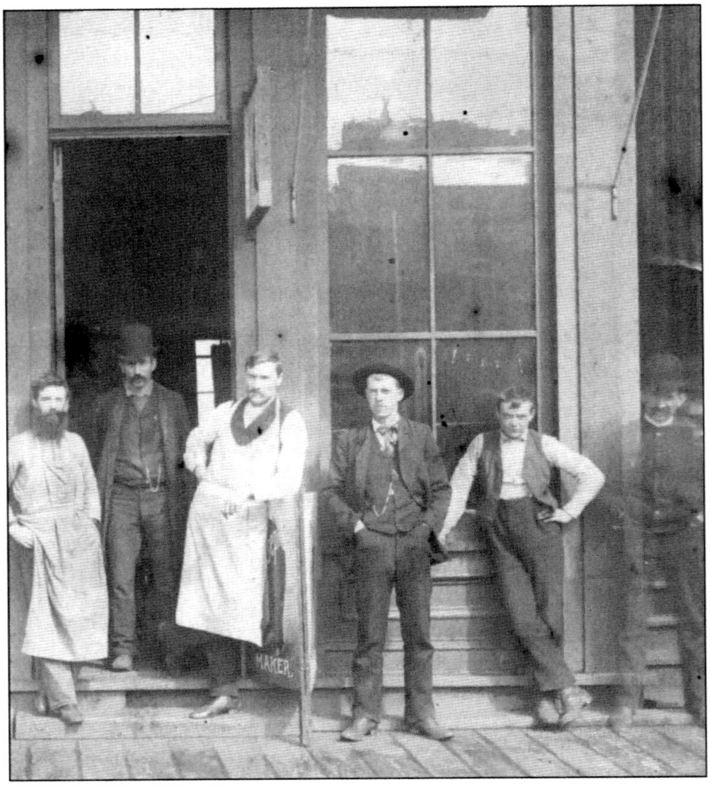

Bootmaker's Shop. This c. 1896 photograph shows Thomas Josephson's boot-and-shoemaking shop that was located at 628 Commercial Street. Josephson moved to this location from Seventh Street. (CRMM No. 030-131.)

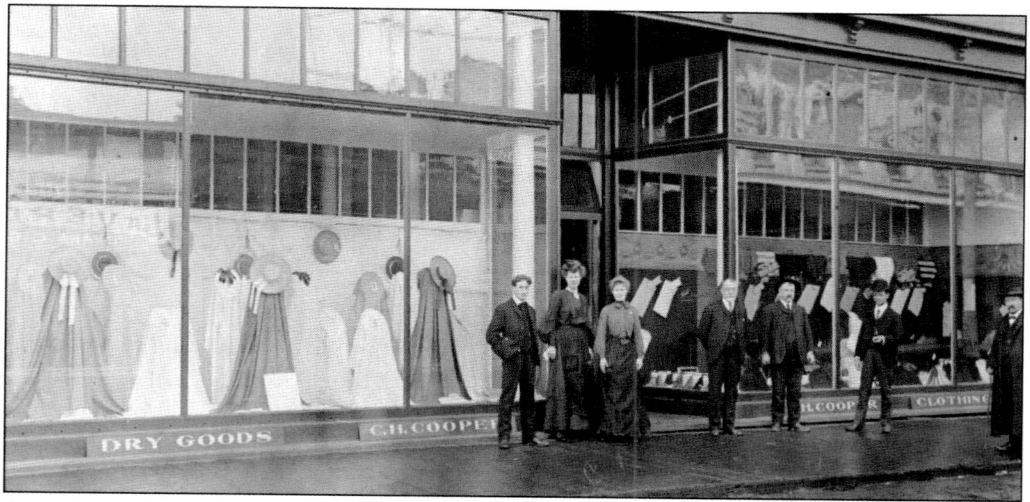

C.H. Cooper's Dry Goods. In addition to dry goods, Cooper sold clothing and furnishings. As with many shops, Cooper's store moved locations. Before it was at this address at 529–533 Commercial it was at 517, 519, 521 on Third Street. In the window at the far left of this c. 1902 photograph, the words "La Verd" are barely visible—part of a sign that was displayed at Will Madison's tobacco shop across the street. (CRMM No. 030-165.)

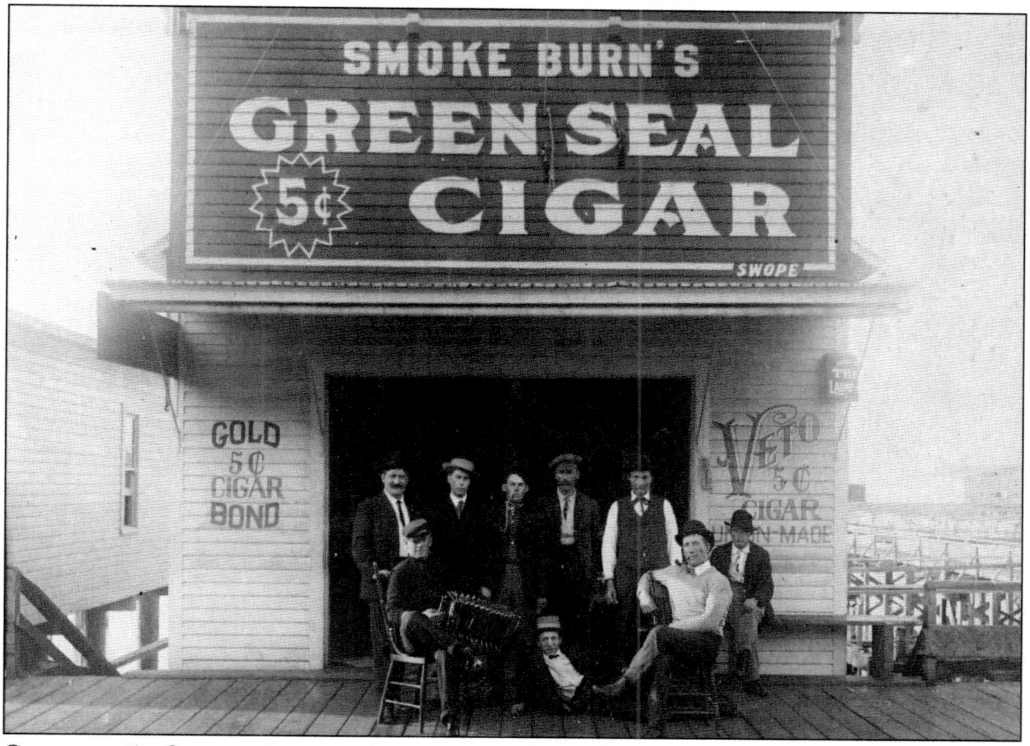

Choice of 5¢ Cigars. A group of men pose in front of John "Jack" Orjala's cigar store in this c. 1906 Frank Woodfield photograph. The shop, located at 1352 Franklin Street (present-day Marine Drive between Twenty-Ninth and Thirtieth Streets), displays an advertisement for local cigar manufacturer J.V. Burn's Green Seal Cigar. In the distance on the right are the net-drying racks of the Columbia River Packers Association fishing depot. On the left of the photograph, one can see how the buildings stood on pilings over the river. (Woodfield collection.)

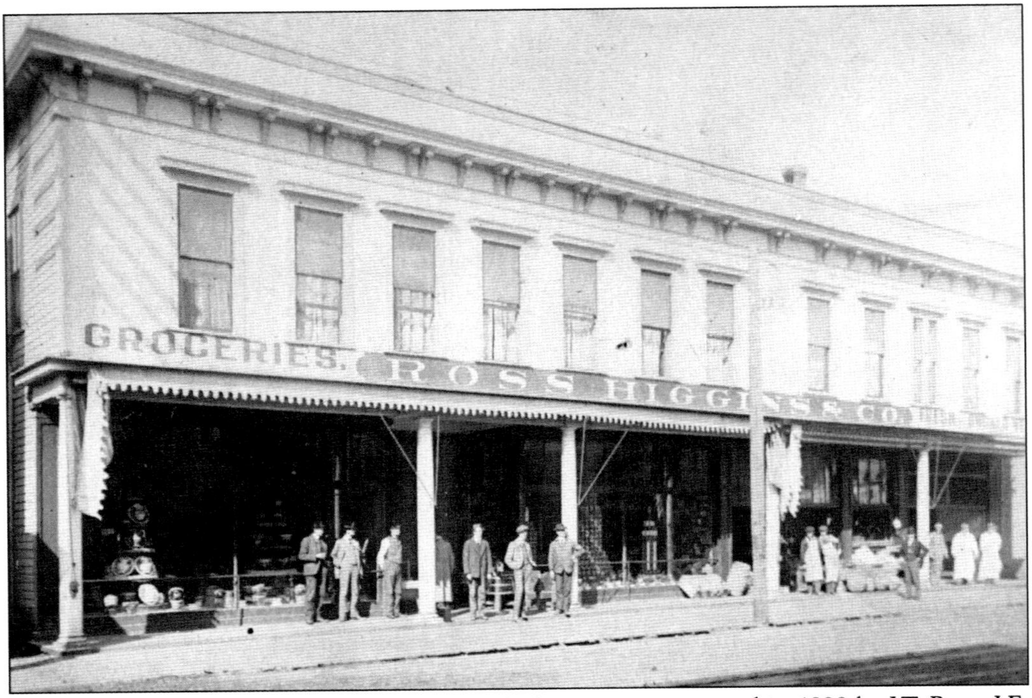

Ross, Higgins & Co., 1906. Ross, Higgins & Co. was incorporated in 1898 by J.T. Ross, J.E. Higgins, H.C. Thompson, E.Z. Ferguson, and C.B. Harden. The building seen here in 1906 was located at 530–542 Bond Street. The business sold groceries and meats. (Woodfield collection.)

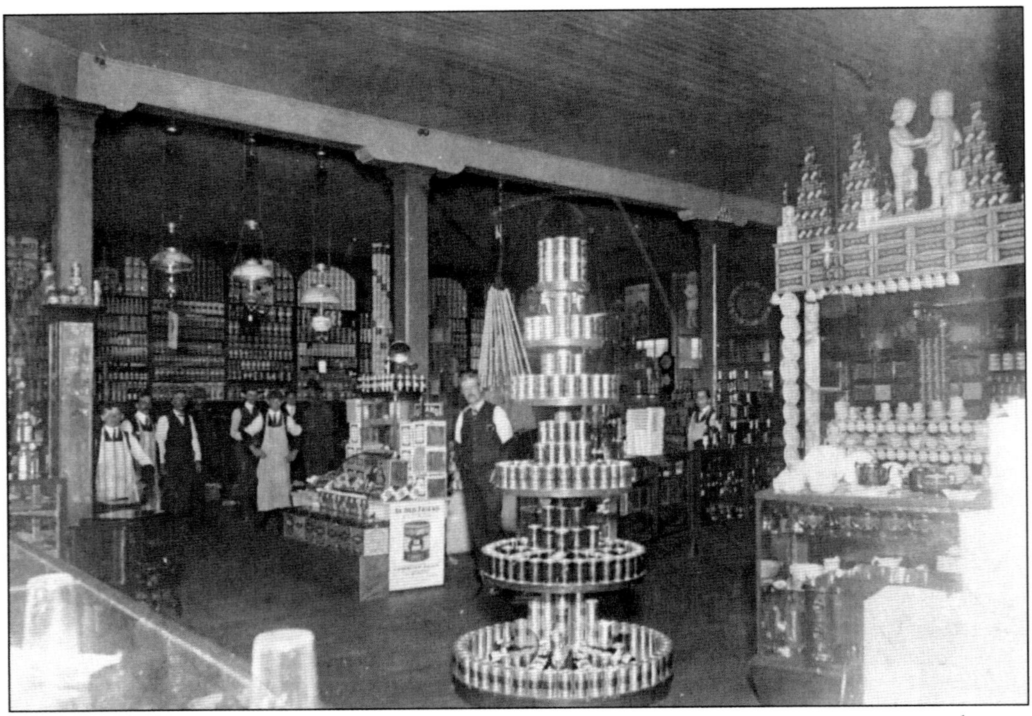

Interior. This interior shot of Ross, Higgins & Co. was also taken in 1906. It is a rare glimpse into the everyday world of the time. (Woodfield collection.)

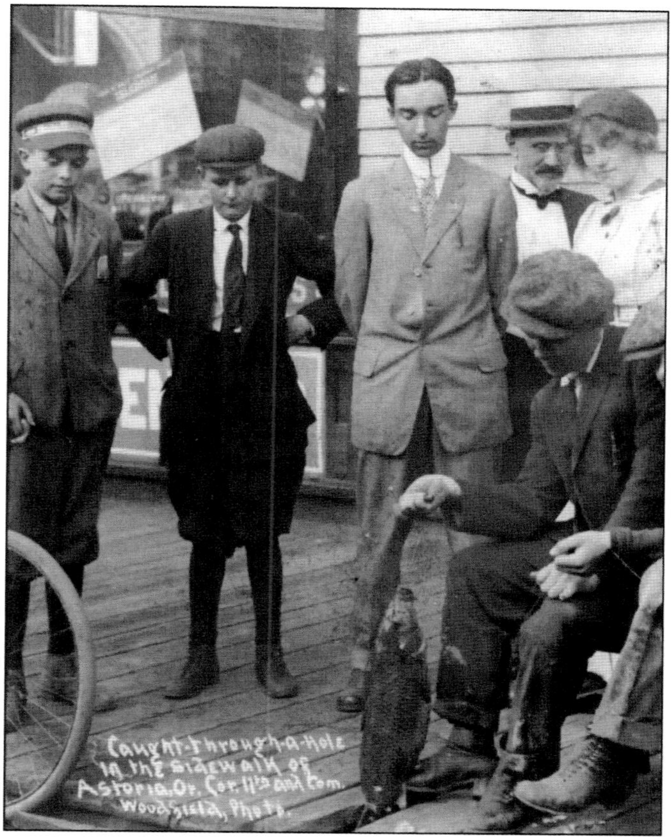

Iconic Image. One of Frank Woodfield's best-known Astoria photographs was taken in 1912 and depicts lucky fisherman Elihu Vasbinder with a three-pound carp he caught through a hole in the sidewalk. Taken in front of the Postal Telegraph, the image includes, from left to right, telegraph messengers Ragnor Johnson and Fritz Peterson, telegraph operator Basil Locke, and Elihu Vasbinder. Mayor Herman Wise stands behind Locke, and Margaret Ross stands behind the seated Elihu, who is next to Bryan Ross. (CRMM No. 030-129.)

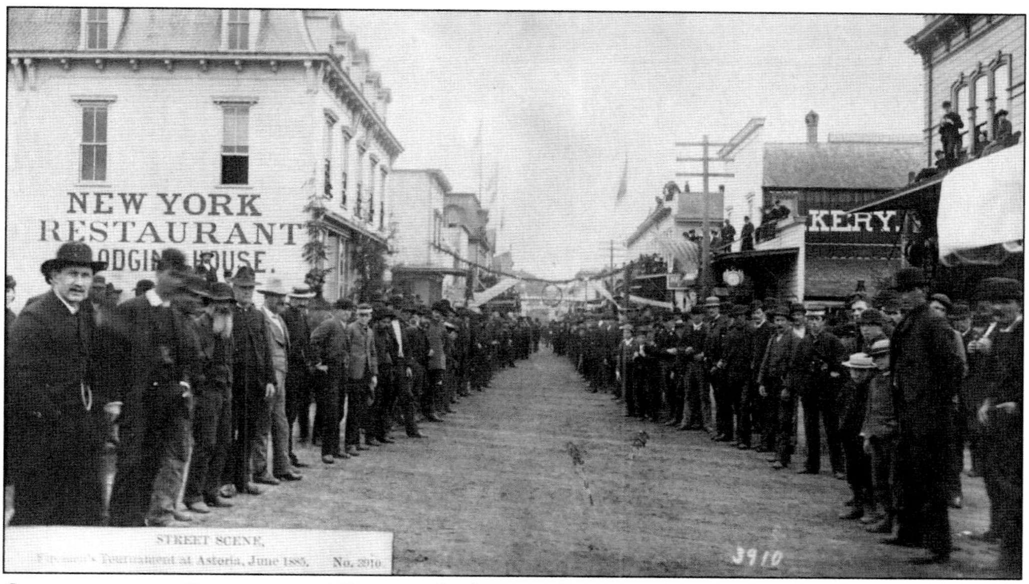

Commercial on Commercial. This view looks west down Commercial Street from Twelfth Street in June 1885. The New York Restaurant and Lodging House on the left was advertised as a new business in the newspaper on January 31, 1885. Across the street is a bakery. Grocers, clothiers, milliners, barbers, jewelers, tobacconists, and saloons were all to be found on Commercial Street. (Woodfield collection.)

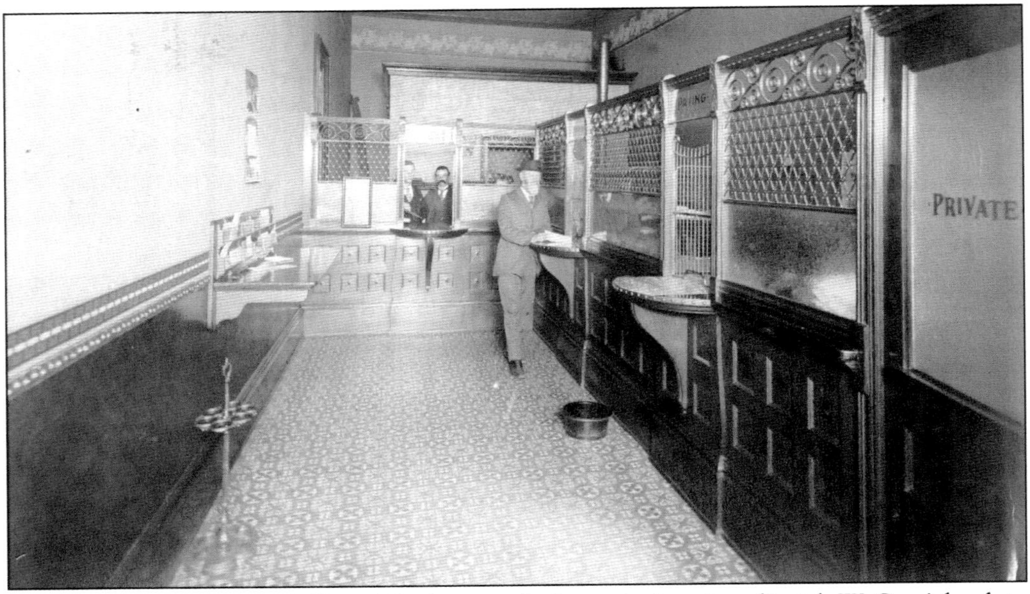

I.W. Case Bank Interior. This 1888 photograph shows the interior of Isaiah W. Case's bank in the International Order of Odd Fellows building at Cass (Tenth) and Squemoqua (Commercial) Streets around 1888. An advertisement in the 1889 Polk Directory for Portland announced that I.W. Case does a "general banking business" with "collections a specialty." The bank failed in 1893, and Case went into the insurance business. (CRMM No. 030-17598.)

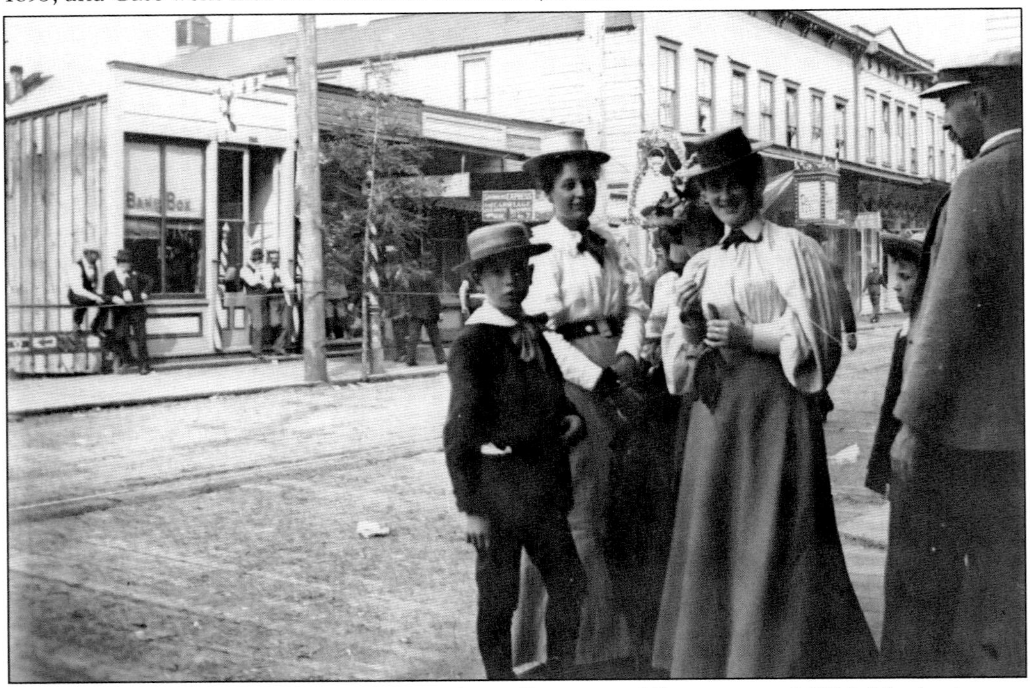

Out and About. A group poses engagingly on Commercial Street around 1896. The businesses on the opposite side of the street, from left to right, are the Band Box Shaving Parlor, unidentified, H.W. Sherman Transfer Company, boot maker Fred Walters, Jack's Cigar Store, the Palace Restaurant, the dressmaking store of Mrs. P.M. Thiel, and Larson and Hillback Grocers. (CRMM No. 420-17260.)

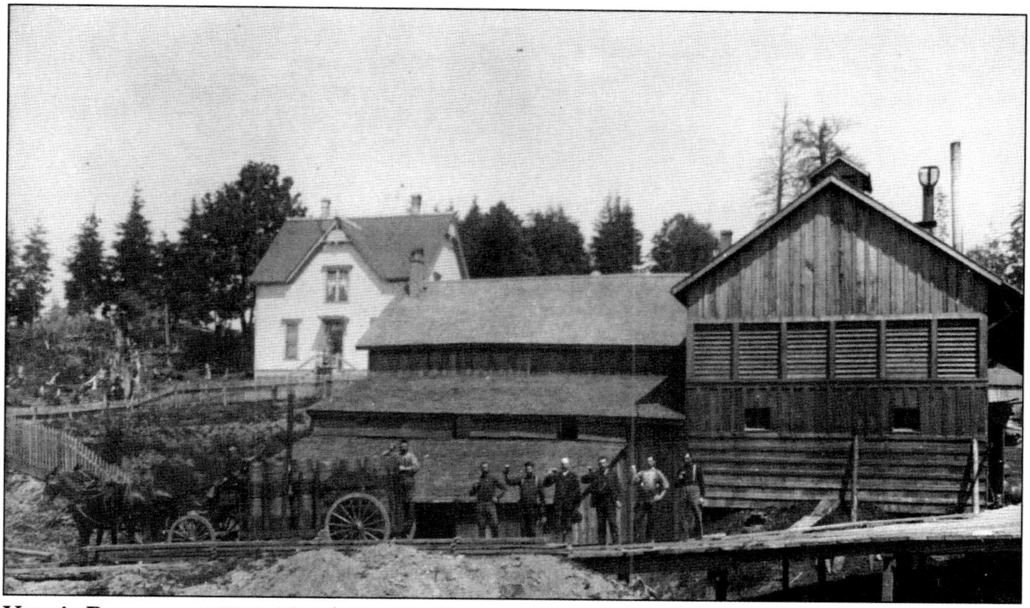

Kopp's Brewery, 1890. North Pacific Brewery employees pose with glasses of beer in hand for this 1890 photograph. Pictured from left to right are driver Nels Simonson, his son Chris (seated on kegs), unidentified, Louis Bosshart, John Kopp (owner), Jake Bosshart (brewmaster), Al Seafeldt, and two unidentified. This Uppertown brewery, established in 1884, was located on Thirty-Fourth Street between Grand and Harrison Streets. Behind the brewery was the Kopp home. (Woodfield collection.)

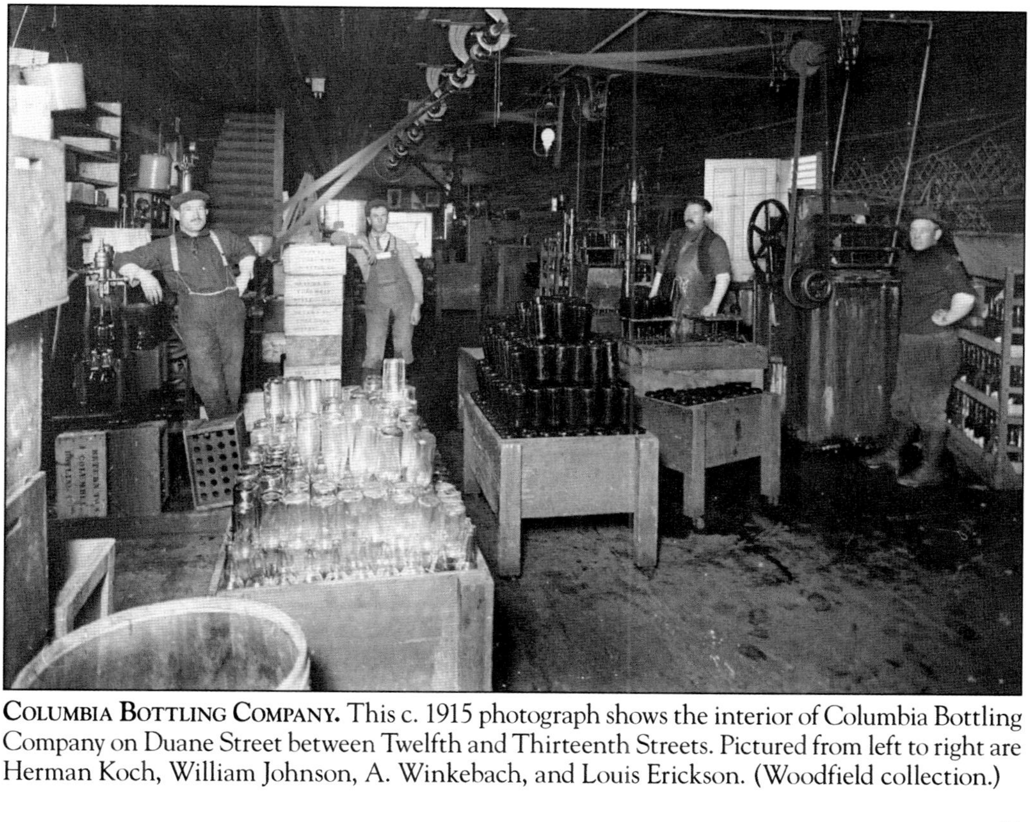

Columbia Bottling Company. This c. 1915 photograph shows the interior of Columbia Bottling Company on Duane Street between Twelfth and Thirteenth Streets. Pictured from left to right are Herman Koch, William Johnson, A. Winkebach, and Louis Erickson. (Woodfield collection.)

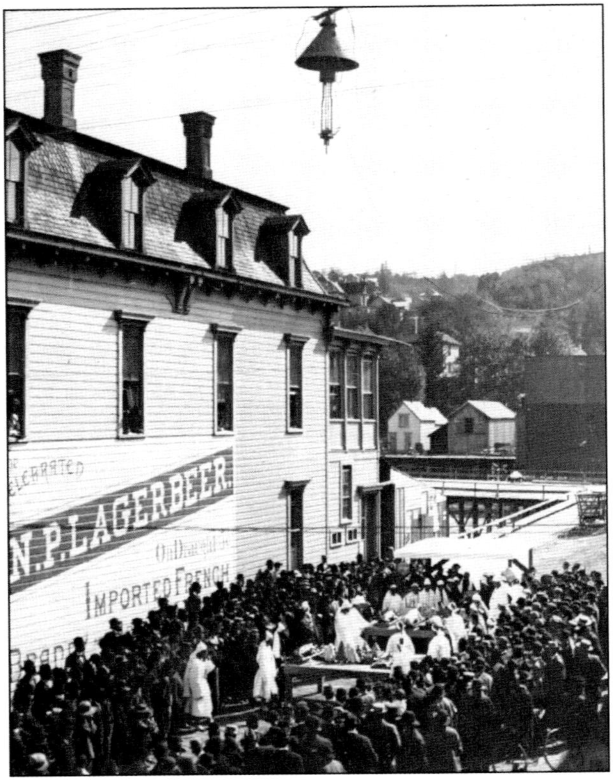

CHINESE FUNERAL PREPARATIONS, 1892. This 1892 photograph shows a crowd gathering to watch professional Chinese mourners, who are dressed in white gowns and making preparations for a burial. The image was taken on the corner of Twelfth and Commercial Streets. On the top of the image is a close-up of one of Astoria's arc lights, which were provided and powered by J.D. Trullinger and were said to have bathed the streets with a brilliant white light at nighttime. The building with the gabled mansard roof is the Cosmopolitan Saloon, which was built on pilings over the tidal flat. (Woodfield collection.)

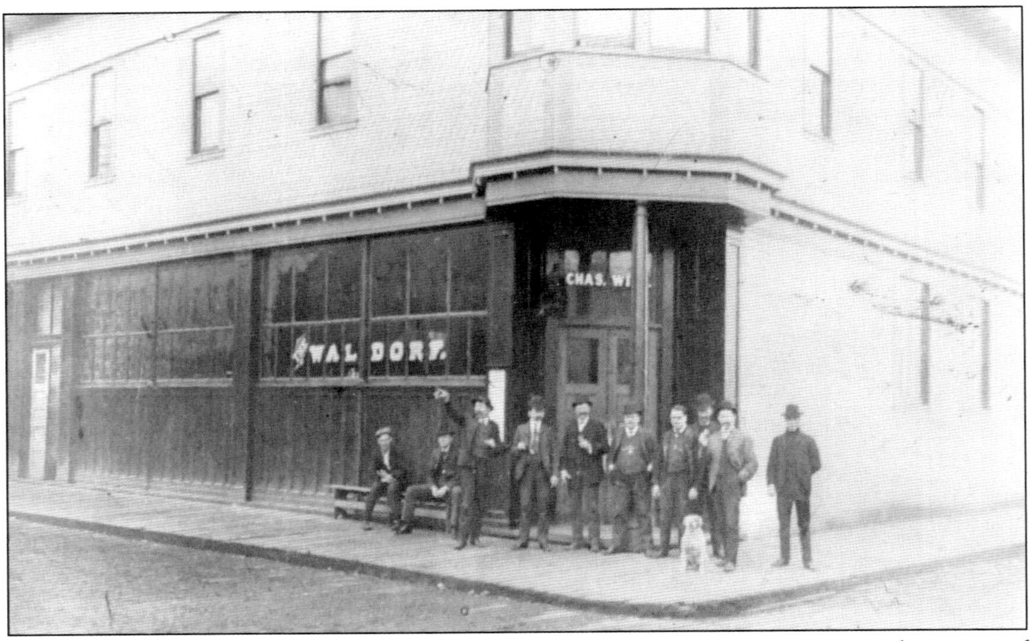

WALDORF SALOON. Charles Wise owned the Waldorf Saloon, seen here in 1907 on the corner of Eighth and Astor Streets. It was only one of several he owned. His Wigwam Saloon had attached female boarding where the ladies could "entertain" gentlemen. Astor Street between Fifth and Tenth Streets had earned the name "swill town" because of the concentration of saloons in the area during the 1870s and 1880s. (CRMM No. 420-17327.)

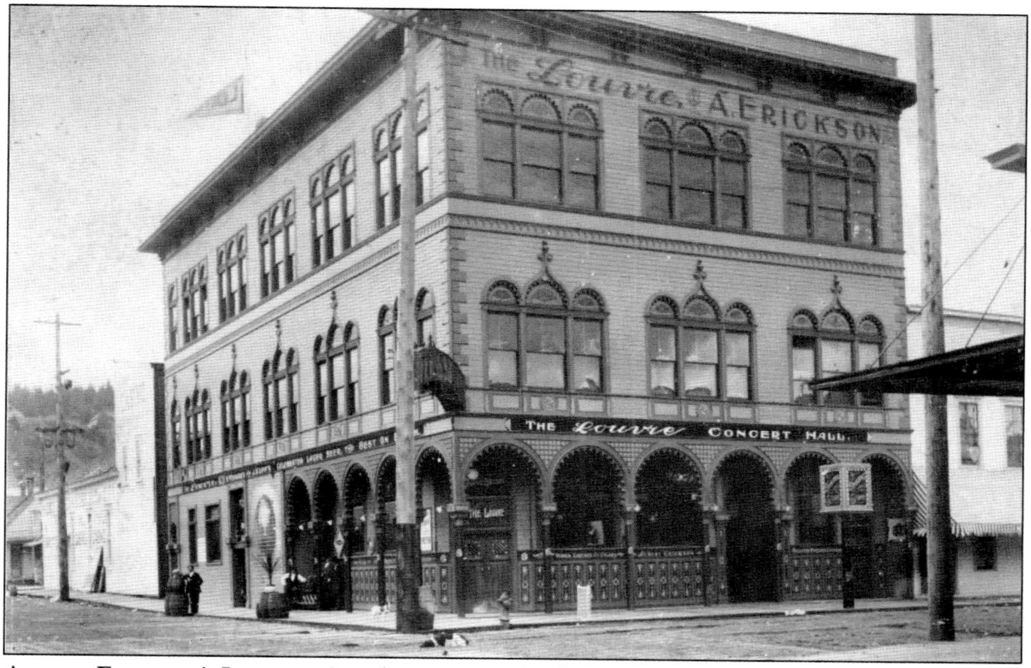

AUGUST ERICKSON'S LOUVRE. An advertisement for the Louvre Concert Hall in the 1896 Astoria Directory claimed that the Louvre was the "finest and best appointed resort in the city." The *Daily Morning Astorian* seemed to agree, reporting that the Louvre was "the most elegant drinking place in Astoria." August Erickson opened his three-story entertainment hall at the corner of Seventh and Astor Streets in April 1896 to great success. The Casino, directly behind the Louvre, is actually a theater. The building at Seventh and Bond Streets was originally constructed as a liberty or spiritual hall around 1867 and served as Astoria's first meeting place. (CRMM No. 030-225.)

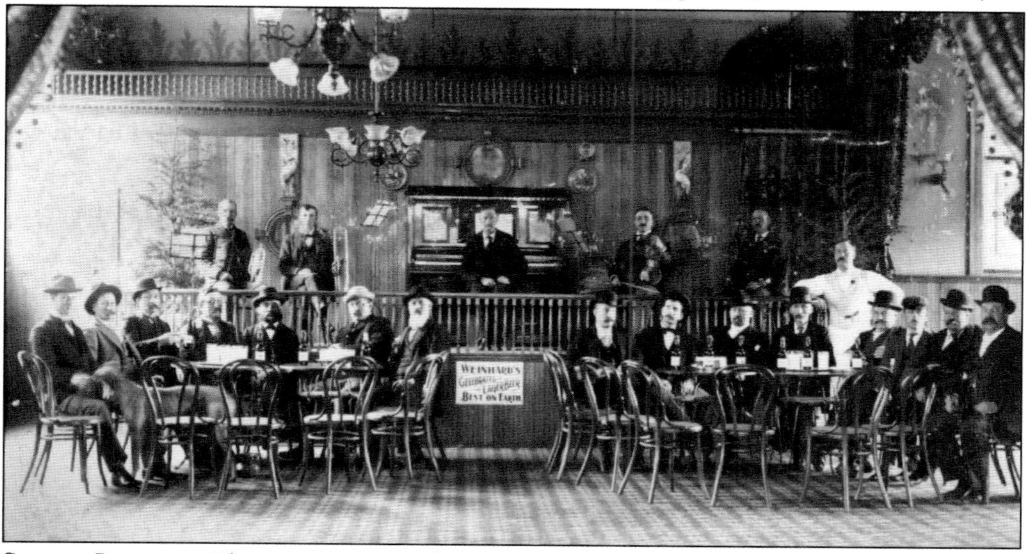

SALOON INTERIOR. This interior view is believed to be from the Louvre, which was reported to have a mezzanine on the third floor. The entertainment hall had pool, billiards, and clubrooms and offered two bars, music, dancing, and even skating. In the photograph, musicians sit on a stage with a sign advertising Weinhard's Beer, one of two beers the bar carried. The other was the local North Pacific Beer. (CRMM No. 420-13243.)

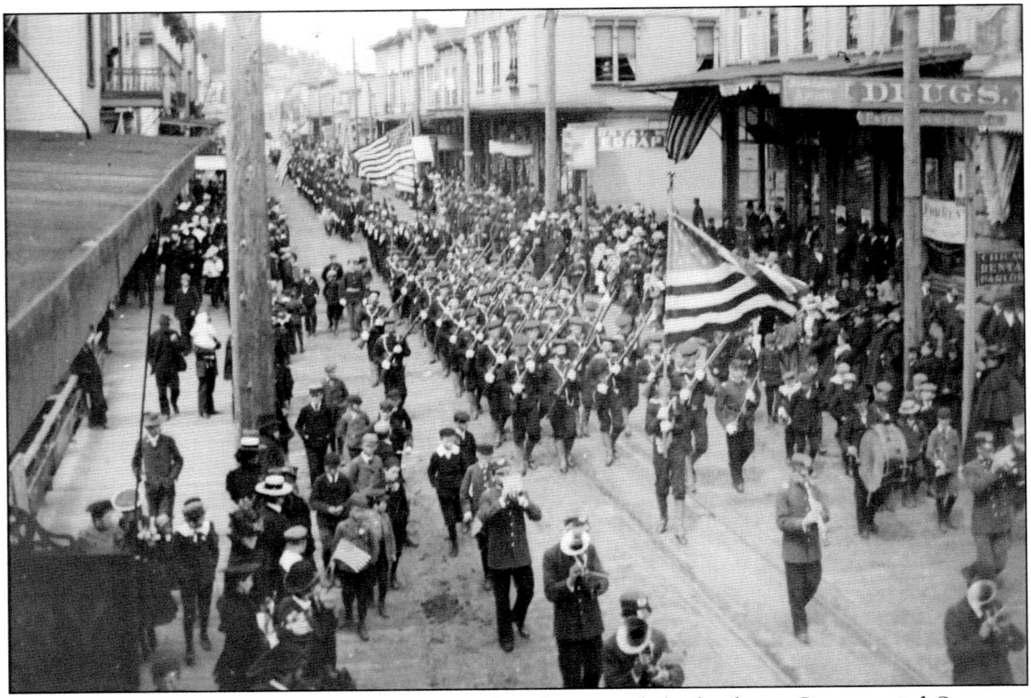

Naval Militia, Second Division, 1898. This photograph looks down Commercial Street at Twelfth Street. The 2nd Division of the Oregon National Guard Naval Militia is about to pass. It was formed during the Spanish-American War and was comprised of many local young men. The Postal Telegraph office near the center right of the photograph is where many of the "fish caught through the sidewalk" images were taken. (CRMM No. 030-169.)

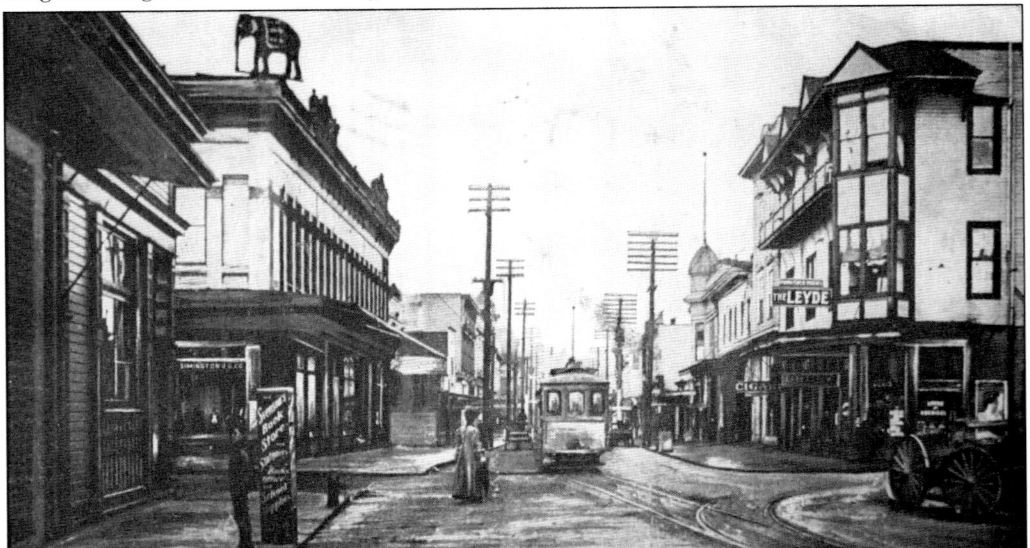

Looking West on Commercial Street, c. 1908. This postcard image dates to around 1908 and shows Commercial Street looking west from Fourteenth Street. The electric trolley provides an interesting contrast with the wagons. On the corner of the closest building on the left of the photograph is Swan Wilson's Saloon. Across Fourteenth Street is the Foard and Stokes Hardware Company, with its distinctive elephant on the roof. (Woodfield collection.)

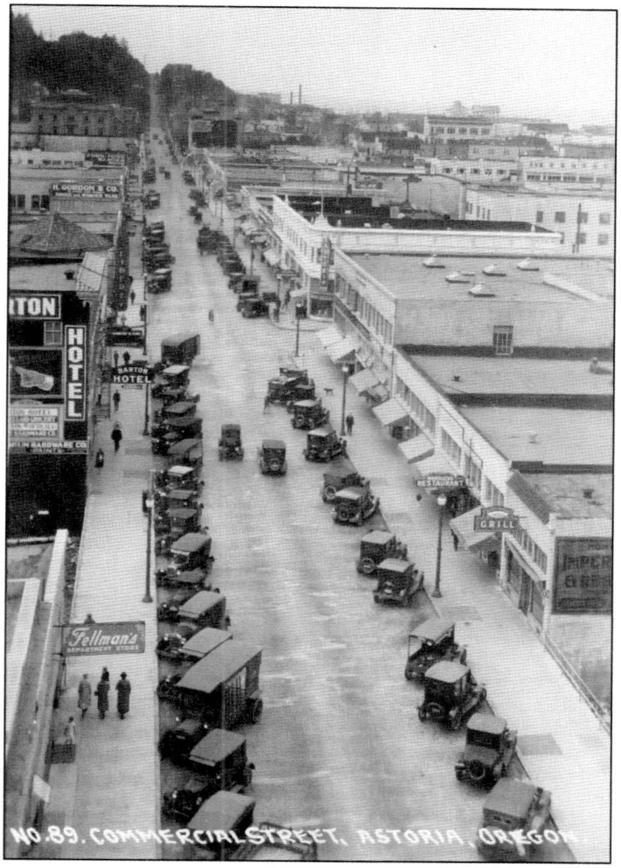

COMMERCIAL STREET FROM ABOVE, C. 1926. This photograph was taken from an upper floor of the new Astoria Hotel looking to the west down Commercial Street around 1926. This was taken four years after the fire. Note that the trolley tracks are missing. During this time, the city decided to run motor coaches instead of the trolleys, thereby bringing the streetcar era to an end. (Clemson collection No. 2011.1.)

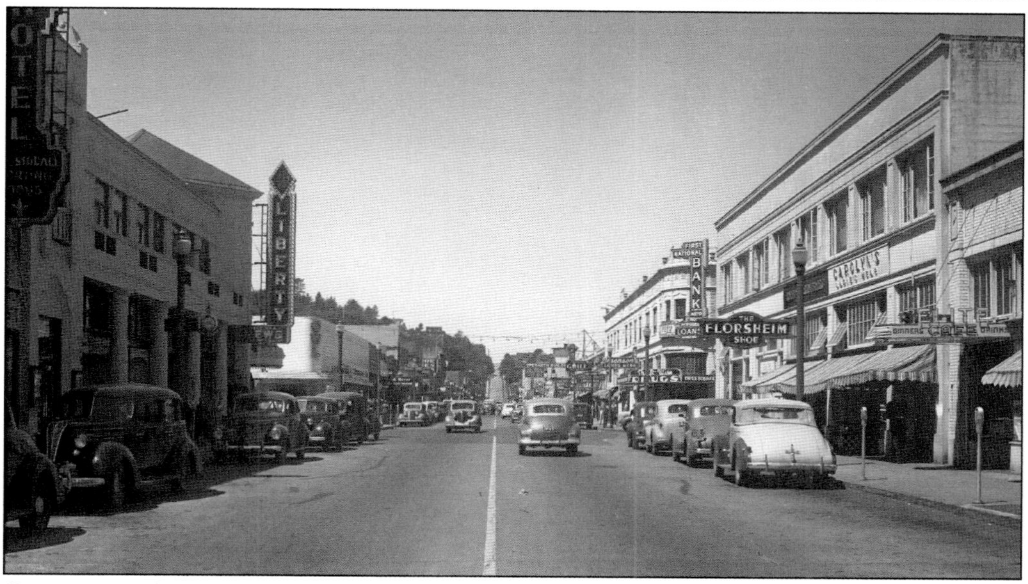

COMMERCIAL STREET LOOKING WEST, C. 1940. This street-level view is also looking west down Commercial Street, about 15 years later than the previous image. The Liberty Theater on the left looks today much like it does in the photograph thanks to efforts to restore the property. (Woodfield collection.)

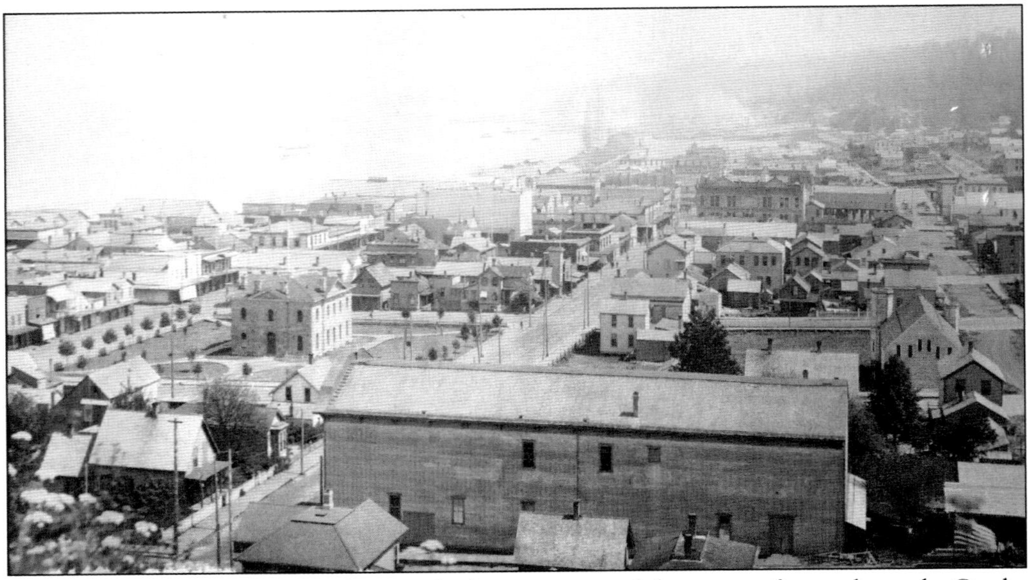

Ross Opera House, c. 1890. This view looking east toward the center of town shows the Crosby House on the lower left. The stone post office is above and to the right, the wooden county courthouse and county jail is farther right, and along the bottom of the image is a long building known as the Ross Opera House. It started out as an indoor skating rink, but in 1888 it was listed as the opera house. It remained as such until October 1892, when the structure burned and was torn down. In its place are two wooden, Italianate residential structures that were built soon after. Both are still standing and are unique to the city. (CRMM No. 030-455.)

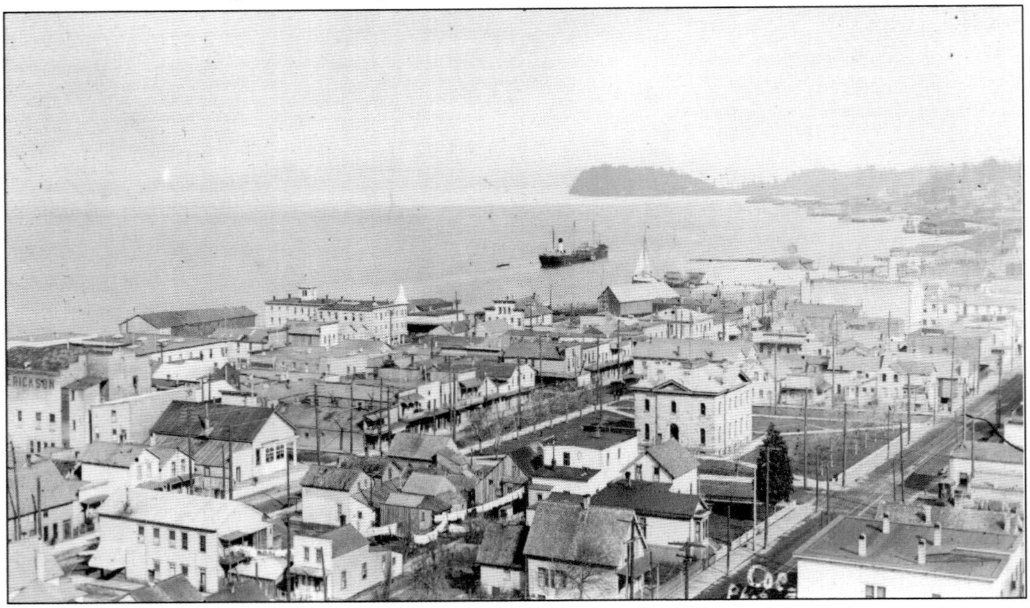

A View of Chinatown. This view looking toward Tongue Point shows Lower Astoria, the main business district, around 1898. The Crosby House is at the bottom center of the photograph, and the post office grounds are well established. Toward the river across from the post office is a street full of small buildings with awnings. Fronting along Bond Street, this block of small businesses and bunkhouses was occupied by Chinese. The Chinese population in Astoria was concentrated along Bond and Astor Streets. (Clemson collection No. 2011.1.)

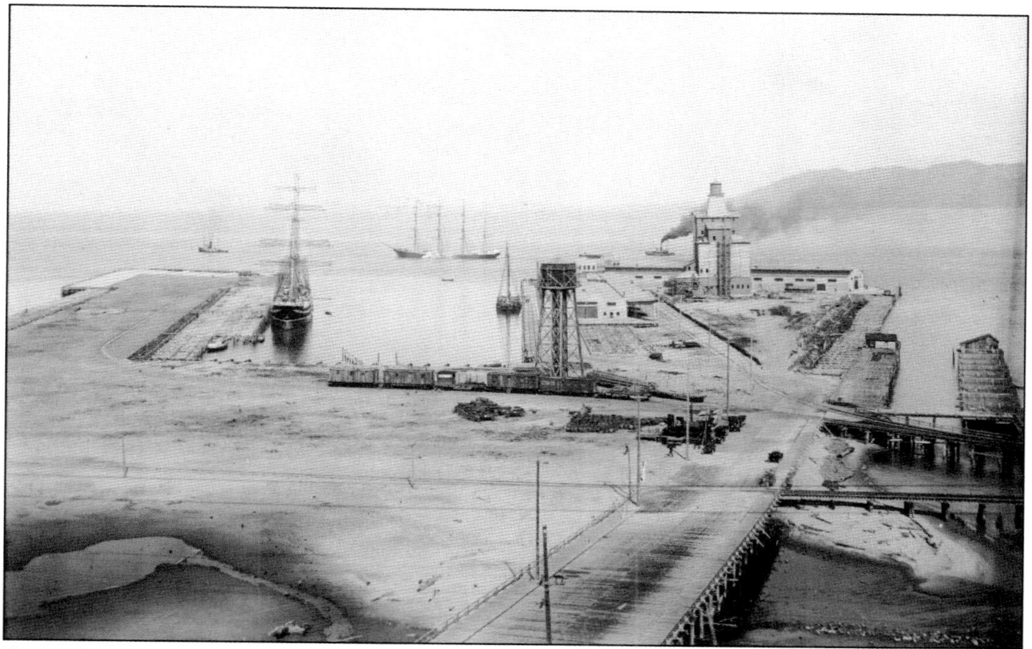

Early View of Port, c. 1917. Established at the west end of town in 1910, the Port of Astoria promoted the maritime and commercial interests of Clatsop County. This c. 1917 photograph shows the warehouse and flouring mill on Pier No. 1 as well as the spur railway lines servicing both piers. The flouring mill was expanded and in continuous use until the 1970s. It was later deemed structurally unsound and was demolished (with great difficulty) in the 1980s. (CRMM No. 036-19513.)

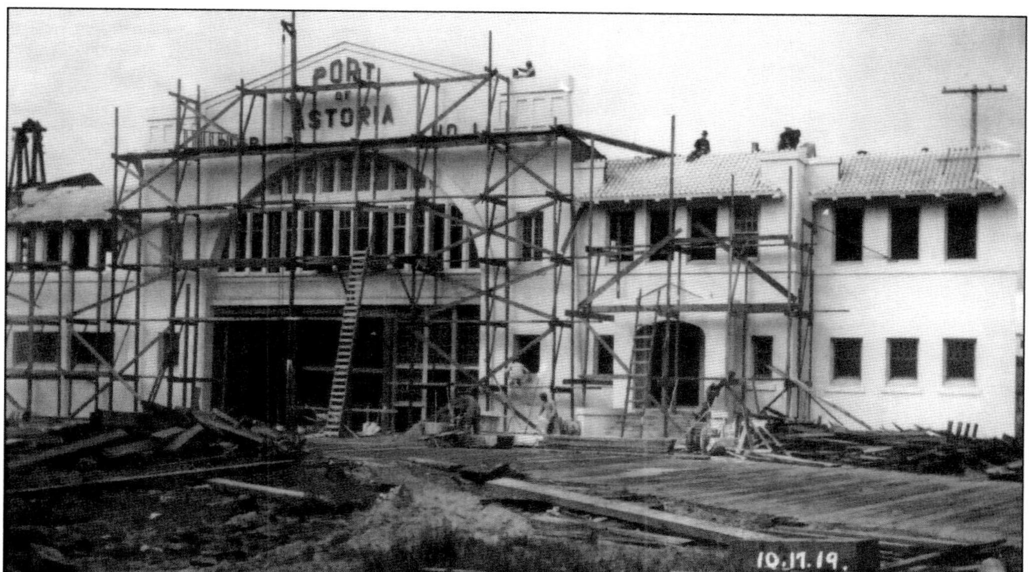

Construction of Pier No. 1. A larger and more imposing warehouse and office building was constructed in 1919 on Pier No. 1. This building was in use until the early 1990s, when it was deemed unsafe and demolished. (CRMM No. 036-19506.)

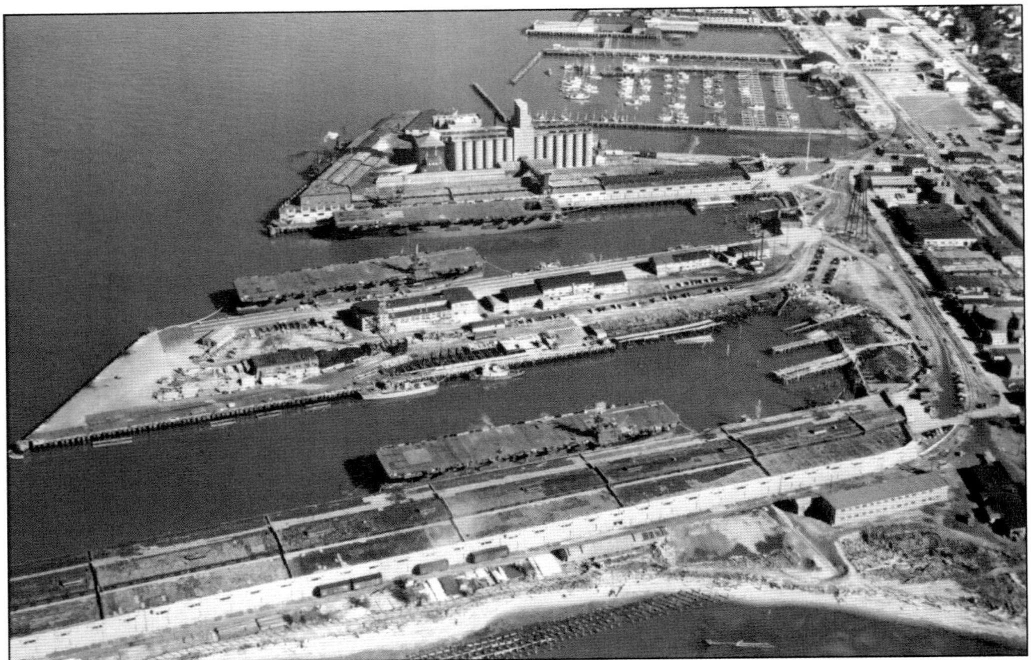

Baby Flattops at the Port, 1944. This photograph shows the Astoria Port docks with the escort carriers *Savo Island* (CVE 78), *Ommaney Bay* (CVE 79), and *Petrof Bay* (CVE 80). They are being fitted out and made ready for combat. The Kaiser Shipyards in Vancouver, Washington, and Portland, Oregon, upriver from Astoria constructed 50 of these vessels for the Navy during World War II. (CRMM No. 036-801.)

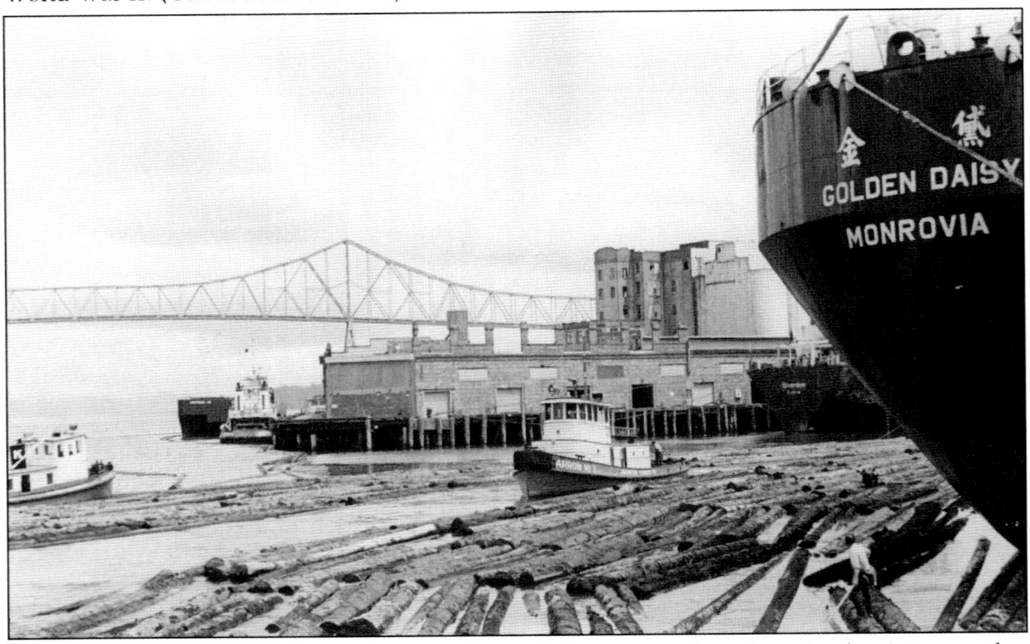

Exporting Logs at the Port. Growing demand for raw wood products in the Asian market during the last quarter of the 20th century provided lucrative business for the Port of Astoria until 1996, when market factors forced the practice to end. In 2010, log exporting to Asia resumed with Oregon logs being sent to Korea. (CRMM No. 291-5795.)

Four

Getting Around Town

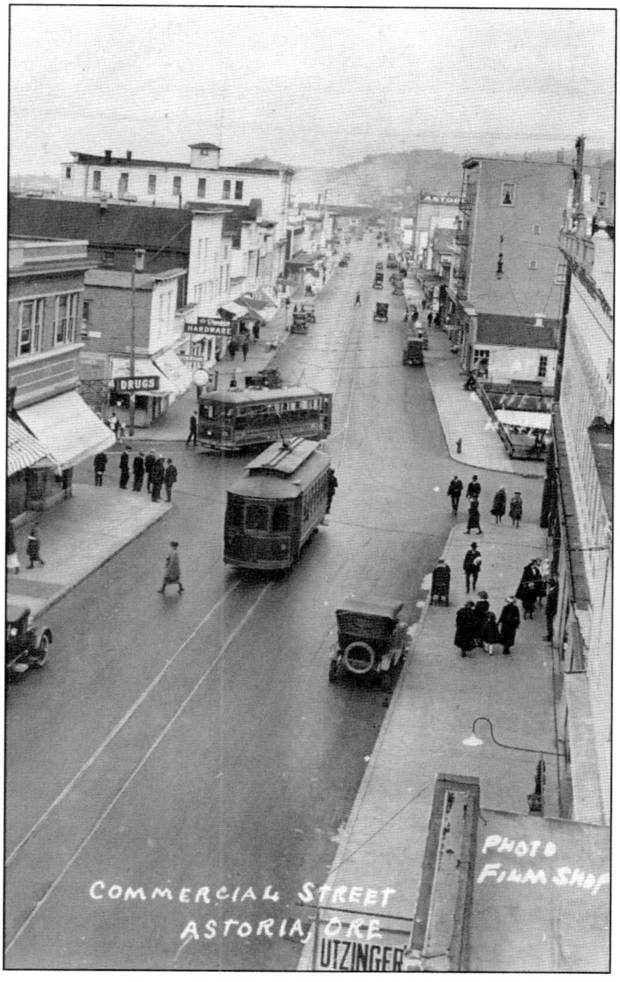

Electricity Drives Streetcars East on Commercial. Astoria's street railway started in 1888 as a horse drawn system. In 1892, the trolleys were converted to run on electricity. From 1904 to 1920, additional electric trolleys were added to the system. The two cars seen in this postcard image from around 1921 are No. 15 (turning the corner at Fourteenth Street) and No. 8 (traveling east down Commercial Street). Trolley service was discontinued when the city brought in a bus line in 1924. (Woodfield collection.)

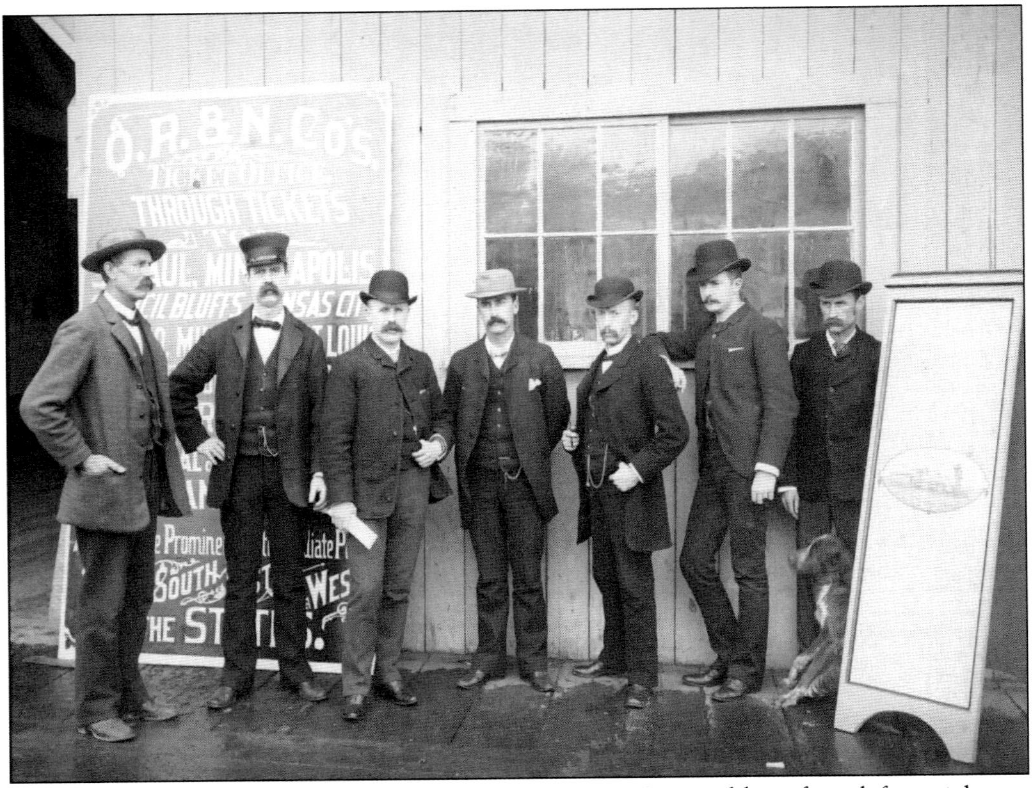

Oregon Railway and Navigation Company, c. 1897. Pictured here from left to right are baggage master John Erickson, receiving clerk A.V. Pendleton, Fred Hewaft, superintendent of Astoria Street Railway F.W. Newell, general agent G.W. Lounsberry, L.W. Garretson, and E.A. Noyes. The Oregon Railway and Navigation Company (OR&N) bought out the former Oregon Steam Navigation Company and continued to link the fertile inland empire with the markets of Portland downriver to Astoria and the world. (CRMM No. 420-9462.)

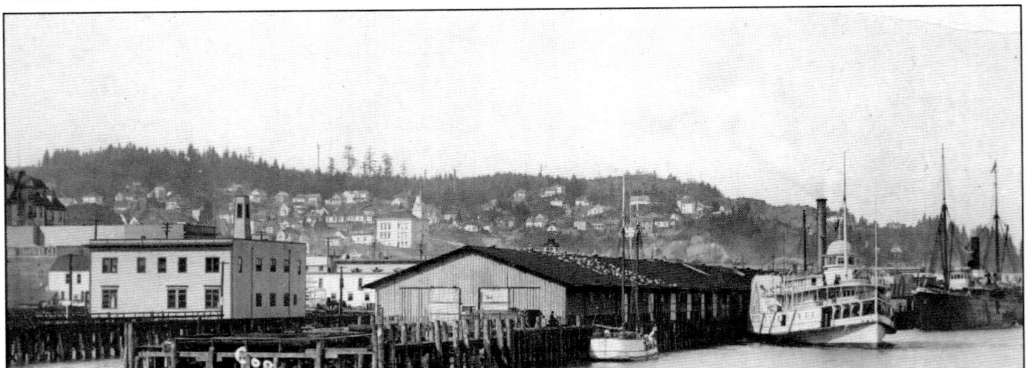

The OR&N Dock, c. 1897. The OR&N Company dock was right in the heart of town at the foot of Seventeenth Street. This was a main hub of transportation that provided access to oceangoing ships, river steamers, and eventually, rail. To the left of the dock is the main fire station, with McClure School visible in the distance on the hill. The sidewheel steamer *T.J. Potter* is just leaving the dock. (CRMM No. 033-16583.)

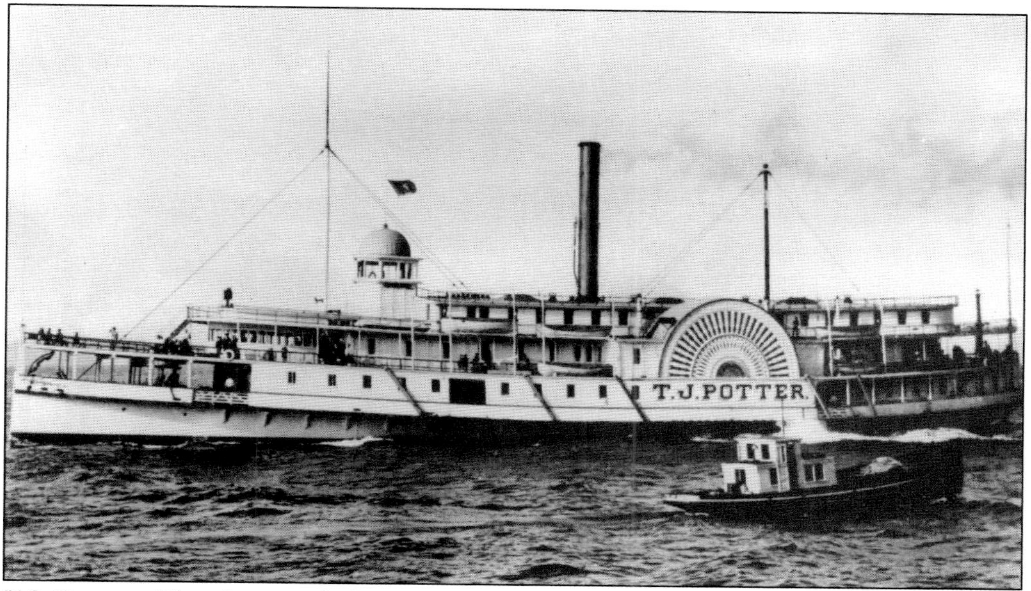

T.J. POTTER. This photograph shows the *T.J. Potter* passing Astoria sometime after 1901. This fast and luxurious boat, the pride of the OR&N Company, made daily runs between Portland and Astoria. It was said that only the best brandy, whiskey, wines, cigars, mixed drinks, and cocktails came across her towel-swiped, mahogany bar. (CRMM No. 566-12689.)

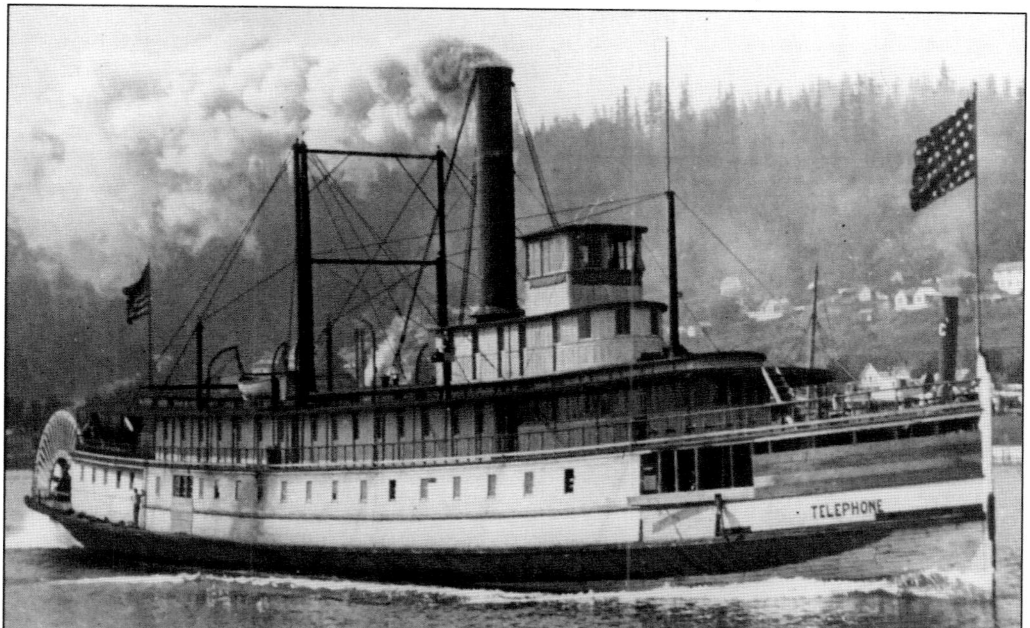

TELEPHONE. The sternwheeler *Telephone* launched on October 30, 1884. On November 20, 1887, on a run to Astoria, the steamboat caught fire. Capt. U.B. Scott beached her at water's edge in Upper Astoria. Through the heroic efforts of Astoria's volunteer fire department, her hull and rigging were saved. Captain Scott showed his appreciation by donating money for the volunteers to buy a team of horses to pull the firefighting apparatus. Up to that point, the apparatus had been pulled by hand. After a rebuild in 1888, the *Telephone* was back on the Astoria run. (CRMM No. 570-13292.)

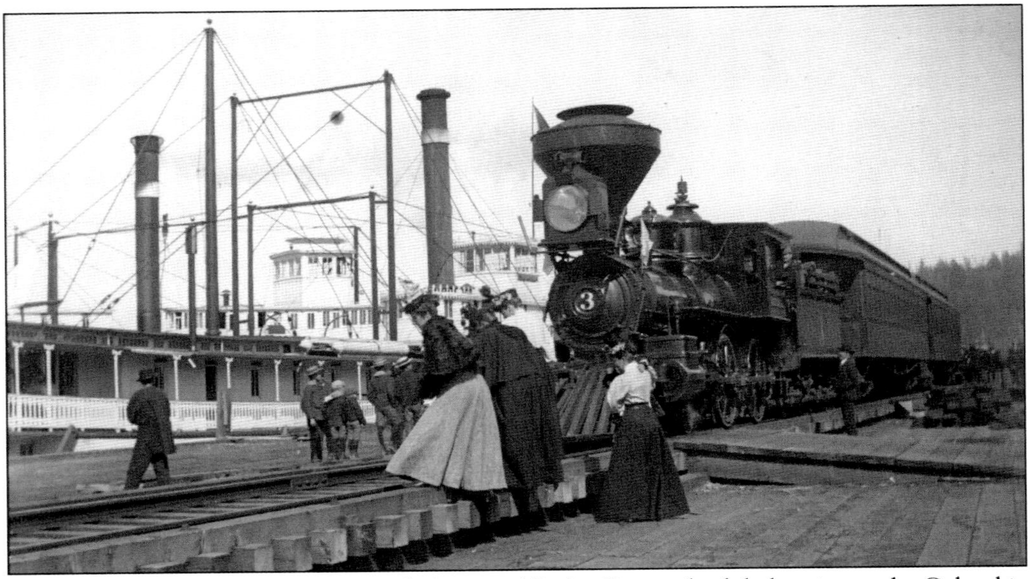

By River and Rail, c. 1900. The *Telephone* and *Bailey Gatzert*, both belonging to the Columbia River and Puget Sound Navigation Company, are seen docked here at Astoria around 1899. The two steamers made daily runs between Astoria and Portland. Passengers would transfer to the Astoria and Columbia River Railroad train at Astoria to head south along the coast to Seaside and Tillamook. The completion of the connection to the Northern Pacific Railway in 1898 provided passengers with an alternative choice for travel. (CRMM No. 570-12995.)

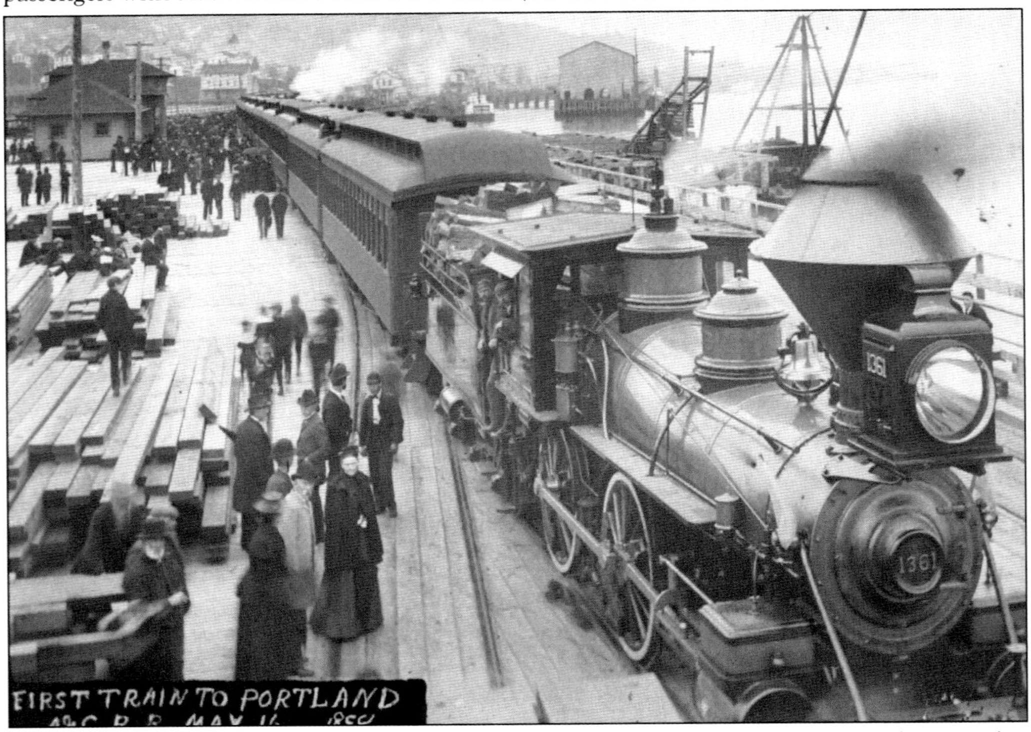

First Train. The opening of the line between Astoria and Portland was celebrated on April 4, 1898, but the first train (shown in this photograph) did not run until May 16. Some 700 people rode the train that day to celebrate its inaugural run. (Woodfield collection.)

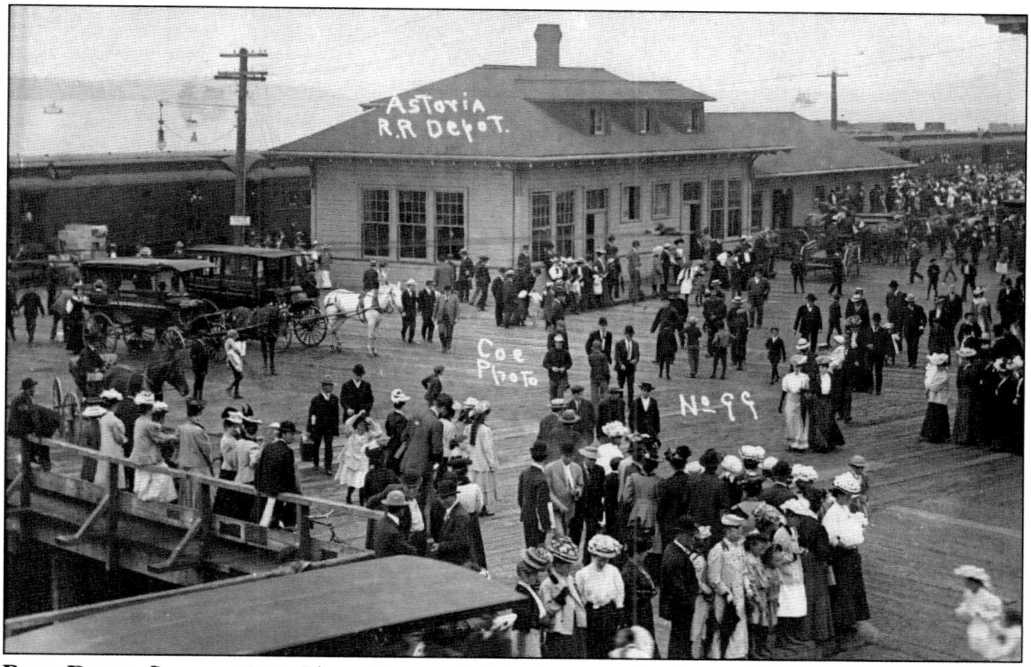

Busy Depot Scene, 1907. Elmer Coe took this photograph of townspeople and arriving train passengers as they gathered at the railroad depot to catch a glimpse of the vice president. Charles W. Fairbanks, vice president under Pres. Theodore Roosevelt, visited Astoria in July 1907. Images taken later in the day show Vice President Fairbanks and his wife riding in a motorized vehicle at this same location. (Woodfield collection.).

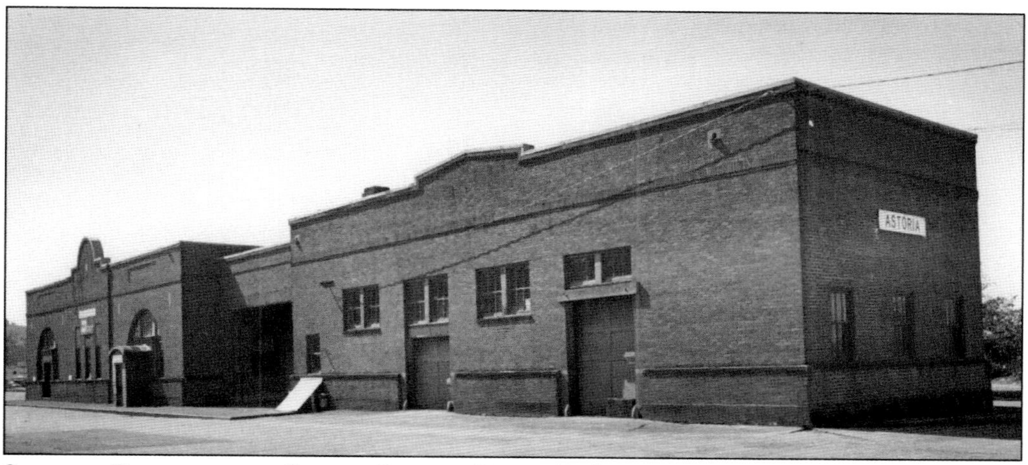

Spokane, Portland, and Seattle Railway Depot. Built in 1925 to replace the wooden structure that burned in the 1922 fire, this brick structure served freight and passenger trains until 1970, when the Spokane, Portland, and Seattle Railway (SP&S) merged with Burlington Northern Railroad. In 1987, Burlington Northern Inc. donated the property to the Columbia River Maritime Museum. The structure is one of only two SP&S depot buildings still in existence. Currently, the museum is exploring means to restore the property. (Larry Gilmore photo, CRMM collection.)

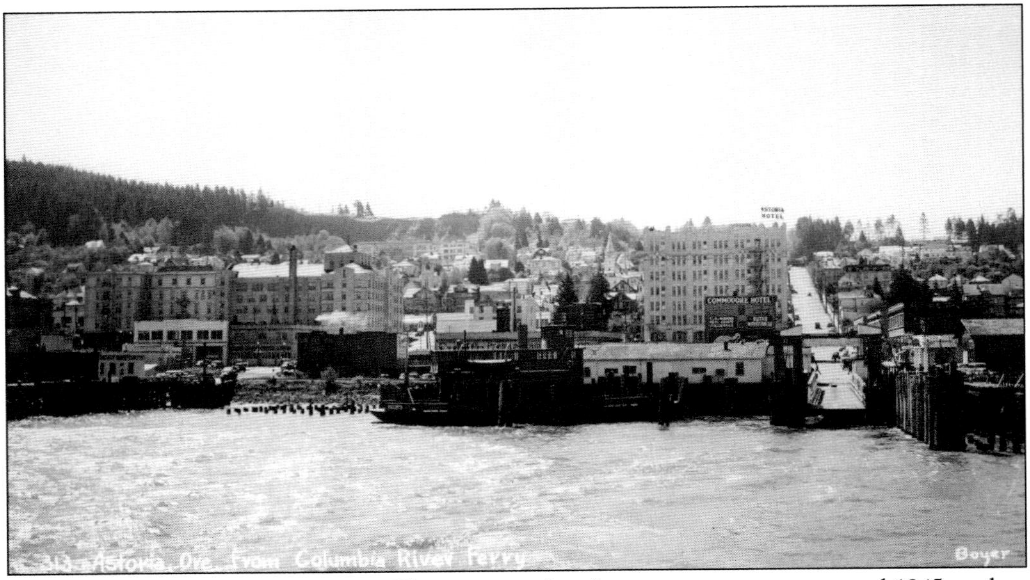

FOURTEENTH STREET FERRY DOCK. This view is what ferry passengers saw around 1945 as they left Astoria for the Washington shore and points north. In the center of the photograph in the shadows is the *Tourist No. 2*. Ferry service was the only means across the Columbia for vehicles until the bridge was completed in 1966. (Clemson collection No. 2011.1.)

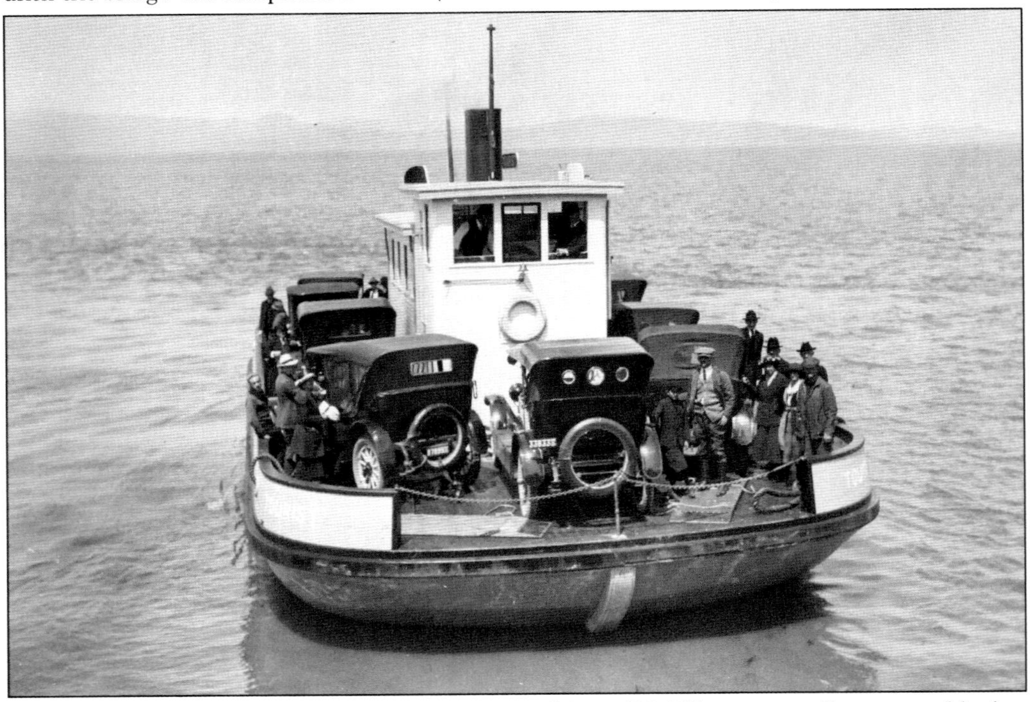

***TOURIST*, 1921.** The automobile was here to stay, and Capt. F.S. Elfving was willing to gamble that more people would travel to the area to make a scheduled ferry service profitable. He commissioned Wilson Shipbuilding Company to build his first boat. The *Tourist*—pictured here on her May 1921 maiden crossing from Astoria, Oregon, to McGowan, Washington—became the first car ferry to traverse the Columbia River at its mouth. A group of Model T Ford enthusiasts motored down for the first ride. (Woodfield collection.)

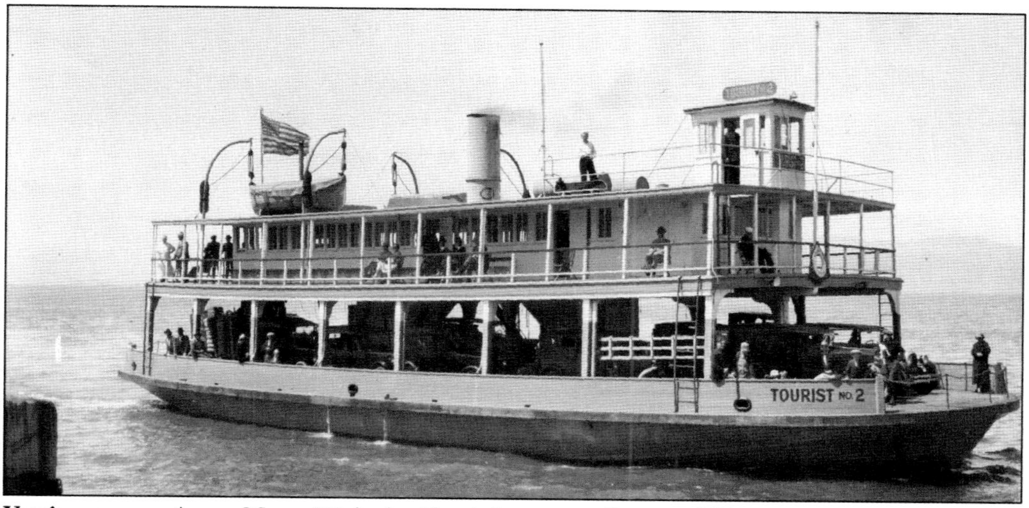

YOU'RE IN THE ARMY NOW. With the *Tourist's* success, Captain Elfving commissioned Wilson Shipbuilding Company to build a second ferryboat in 1924, and he fittingly named it the *Tourist No. 2*. It served its original purpose until war was declared in 1941 and it was pressed into service as a minelayer and tender at the mouth of the Columbia River. Renamed the *Octopus*, she served in that capacity until the end of the war, at which time she was converted back for ferry service. (Woodfield collection.)

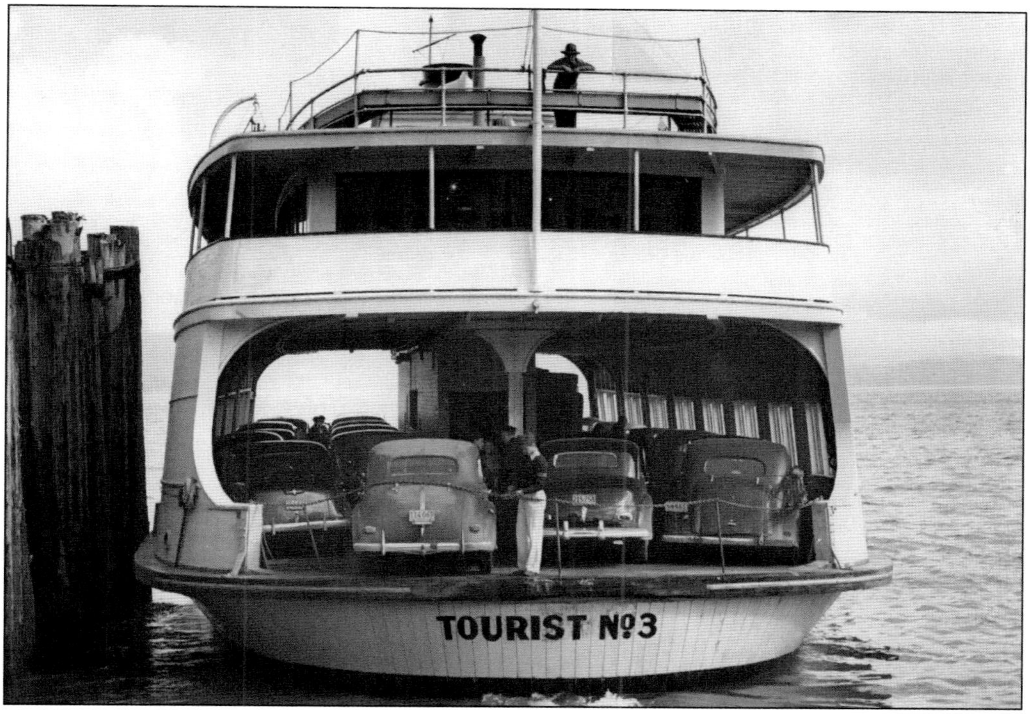

TOURIST NO. 3. The largest of Captain Elfving's ferries, *Tourist No. 3* was built by Astoria Marine Construction Company in 1931. Elfving's success had not gone unnoticed. A rival company began running the *North Beach* from the foot of Seventeenth Street. Elfving's originated at the foot of Fourteenth Street. The two companies were locked in such a fierce competition that their disputes became known as the Ferry War. Captain Elfving eventually solved the problem by buying out his competitor in 1933. (CRMM No. 140-16562.)

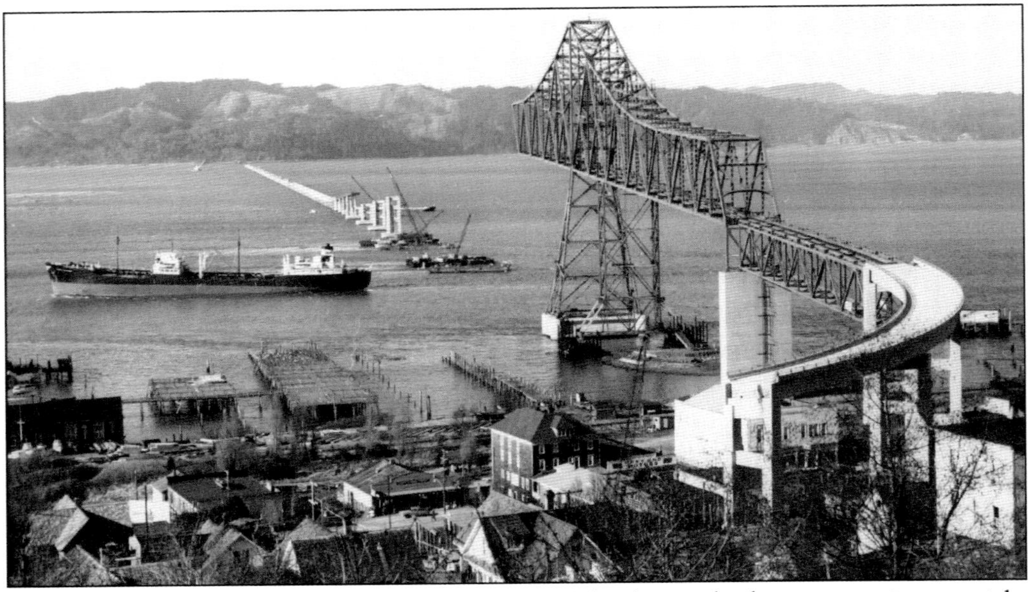

Astoria Bridge Under Construction, c. 1964. The Astoria bridge construction cut right through the Uniontown neighborhood. Peeking out from under the onramp, the white building is Union Hall (or Suomi Hall), the civic center of Uniontown. The cofferdams are in place in the river, and the main support piers are almost ready to be poured. The main truss is being extended across to the other pier and, when complete, will be the longest single span bridge to date. (CRMM No. 031-373.)

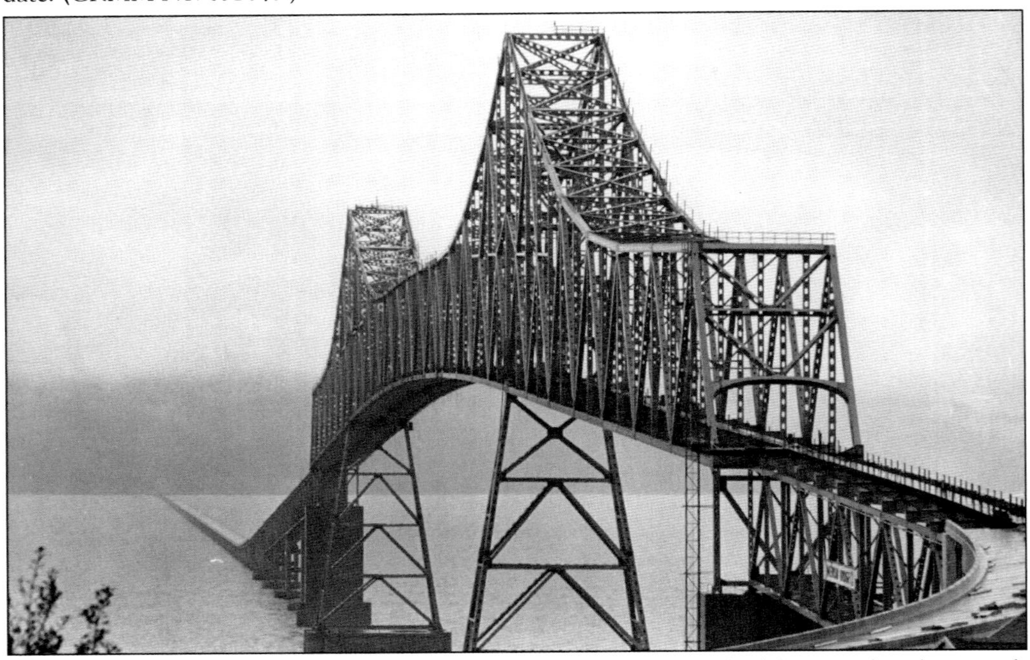

Bridge to Nowhere. Almost complete, the bridge deck is still being laid down in this photograph from 1965. The "bridge to nowhere," as it was called, extends 4.2 miles across the Columbia River from Astoria to Megler, Washington. It connected southwest Washington with Oregon and created a direct route down highway 101 along the coast. It spelled the end of the ferry service across the river at Astoria. (CRMM No. 031-372.)

Five

FIRE!

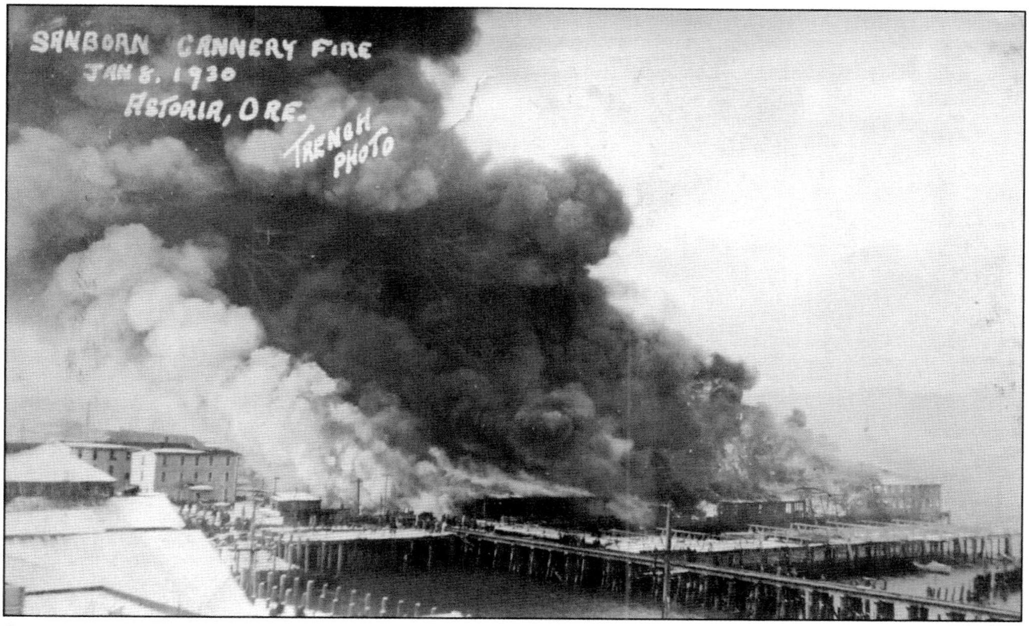

SANBORN CANNERY BURNS, 1930. The Sanborn Cannery burned on January 8, 1930. This dramatic photograph shows the entire plant involved. Located at 466 Bond Street in an area known as Uniontown, The Sanborn-Cutting Company was one of the largest and most modern salmon packing plants in the world. (CRMM No. 072-1760.)

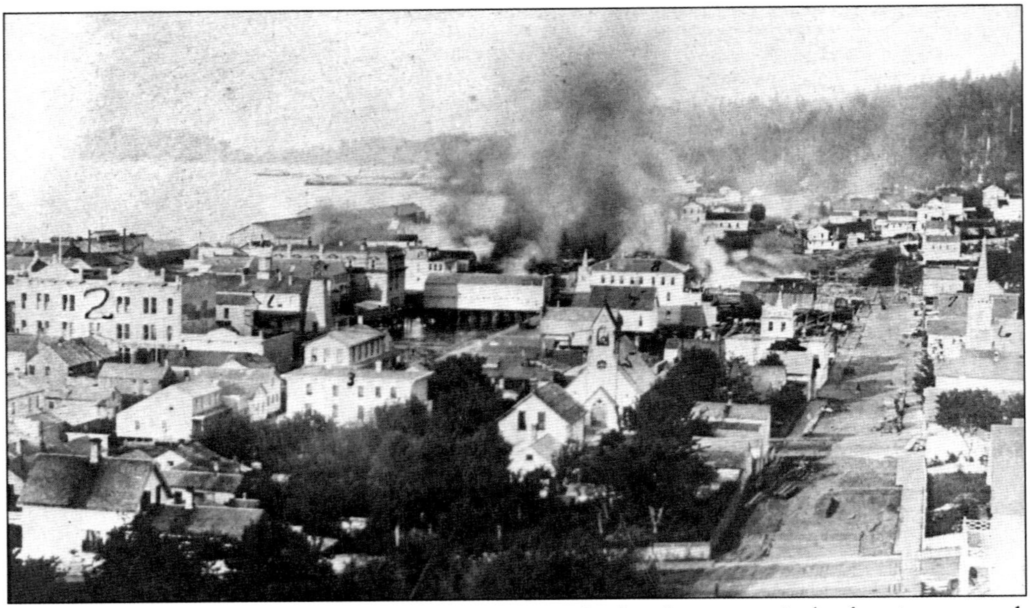

Ferrell's Sawmill Burns, 1883. In his 1880 report, the fire department's chief engineer stated, "The year has been one of general good fortune to the city, so far as losses by fire are concerned." The city would not be so fortunate in 1883. In the early evening of July 2, the sawmill, formerly owned by Ferdinand "Dad" Ferrell and located at Fourteenth Street, caught fire. The OR&N dock and the businesses on Commercial Street, between Fourteenth and Seventeenth Streets, were destroyed as well. (Woodfield collection.)

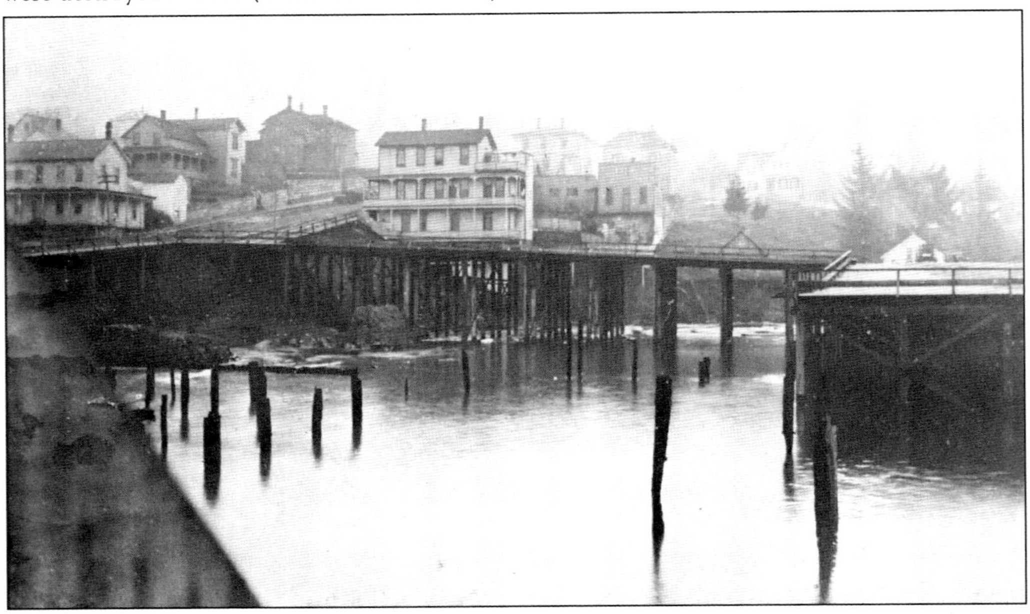

Site of the 1883 Fire. This is the site of the 1883 Clatsop Mill fire that burned out the area surrounding the mill, leaving these charred pilings behind. At the left is a house built by Ferdinand Ferrell, the previous owner of the mill, in the 1870s. It stands today and is an apartment house. At the water near the center left is Shark Rock, where survivors of the wrecked USS *Shark* etched their memorial. The top piece of the rock that bears their inscription is on display in the Columbia River Maritime Museum. (Woodfield collection.)

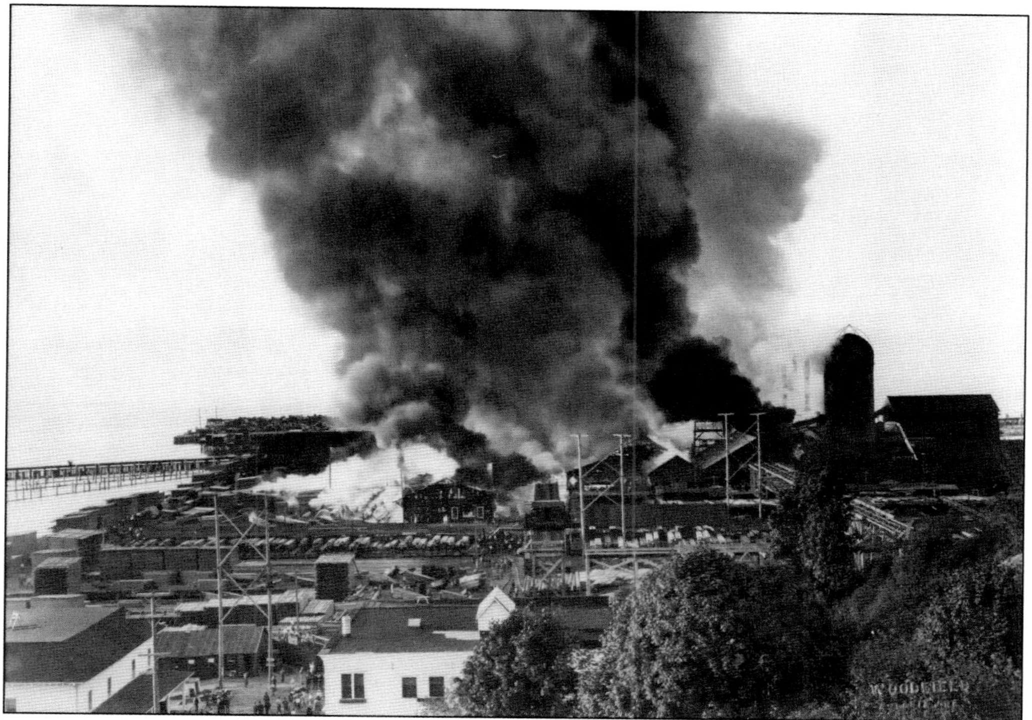

Hammond Mill Fire, 1922. Hammond Mill in Alderbrook, at the east end of town, burned on September 11, 1922. The mill employed a diverse workforce, and its closure affected many, in particular, the Sikh workers from India. They lived four men to a bunkhouse in 12 bunkhouses down a street near the mill that came to be known as "Hindu Alley." When the mill closed, they were forced to move to find other work. (CRMM No. 262-5534.)

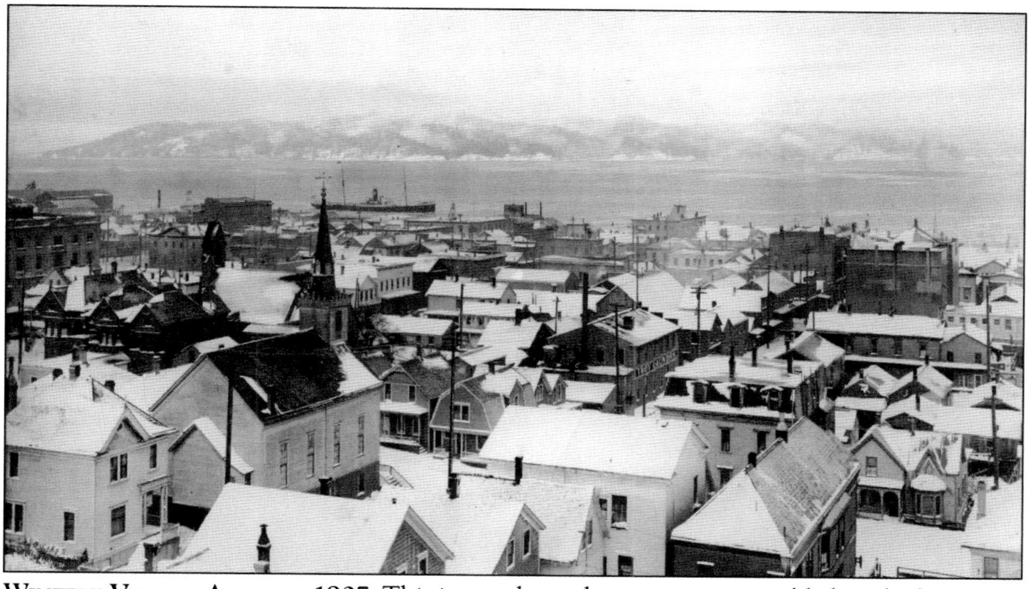

Wintery View of Astoria, 1907. This image shows downtown as it was likely to look some 15 years later on the eve of the December 1922 fire that destroyed 32 blocks in the heart of the city. Nearly everything to the right of the post office and courthouse on the far left of the photograph was destroyed. (CRMM No. 030-222.)

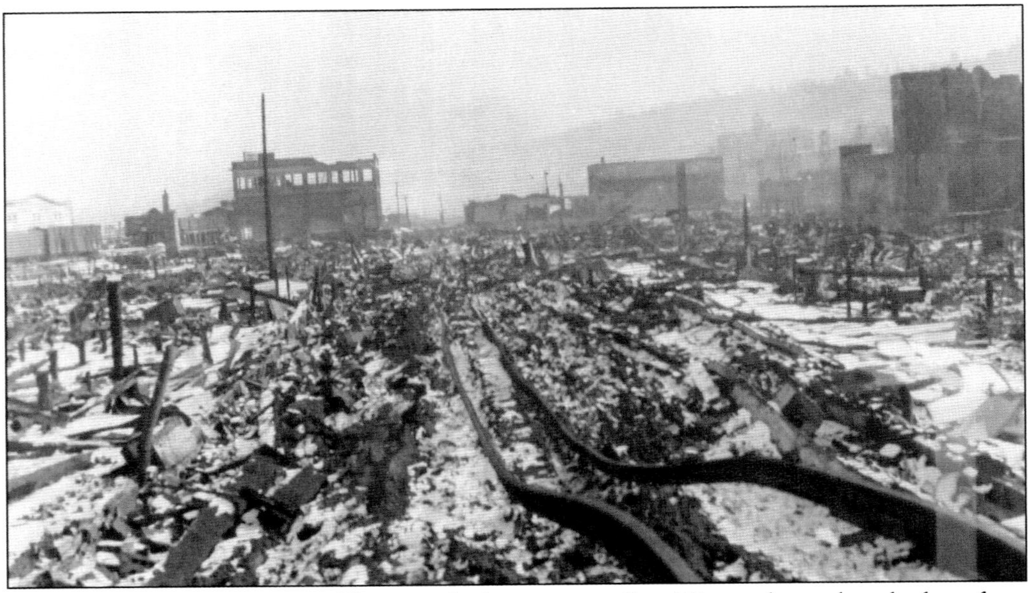

Bond Street Looking East. This view looking east on Bond Street shows that the heat from the flames of the 1922 fire was intense enough to twist the trolley tracks. The streets, built on wooden pilings, burned along with the structures. (CRMM No. 032-463.)

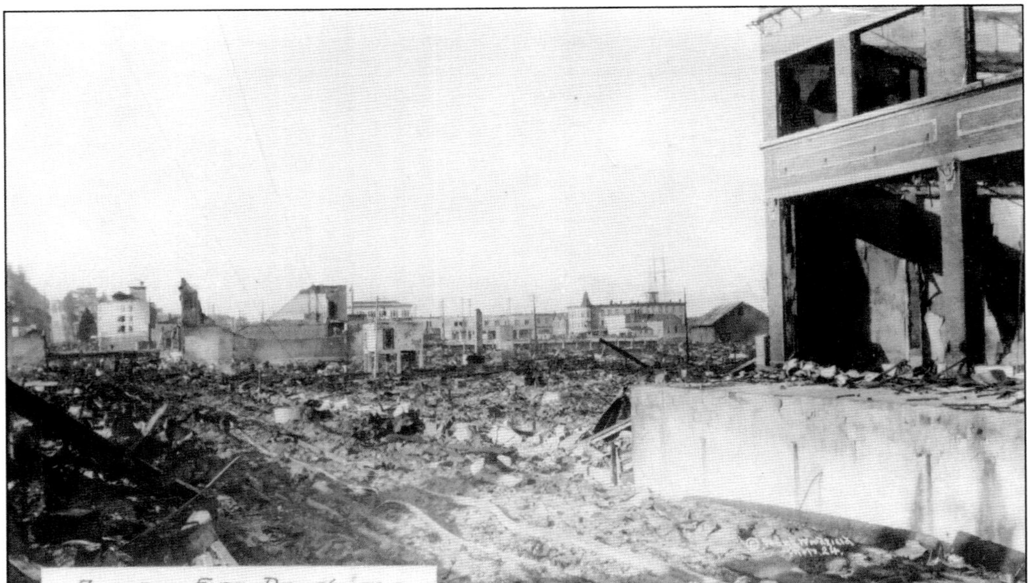

Looking Northwest at Fourteenth and Commercial Streets. This is the 24th photograph in a series of images taken by photographer Frank Woodfield documenting the aftermath of the conflagration. It looks west from Fourteenth and Commercial Streets, showing the spared buildings of Astor Street. (CRMM No. 032-473.)

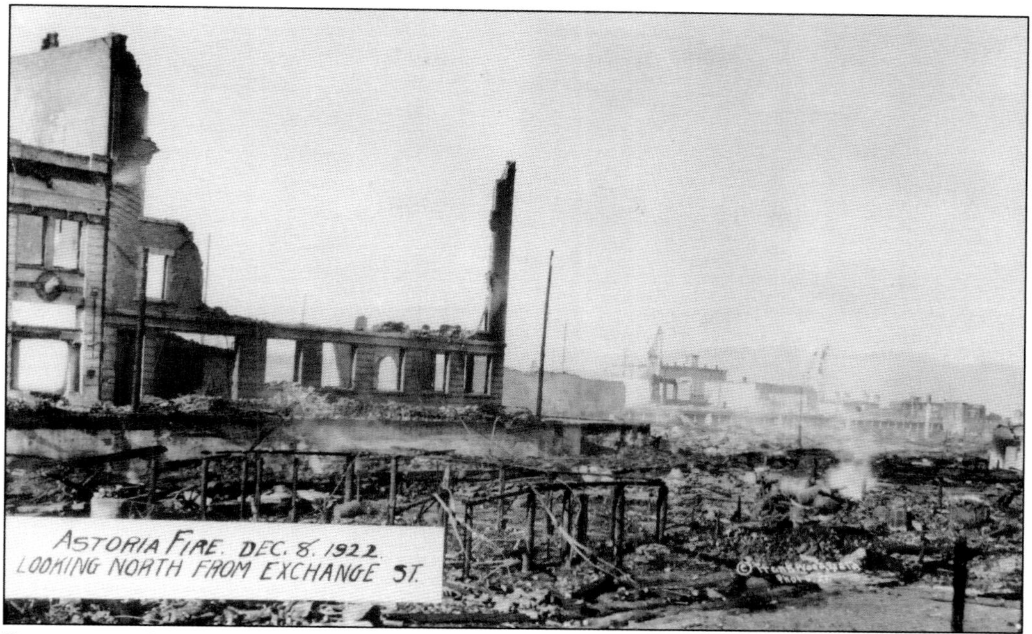

REMAINS OF ASTORIA SAVINGS BANK. The town was still smoldering. This photograph, part of the Frank Woodfield series, looks north from Exchange Street. The debris in the foreground was formerly Eleventh Street. The two structures on the left of the photograph are the Elks Building (identifiable by the mounted elk head on the exterior) and Astoria Savings Bank. (CRMM No. 032-466.)

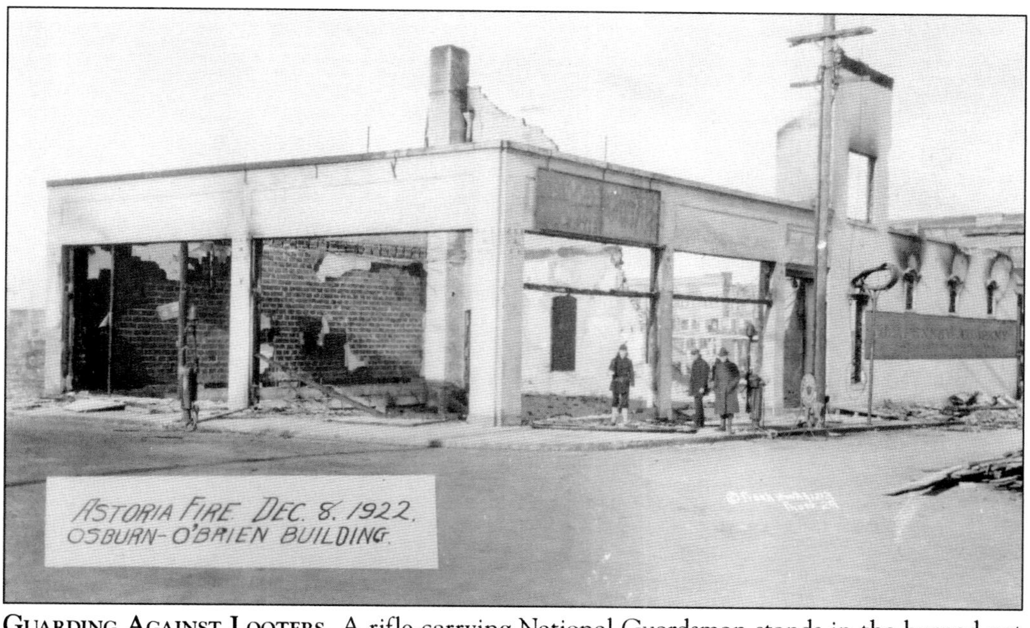

GUARDING AGAINST LOOTERS. A rifle-carrying National Guardsman stands in the burned-out shell of the Osburn-O'Brien Building. The Guard was called in to control looting and keep order. Osburn and O'Brien rebuilt. Unfortunately, they lost the building during the Depression. (CRMM No. 032-465.)

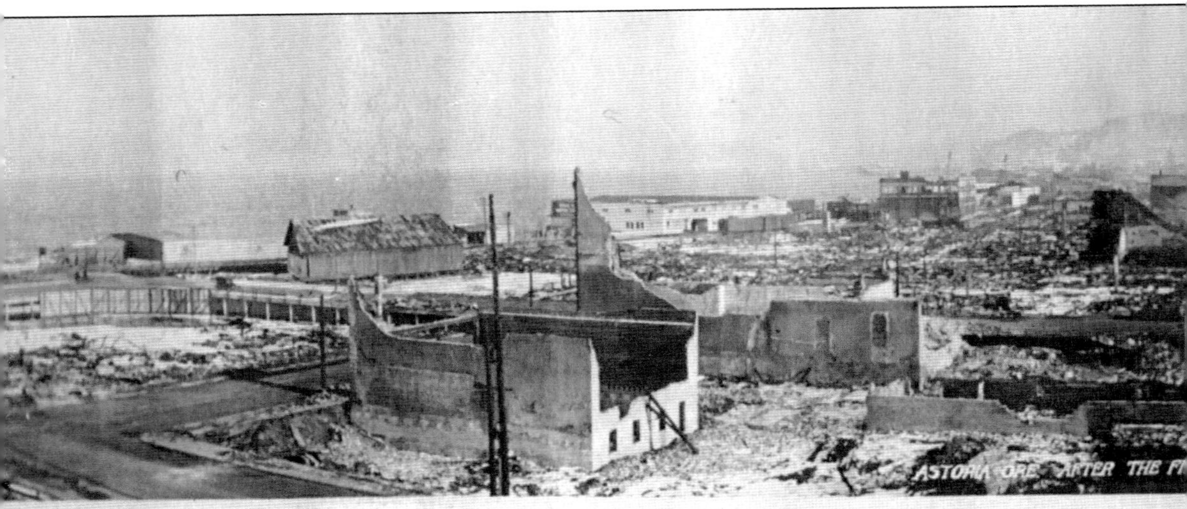

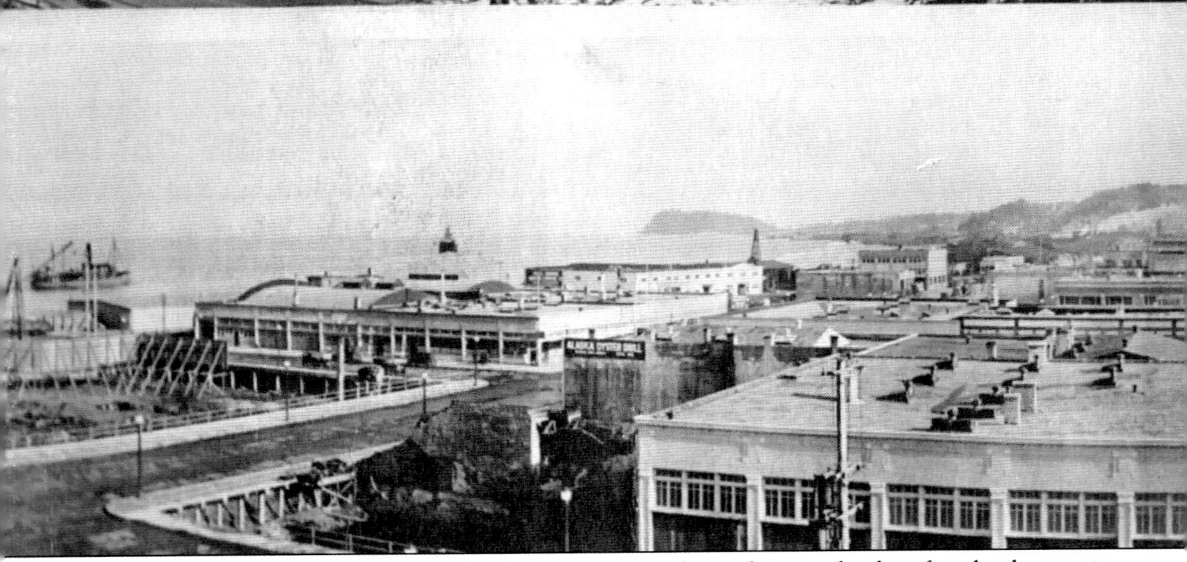

Panoramic Views of the City. The above panorama shows the area the day after the devastating fire in 1922. Practically the entire business district was destroyed, including banks, merchandisers, hotels, restaurants, and saloons. The city and county government buildings, as well as the post office, were spared. The outlying residential neighborhoods were also safe. The bottom photograph

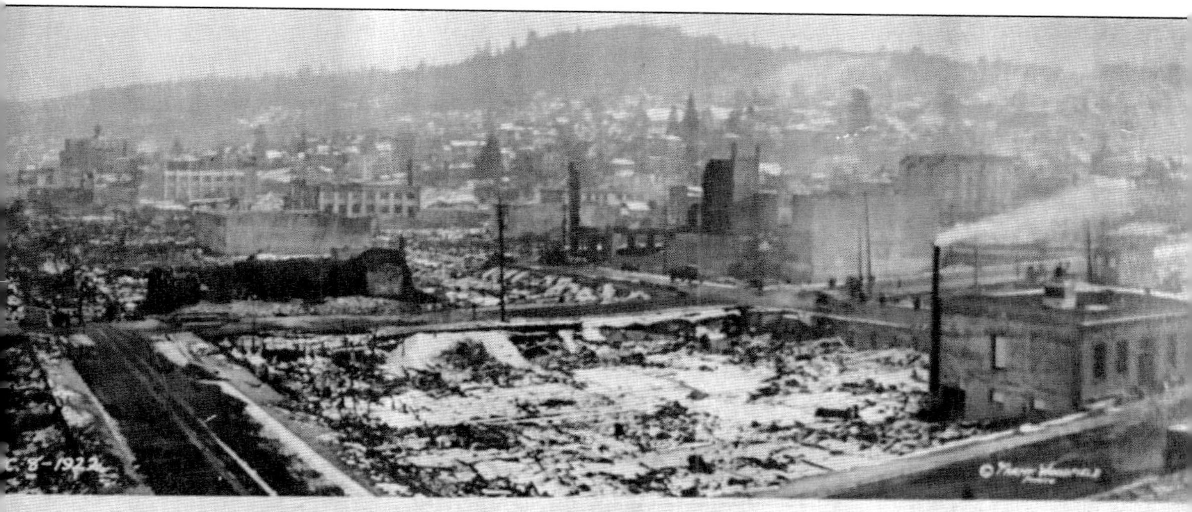

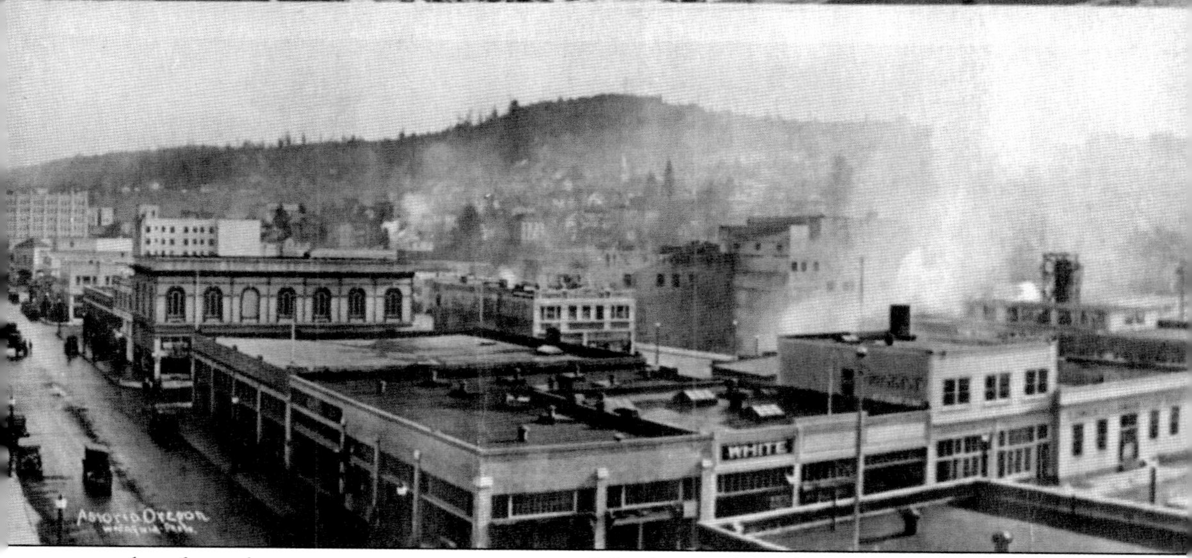

was taken from the same vantage point on top of the Spexarth Building that survived the fire and shows the city roughly five years later. Astoria was quickly rebuilt, this time out of bricks and cement. (CRMM No. 032-481.)

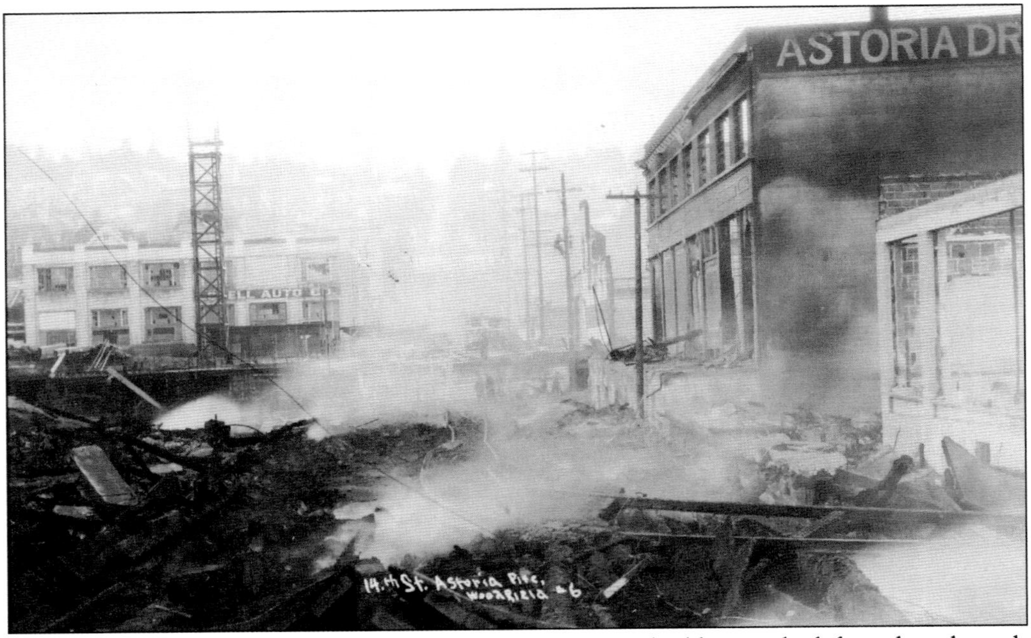

LOOKING SOUTH ON FOURTEENTH STREET. The Lovell Auto building to the left made it through the firestorm due to heroic efforts of citizens to douse embers and flames as they drifted onto the structure. The building owner prevented railroad workers from igniting dynamite, intended to blast firebreaks in the path of the flames, sparing the building. The masonry building on the right, with the "Astoria Drug" sign, lost its roof and was completely gutted by the fire. Both buildings were repaired and still stand today. (CRMM No. 032-475.)

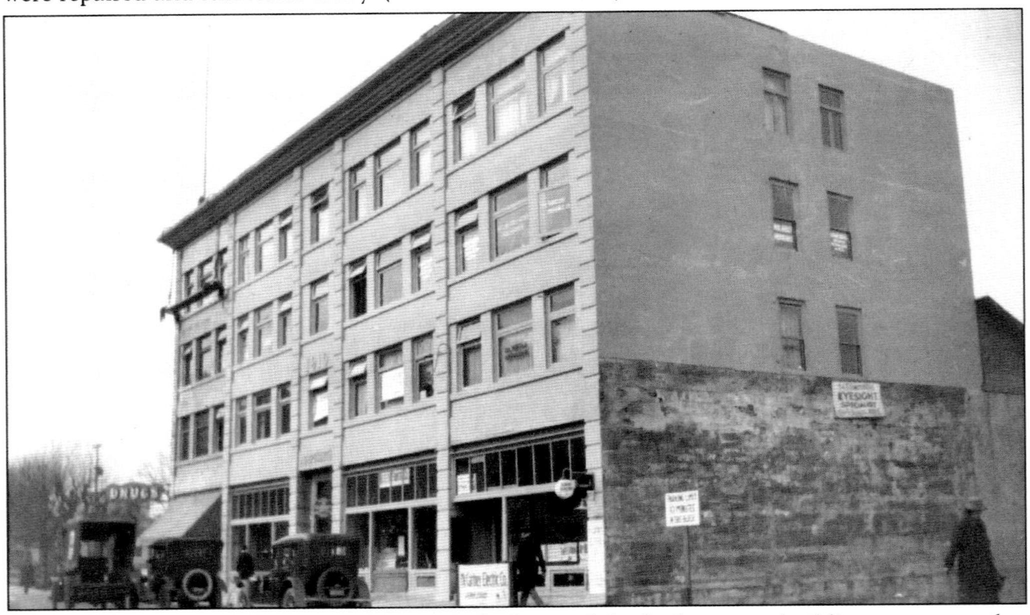

SPEXARTH BUILDING. From 1909 to 1910, A.G. Spexarth had a four-story building constructed at the corner of Eighth and Commercial Streets. The structure's reinforced concrete walls and floors helped it survive the 1922 fire that destroyed much of the city's downtown businesses. The roof provided an accessible vantage point from which to photograph the devastation and recovery, as seen in the previous two-page spread. (CRMM No. 030-155.)

Six

Festivities and Fun

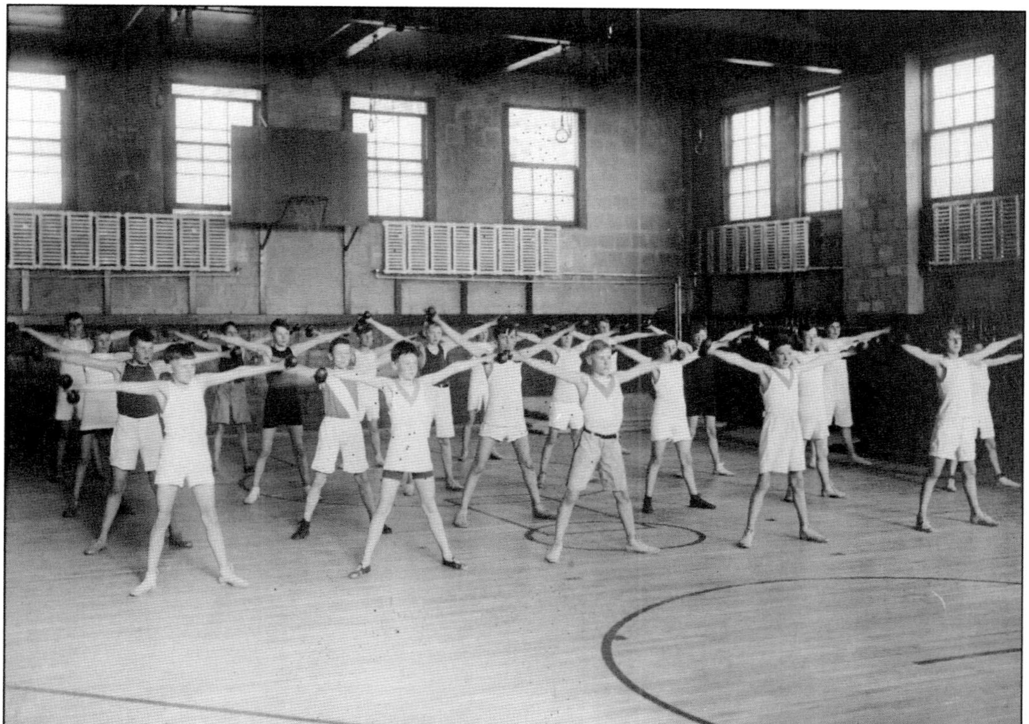

YMCA, 1915. This 1915 photograph shows a group of young boys working out with weights at the YMCA. The YMCA building was constructed at the southeast corner of Twelfth and Exchange Streets in 1914. (CRMM No. 420-9701.)

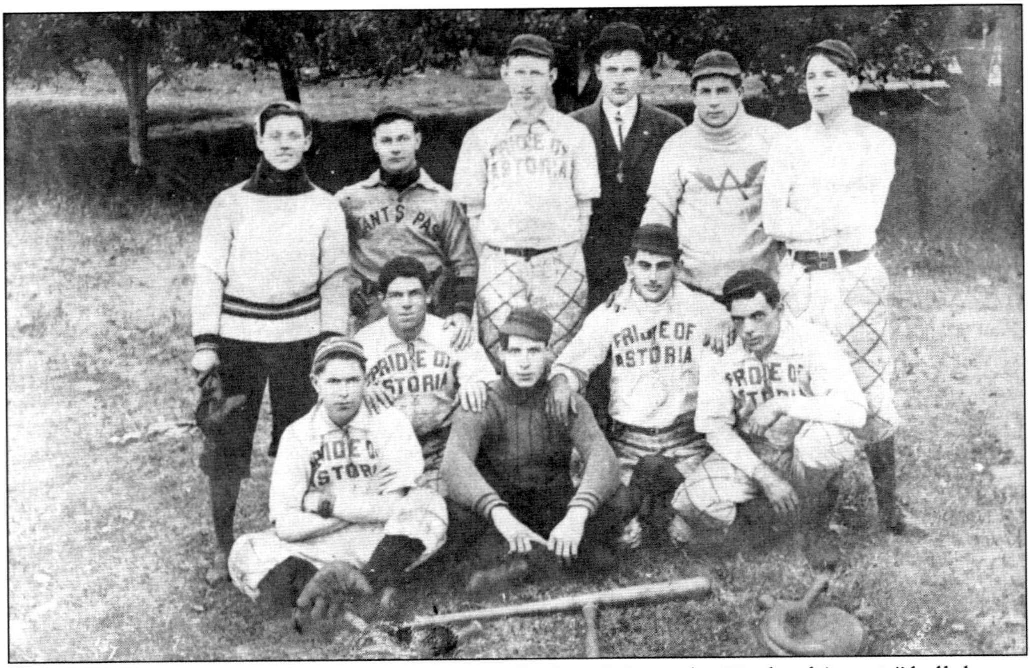

PRIDE OF ASTORIA. There is little information to be found about the "Pride of Astoria" ballplayers. This photograph was taken around 1900. They looked like a tough team to beat, and a few of the players were reputed to be some of the "bad boys" in town. (Woodfield collection.)

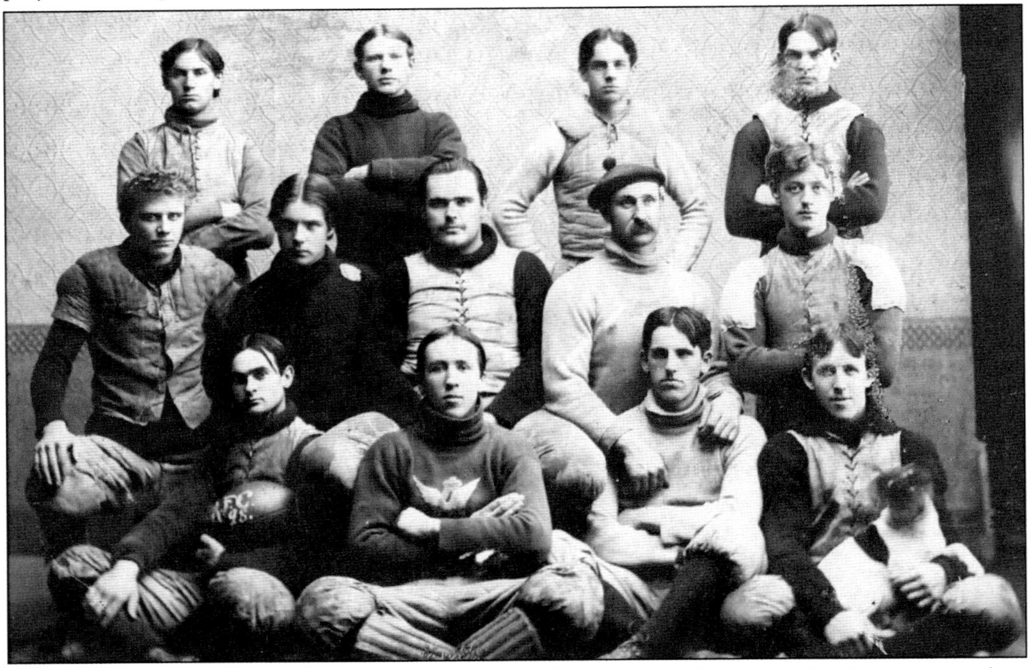

ASTORIA FOOTBALL CLUB. The Astoria Football Club members of 1898 pose for the photographer. The players, pictured from left to right, are (first row, seated) Dan Allen, Win Crosby, ? Abercrombie, and Roscoe Caselle; (second row, kneeling) Sig Young, Ross Trullinger, ? Knapp, Tom Spencer, and Ted Sutton; (third row, standing) Bill Jones, J. Buffington, Park Upshur, and Nat Tallant. The identity of the dog is unknown. (Woodfield collection.)

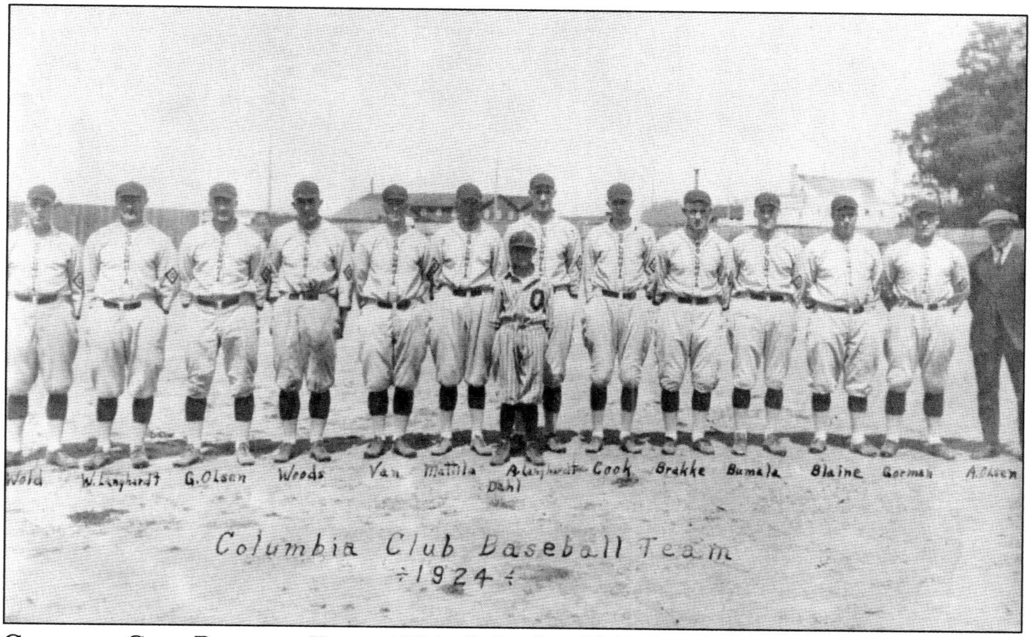

Columbia Club Baseball Team, 1924. Columbia Club's Baseball Team of 1924 poses for a team photograph at Columbia Field. The field was located on the block bordered by Thirty-Fifth, Thirty-Sixth, Duane, and Exchange Streets. It was constructed in 1922 by dumping 500 cubic feet of fill across the tidal flats. The Columbia Club was a private athletic organization created in Uppertown in 1910. The club served a predominately Scandinavian membership, but included Icelanders, Finns, Germans, Italians, and Greeks as well. Columbia Club's first organized baseball team was formed in 1915. (Woodfield collection.)

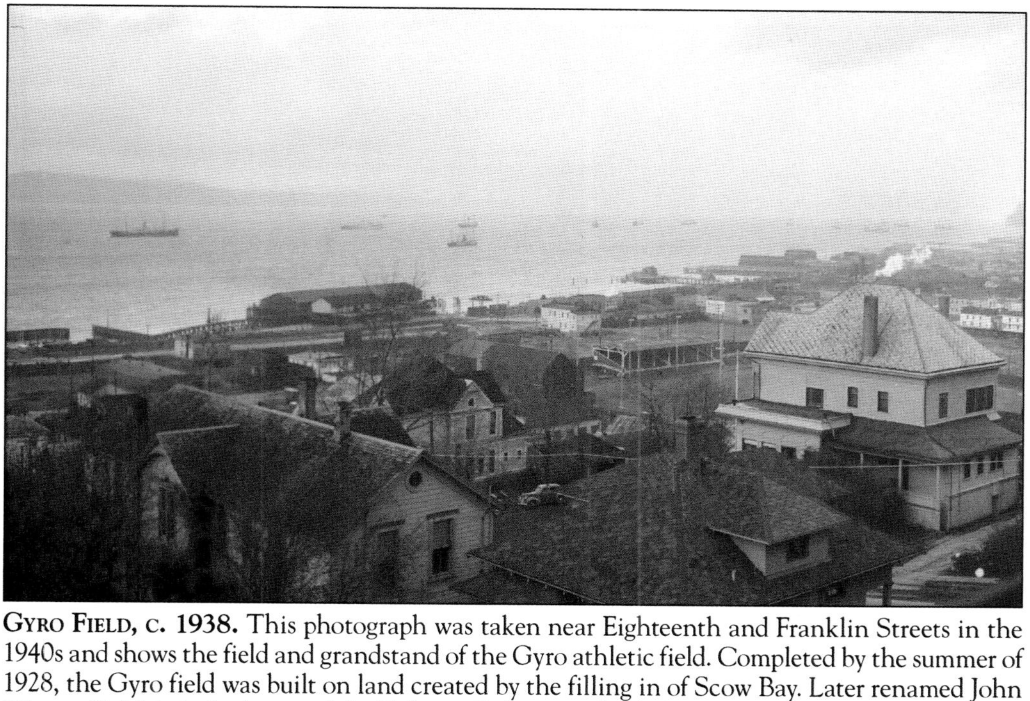

Gyro Field, c. 1938. This photograph was taken near Eighteenth and Franklin Streets in the 1940s and shows the field and grandstand of the Gyro athletic field. Completed by the summer of 1928, the Gyro field was built on land created by the filling in of Scow Bay. Later renamed John Warren Field, it is the home of the Fighting Fishermen football team. (Woodfield collection.)

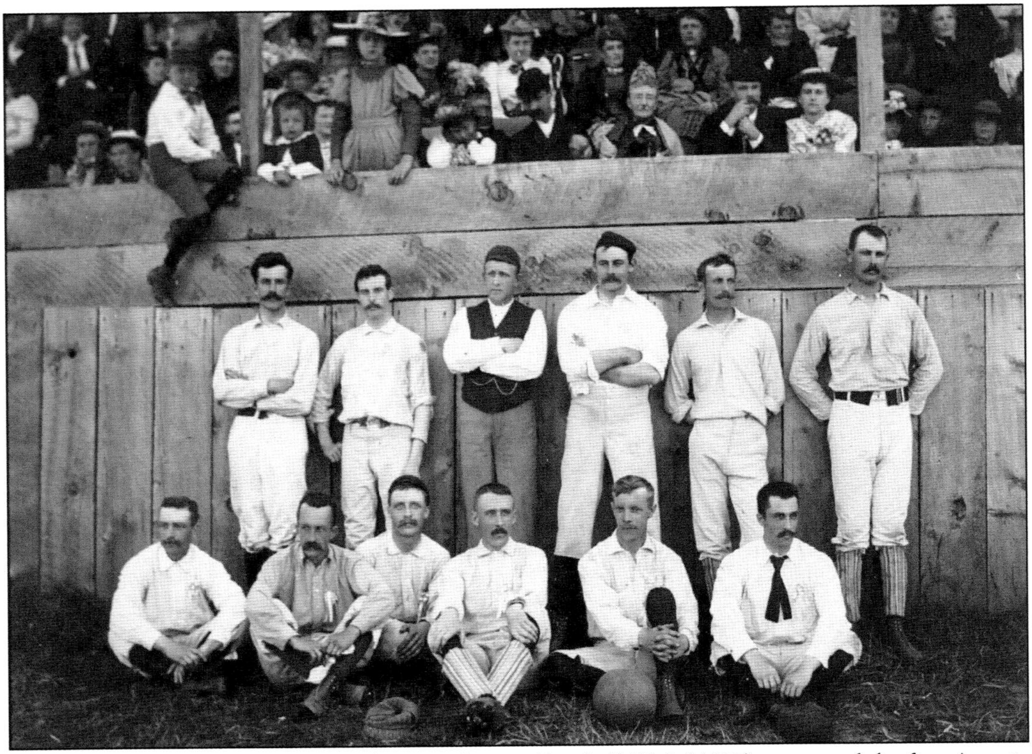

Astoria Football Club, 1894. The 1894 Astoria Football Club (AFC) sponsored the first Astoria Regatta. The event was conceived by E.J. Smith, editor of the *Morning Astorian*. Smith shared the idea with Frank M. Gunn, a businessman and secretary of the AFC. Although a football club sponsoring such an occasion might seem odd at first, it is important to note that the club, which offered more than just football, participated in almost every event that took place in the city. Their membership included several mid-town business people as well. (Woodfield collection.)

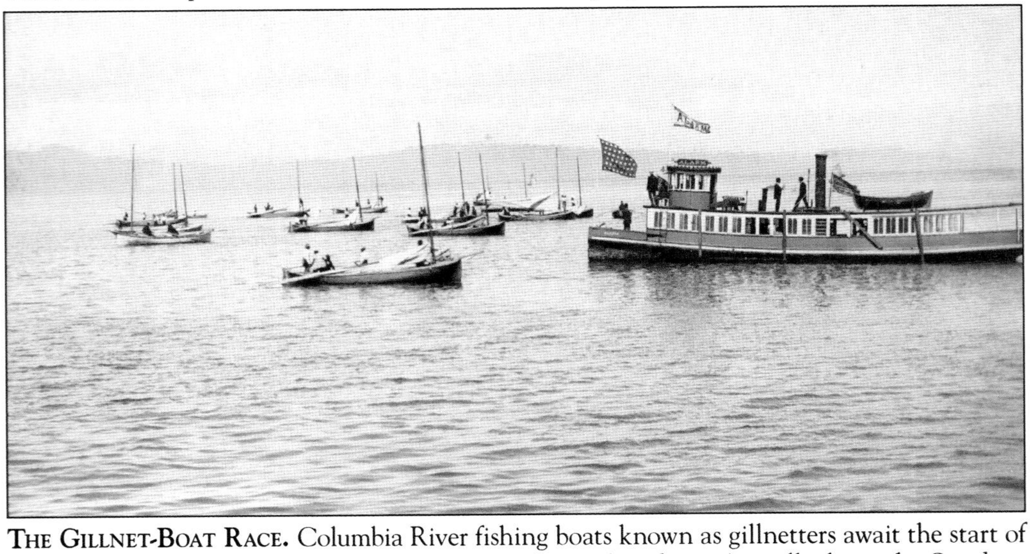

The Gillnet-Boat Race. Columbia River fishing boats known as gillnetters await the start of their race on August 21, 1894. The larger boat at right is the *Alarm*. A smaller boat, the *Occident*, is behind the *Alarm*. The fish boat race was a featured event at this first Astoria Regatta. (CRMM No. 033-483.)

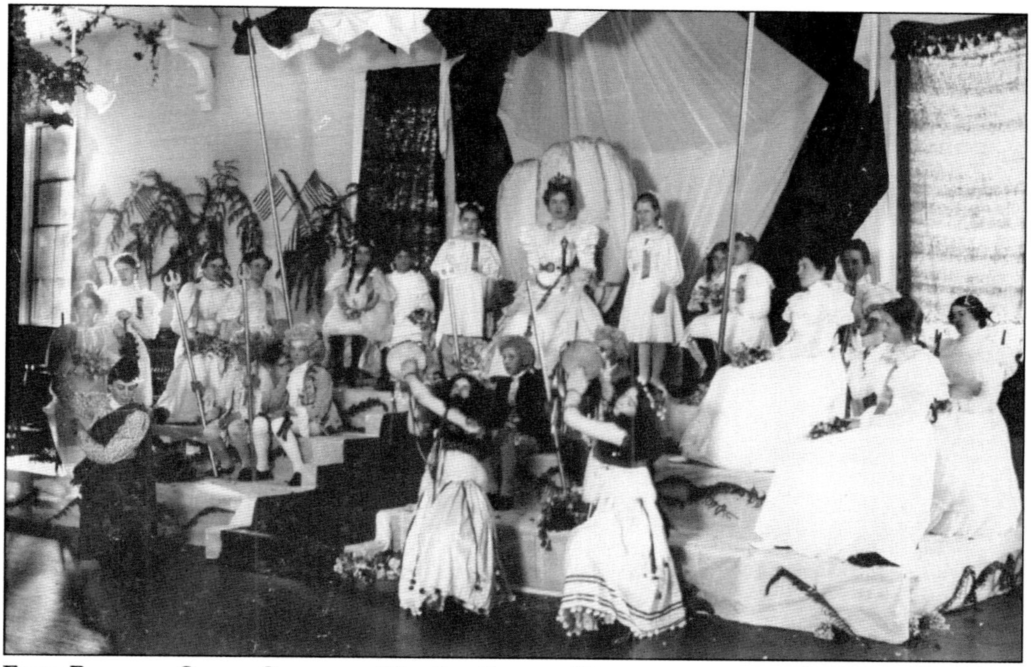

First Regatta Queen Crowned. The first Queen of Regatta was crowned in 1897. The honor went to Lydia Gosselin, who is seen here seated on her throne with her attendants surrounding her. (Woodfield collection.)

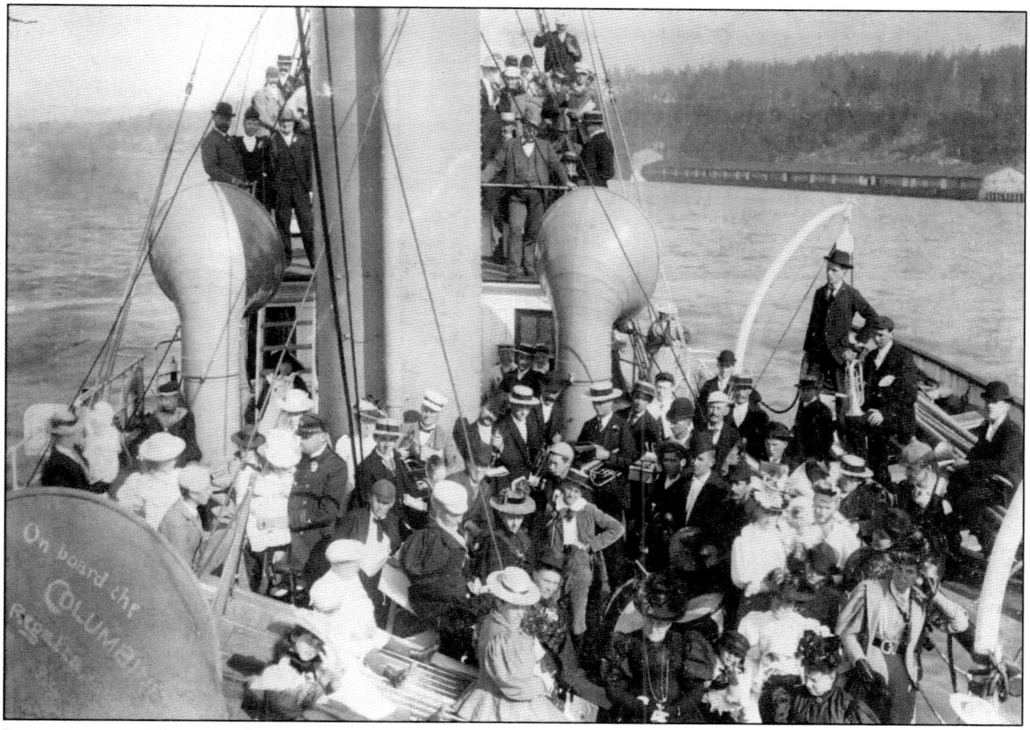

Lighthouse Tender Columbine. Regatta revelers enjoy a pleasure cruise complete with brass band aboard the lighthouse tender *Columbine* in this photograph taken around 1900. (CRMM No. 033-586.)

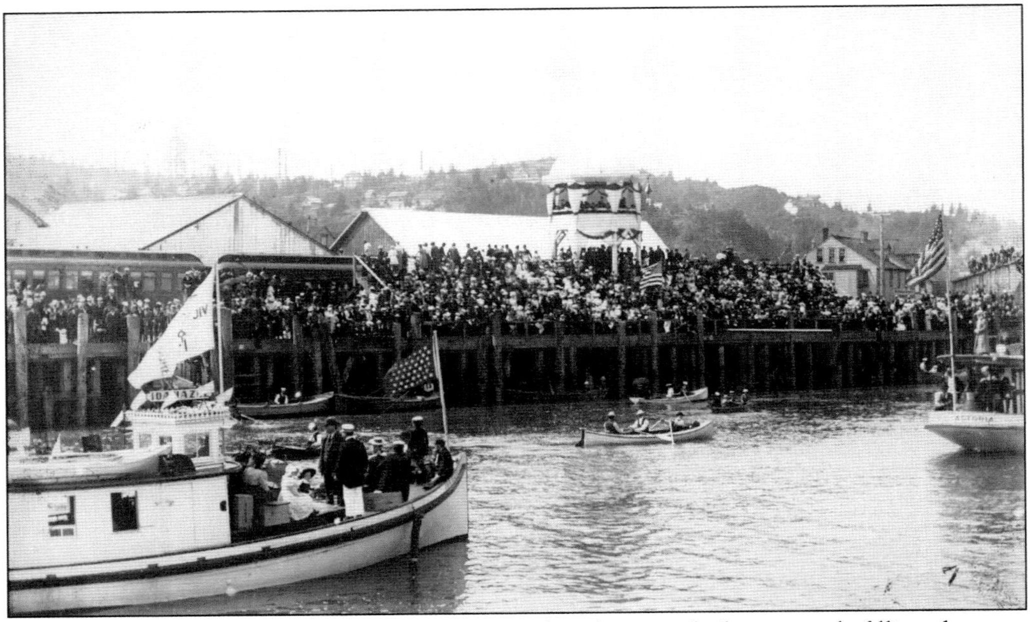

Regatta Grandstand on Sixteenth Street. This photograph shows people filling the seats at the regatta grandstand as the *Ida Hazel* (left foreground) and the *Electric* (right foreground) motor by. (CRMM No. 033-571.)

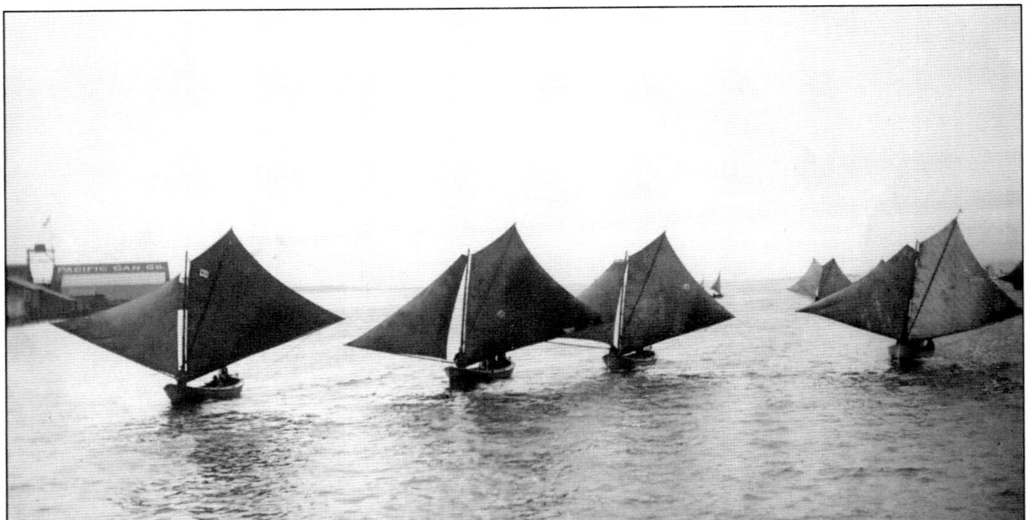

Gillnetter race, 1906 Regatta. For this race during the annual regatta, sailing gillnet boats would mount extra sails and run "wing and wing" for the downwind leg of the race. Many who witnessed this event likened their appearance to butterflies on the wind; hence the name "Butterfly Fleet." (CRMM No. 033-534.)

COMMANDER OF REGATTA. Chris Mensinger was named commander of regatta and posed with his cigar rather precariously for this photograph while sitting on a paper moon. (CRMM No. 420-9710.)

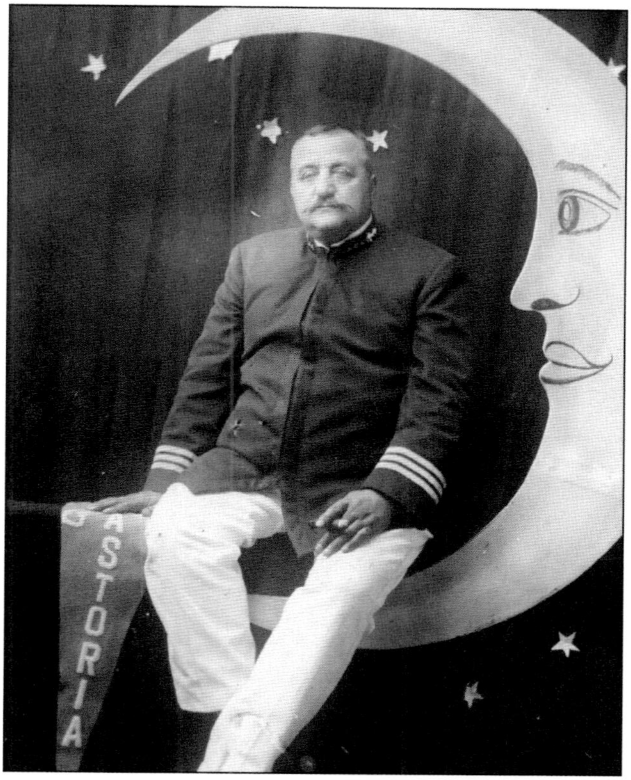

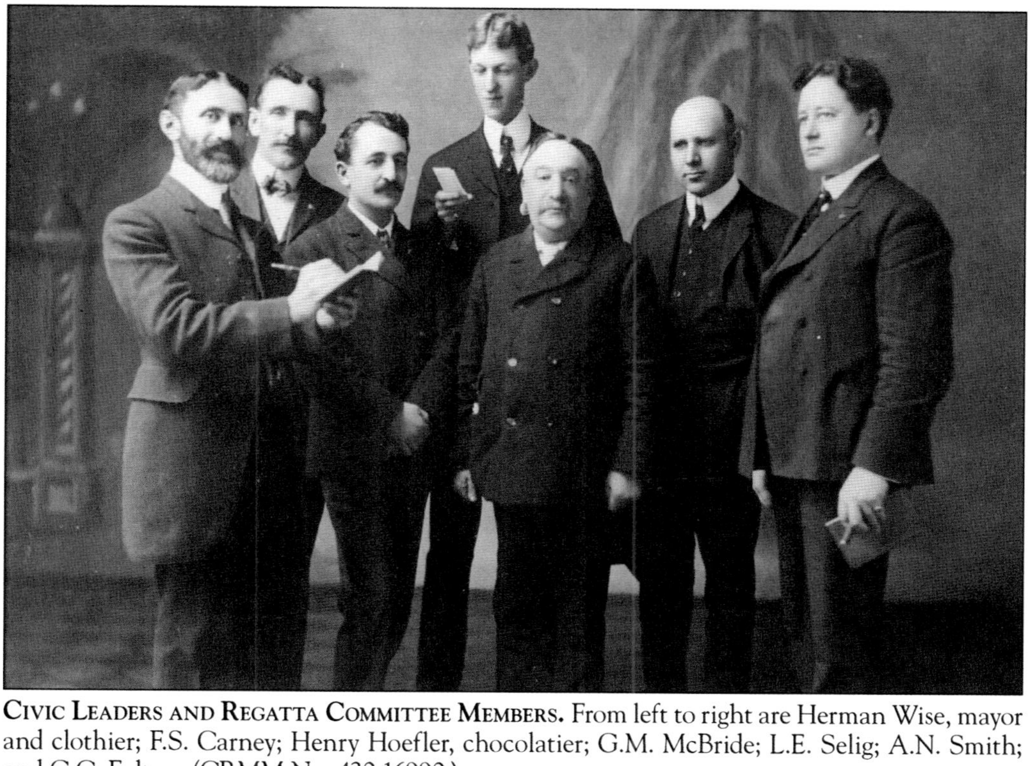

CIVIC LEADERS AND REGATTA COMMITTEE MEMBERS. From left to right are Herman Wise, mayor and clothier; F.S. Carney; Henry Hoefler, chocolatier; G.M. McBride; L.E. Selig; A.N. Smith; and G.C. Fulton. (CRMM No. 420-16990.)

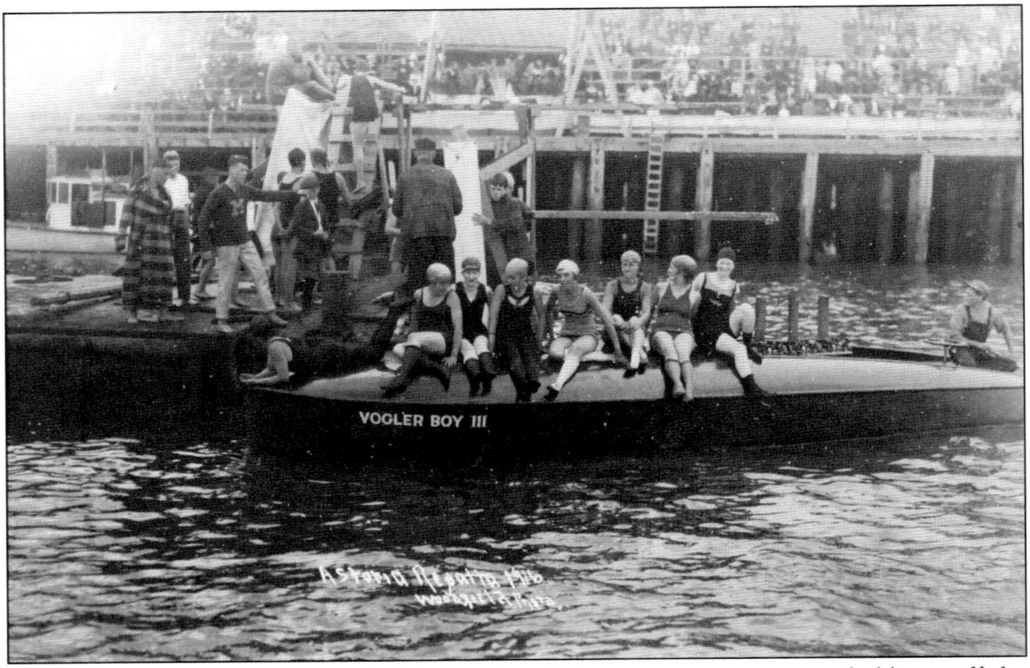

Astoria Regatta Dive Competition, 1916. This competitive event was held just off the viewing grandstand at the foot of Sixteenth Street. The photograph shows women waiting their turn aboard the speedboat *Vogler Boy III* and men making their way up the diving platform. (CRMM No. 033-626.)

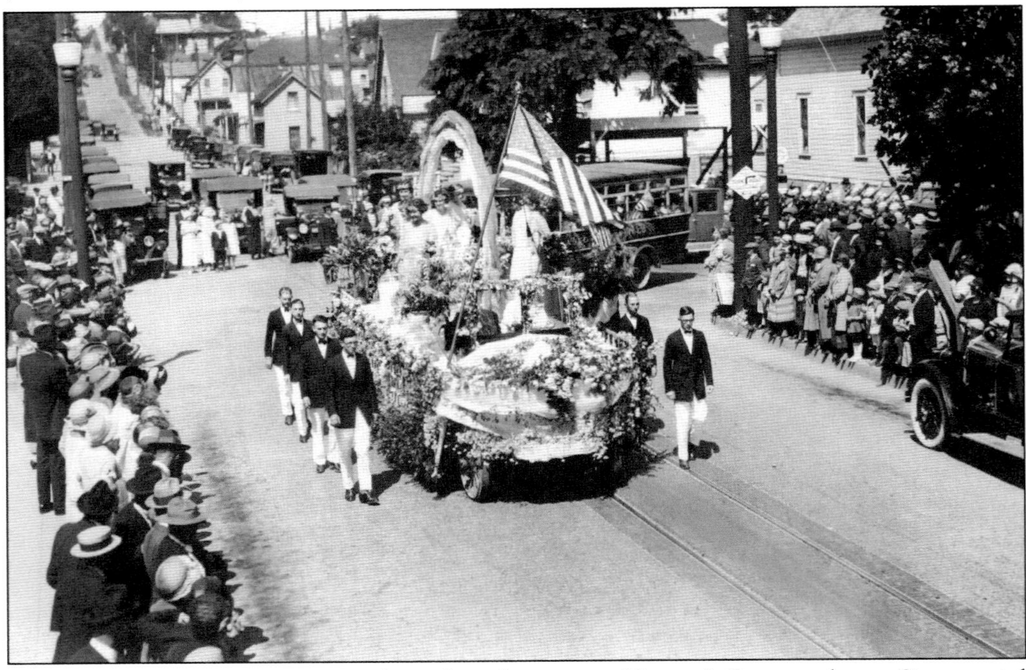

Regatta Queen's Float, c. 1920. Rounding the corner of Seventh Street and onto Commercial Street with the Queen's Float under escort is future Columbia River Maritime Museum founder and its first director Rolf Klep. He is visible as the second to the back and from the front on the right side of the float. (CRMM No. 033-625.)

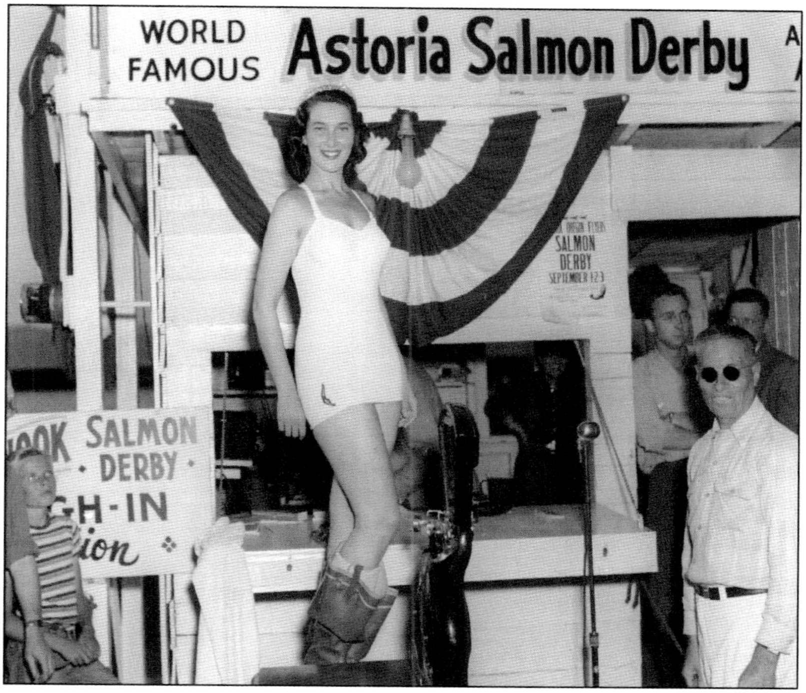

Salmon Derby Beauty. She caught more than fish with her Jantzen Beach swimwear and waders. This Salmon Derby royal representative was part of the effective advertising campaign that promoted the event in 1951. (CRMM No. 034-774.)

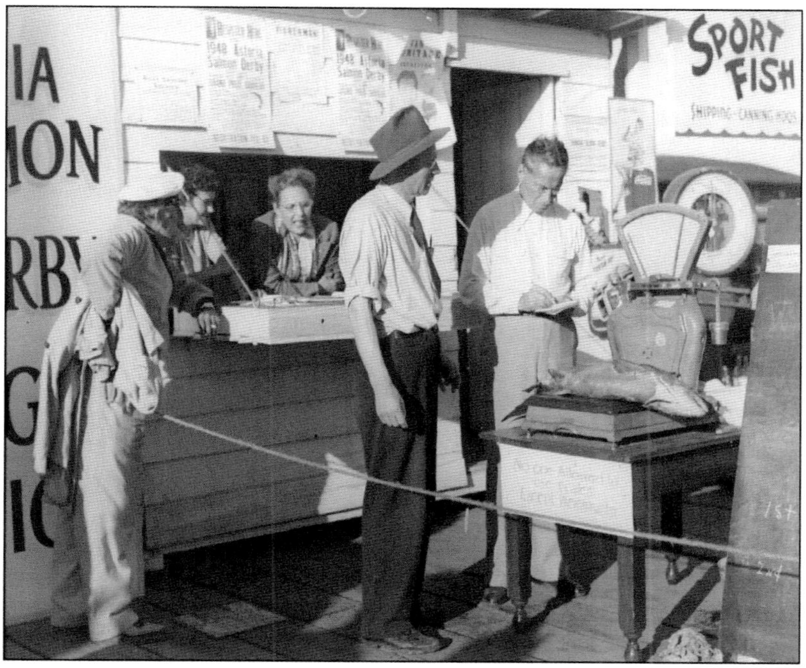

Salmon Derby, 1948. The first Salmon Derby was held in 1937 and coincided with the last day of the Astoria Regatta festival. Amateur anglers paid an entrance fee for a chance to win a cash prize for the largest fish caught. In 1948, the entrance fee was $2, and the grand prize was $1,000. (CRMM No. 034-777.)

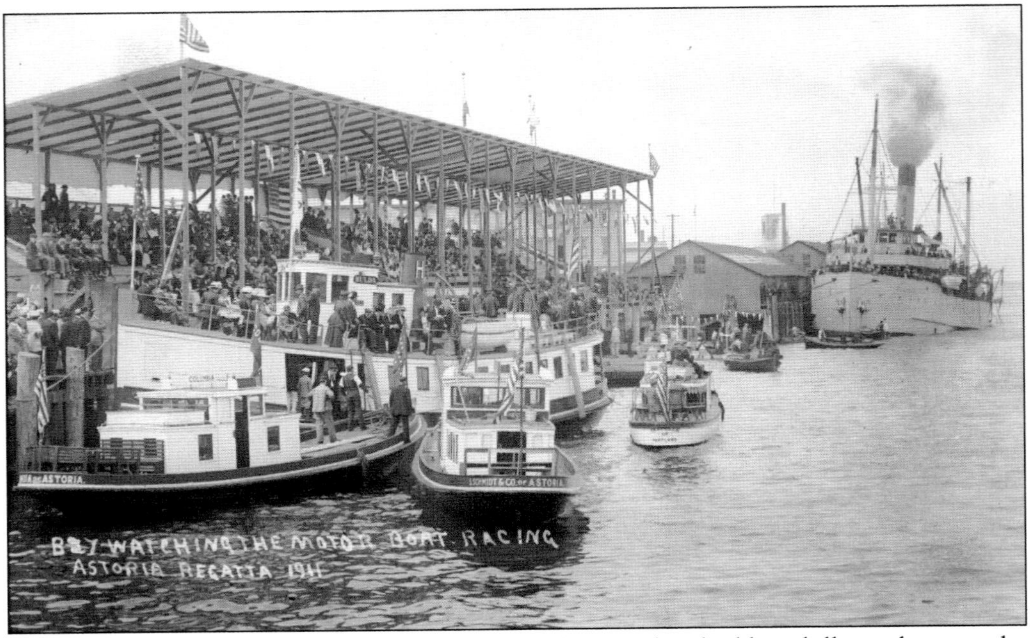

CENTENNIAL REGATTA, 1911. Many fine examples of Astoria boatbuilding skills are shown to the left of center in this image. On the far right of the photograph is the government dredge *Clatsop*, launched three years earlier at Newport News, Virginia. It was tasked in Astoria to dredge the channel over the bar to a depth of 26 feet. It hauled 2,352,787 cubic yards of material in 1911. In 1922, during the great fire, it aided the firefighters by pumping river water onto the flames. (CRMM No. 038-16584.)

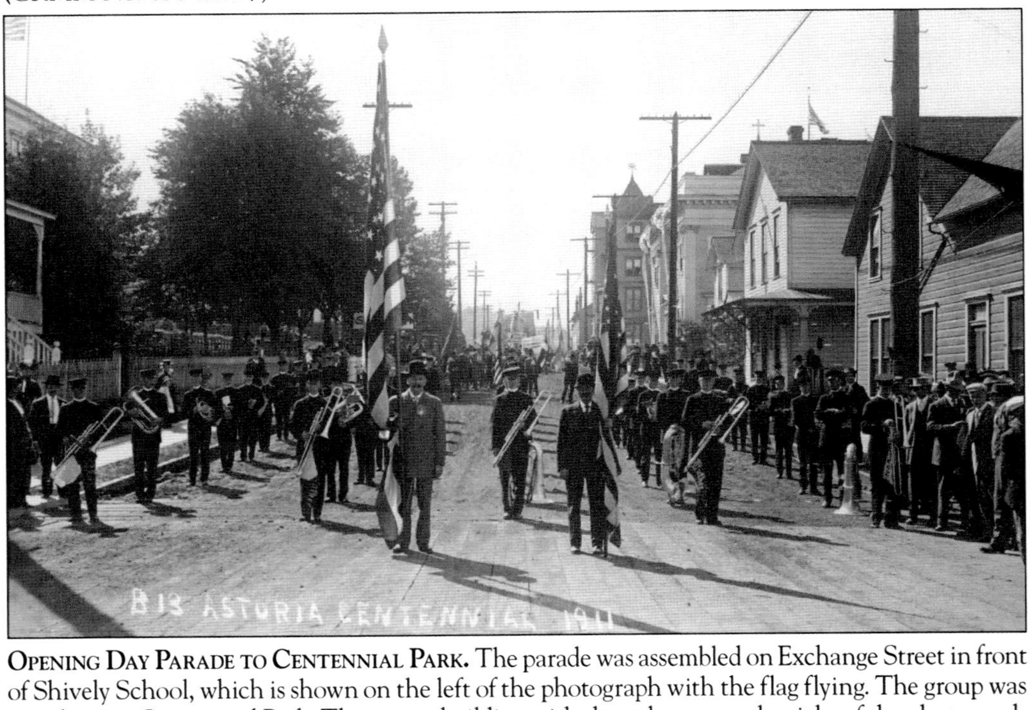

OPENING DAY PARADE TO CENTENNIAL PARK. The parade was assembled on Exchange Street in front of Shively School, which is shown on the left of the photograph with the flag flying. The group was marching to Centennial Park. The square building with the columns on the right of the photograph is the six-year-old city hall, and behind it is St. Mary's Hospital. (CRMM No. 030-151.)

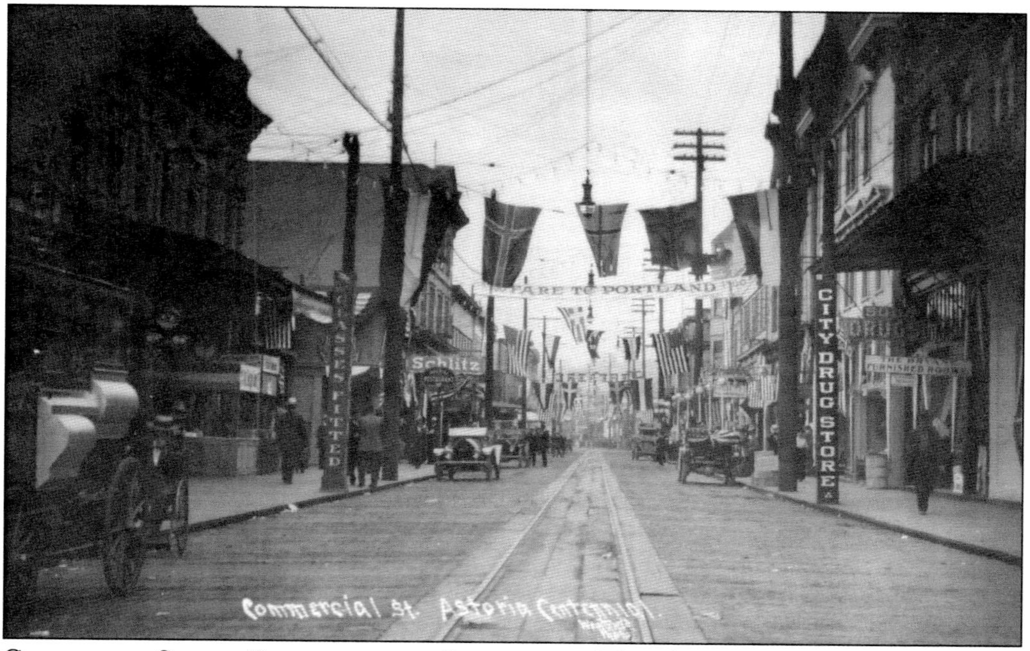

COMMERCIAL STREET DECORATED FOR CENTENNIAL. This photograph shows Scandinavian and American flags hanging over Commercial Street looking east from Eleventh Street. In the photograph, there are more than 12,000 electric lights that the Pacific Power and Light Company provided to illuminate the celebration. Hanging above the center of the street are arc lights used for general street illumination. (CRMM No. 030-154.)

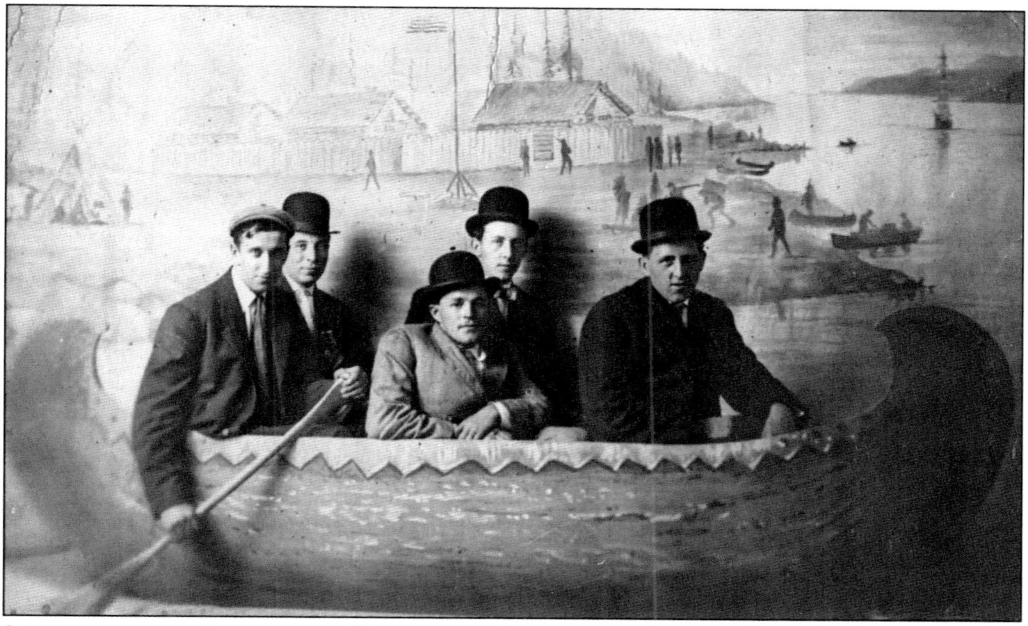

SOUVENIR OF THE CENTENNIAL. These men pose in front of an artist's rendition of early Astoria, paddling a less-than historically accurate canoe. During this time, photography was becoming more accessible to the mass market, and souvenir photographic postcards were quite the rage. Photographers like Coe, Woodfield, Bratt, and Trench were responsible for much of the visual documentation from this period. (Woodfield collection.)

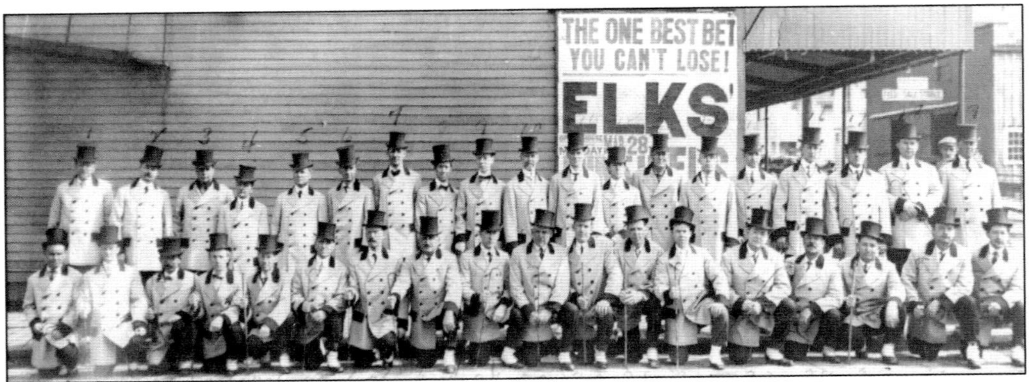

Astoria Elks Formally Presented. Service and fraternal organizations were very popular in Astoria and many of the city's movers and shakers were members of more than one. The lodges and halls of several of these organizations were some of the first buildings rebuilt after the fire in 1922, a true testament to their loyal and active membership. (CRMM No. 420-17261.)

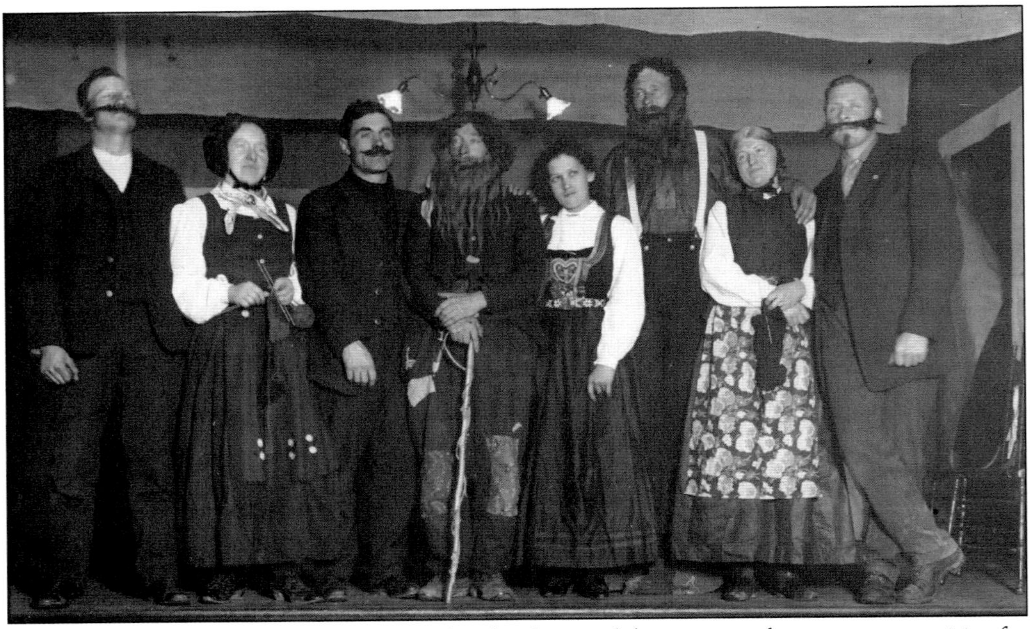

Idun Dramatiske Klub (Drama Club). The drama club was one of many opportunities for recreation before the days of television. These people chose live theater as a creative outlet. Pictured here from left to right are Lars Leiknes, Miss Olsen, Haral Bjorg, Johannes Harun, Sigrid Dybvik, Ole Groting, Anna Mikalsen, and Martin Landro. (CRMM No. 420-9832.)

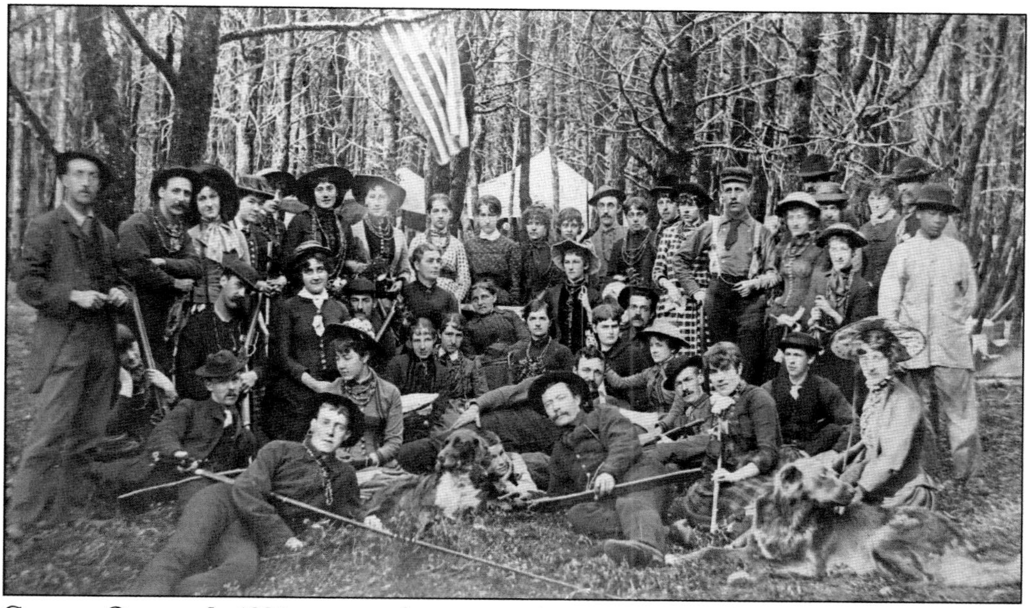

GENTEEL OUTING. In 1884, a group of prominent Astorians ventured to the beach to camp for a week. The entire experience was written about rather poetically in the local paper. The article described the people who visited, the meals they enjoyed, and the activities they were engaged in. Vacationers regularly came down from Portland by steamboat and transferred to wagons just south of town to head overland to the Clatsop beach. This practice gave rise to the vacation-resort nature of the Seaside and Gearhart communities south of Astoria. (CRMM No. 420-9834.)

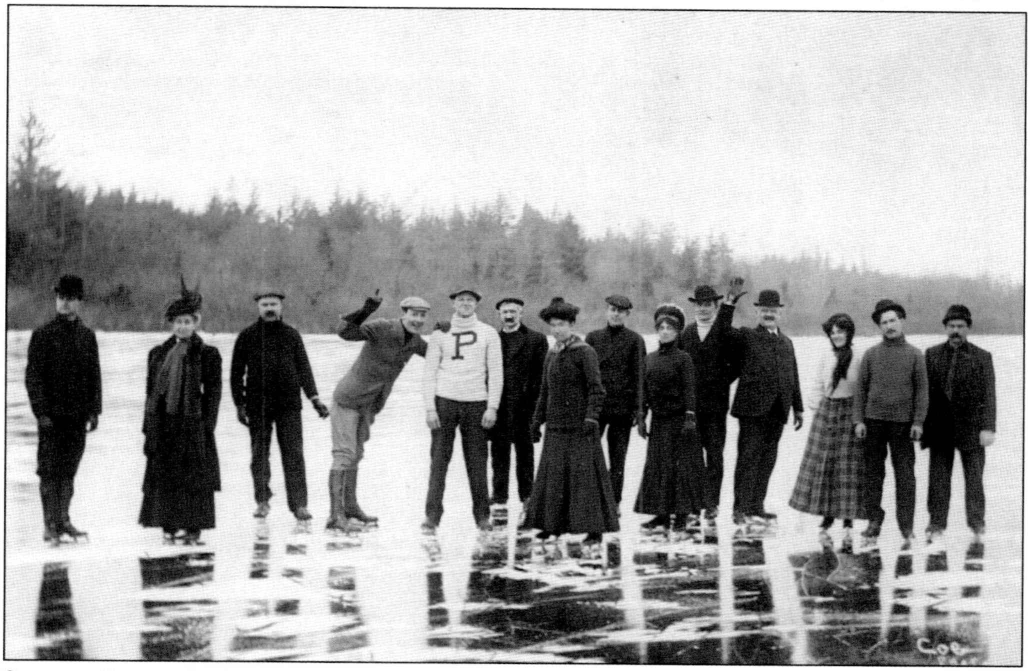

SKATING PARTY. On January 17, 1907, a group ventured to the frozen Smith Lake near Warrenton. The party included, from left to right, Dan Allen, Isabelle Higgins, Albert Dunbar, Del Scully, Harry Flavel, Henry Wedikin, Margaret Higgins, Jimmy Robb, Jennie Curtis, Jack Bay, and Sam Schmidt. The last three are unidentified. (Woodfield collection.)

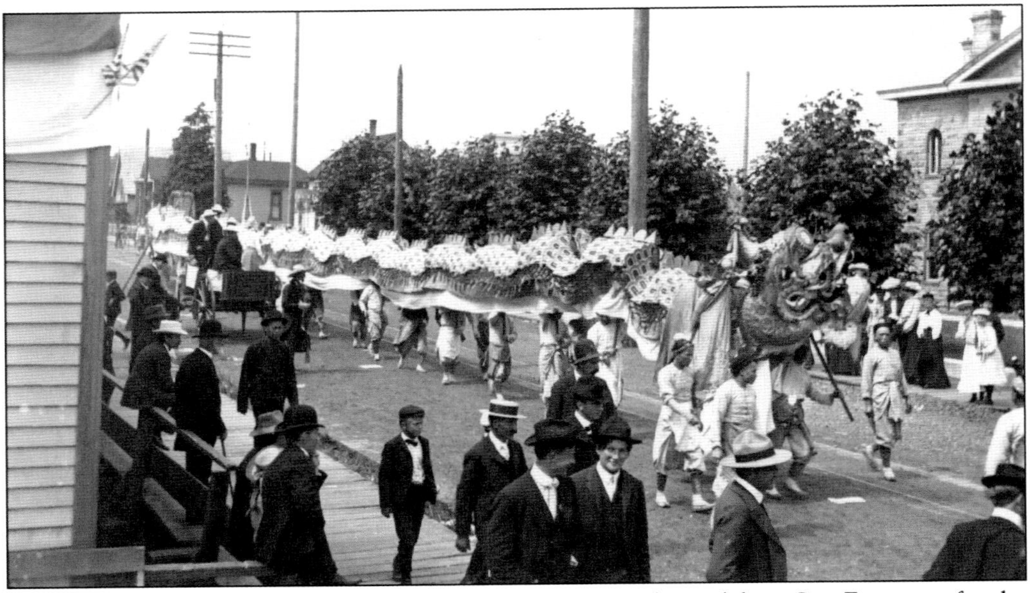

CHINESE DRAGON PARADE. A special Chinese dragon was shipped from San Francisco for the Regatta parade in 1900. It was quite the sensation. This photograph shows it passing in front of the post office, headed east on Commercial Street. (Bernier collection.)

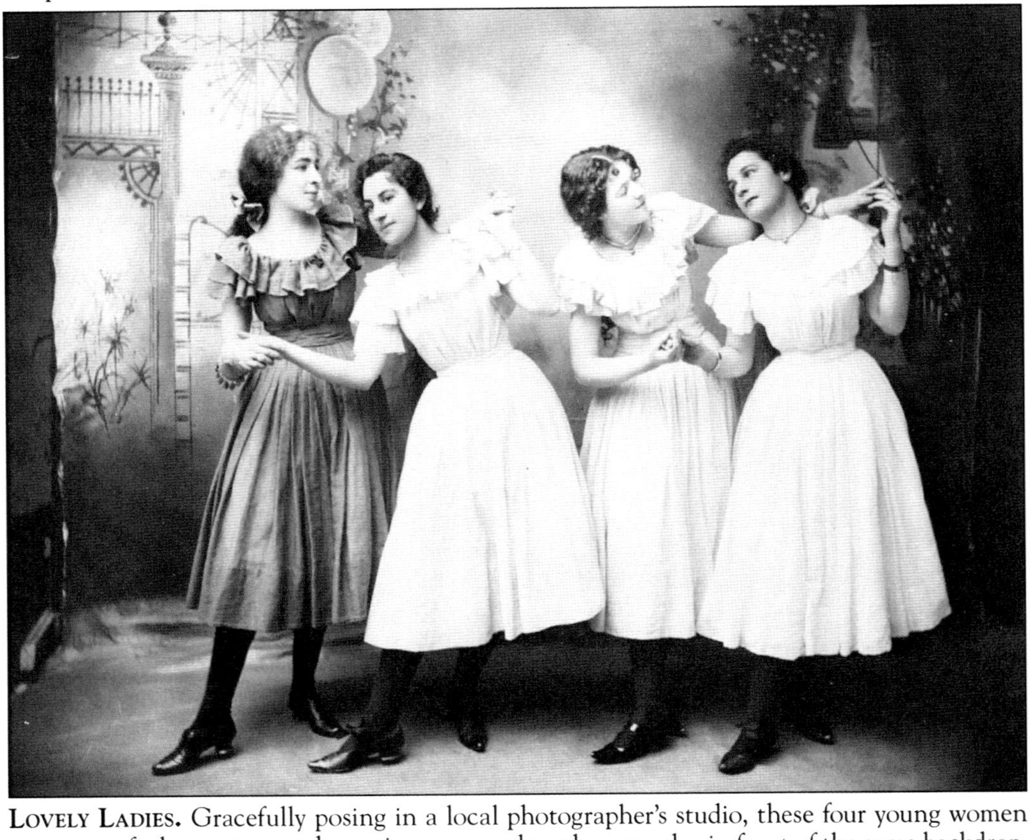

LOVELY LADIES. Gracefully posing in a local photographer's studio, these four young women were part of a larger group, whose picture was taken the same day in front of the same backdrop. (Woodfield collection.)

Seven

Harvesting the Land and Sea

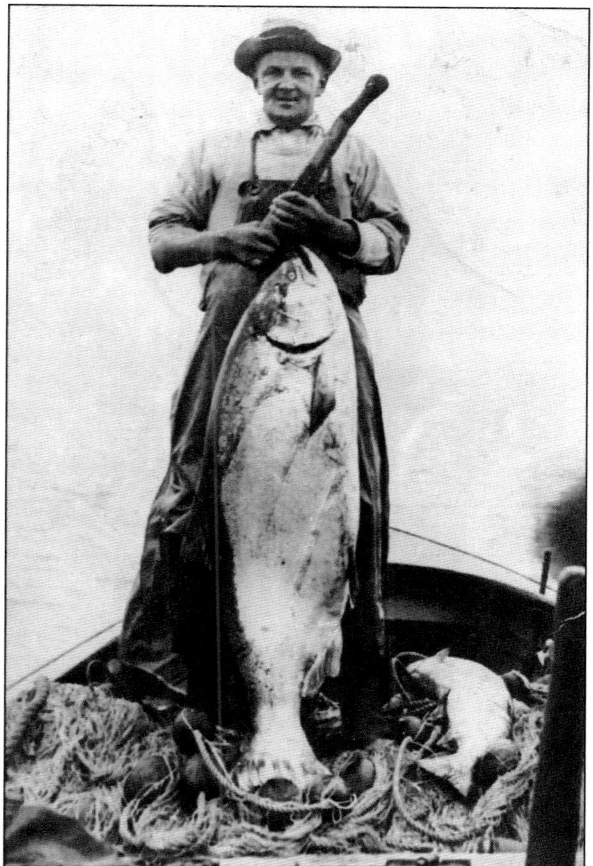

Fish Tale. This well-known Woodfield photograph shows Jalmar Wilson with his catch. The Chinook salmon hooked on May 26, 1936, on the river opposite the Flavel dock weighed in at 82.5 pounds and measured 56 inches in length. The fishing boat belonged to the Union Fishermen's Cooperative Packing Company. Frithiof Kankkonen, general manager of the business, had the salmon packed in ice and shipped to the White House, where it was served to Pres. Franklin D. Roosevelt. (CRMM No. 160-2750.)

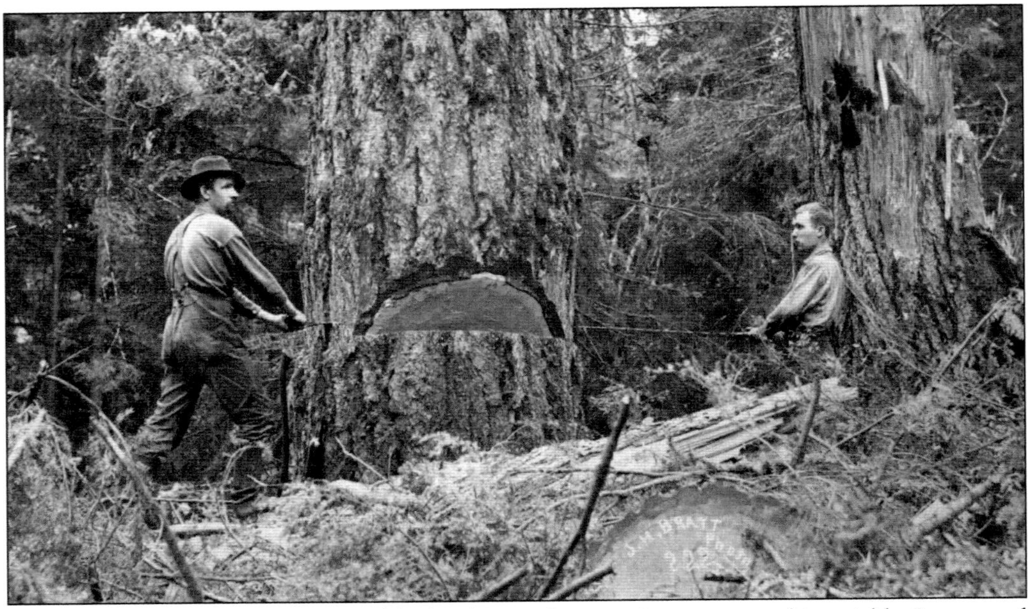

Backbreaking Work. The demand for lumber products in Astoria seemed insatiable. It was used to construct streets, buildings, ships, boats, and thousands of boxes and crates that were used to ship canned fish to the rest of the world. Consequently, loggers were kept busy supplying the material for the mills. Up until World War II, the methods shown above were the standard. Axes, crosscut saws, and wedges were used to fell tremendous trees into the water for easy transport to the mills. (CRMM No. 262-5453.)

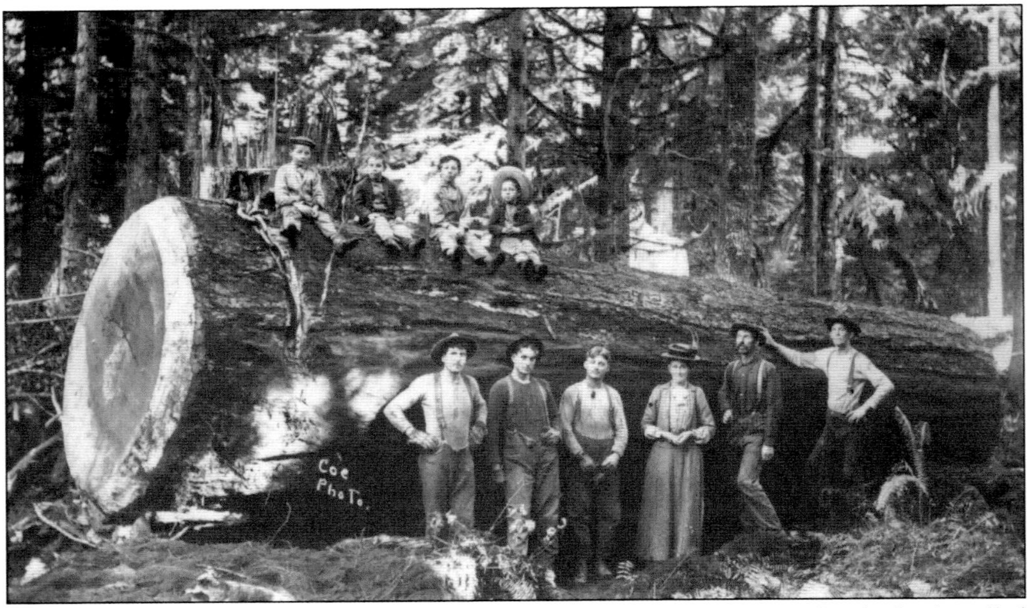

Posing with Their Trophy. When trees could not be felled into the water, they had to be rolled there. Often, they were chained and dragged over skid roads by teams of oxen to the water's edge. Trees harvested at this time (1870s–1890s) had grown tall and thick and were clear of knots. Many of the buildings in Astoria still hold some of the lumber from these trees. The children on the log are unidentified. Standing from left to right are unidentified, Chet Forrester, unidentified, Mrs. Okerstedt, Mr. Okerstedt, and Victor Olson. (CRMM No. 262-5480.)

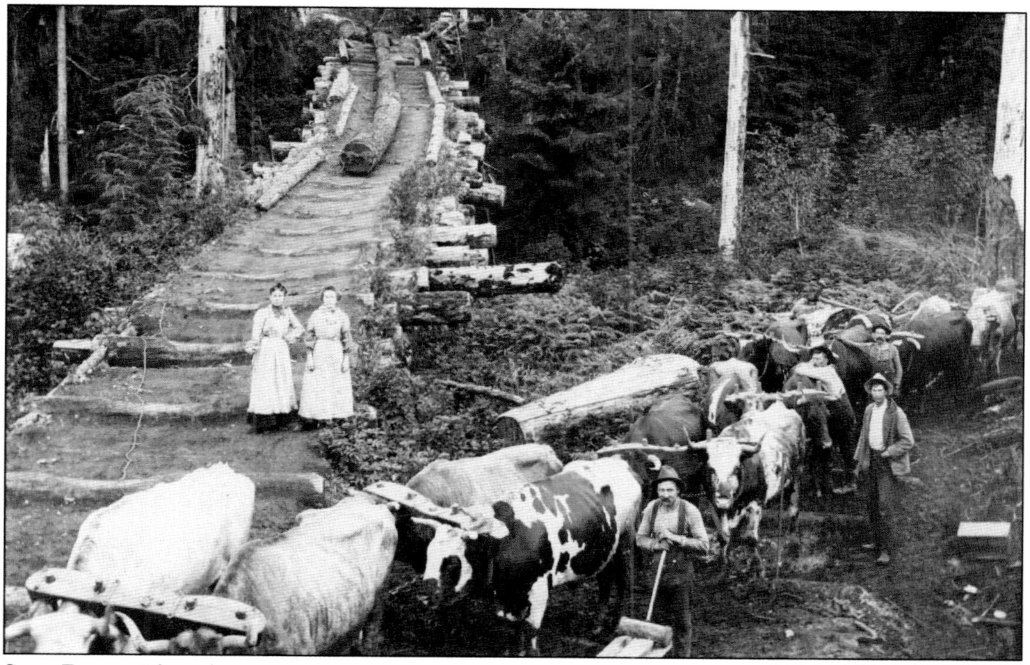

Skid Road. This photograph shows a skid road in action. Short logs were laid down every 8 to 10 feet across the path, and logs were hauled to the center of the road. Oxen teams were yoked up and chained to the logs and then driven by a bull whacker with a whip to get the logs to the water to float to the mill. (Woodfield collection.)

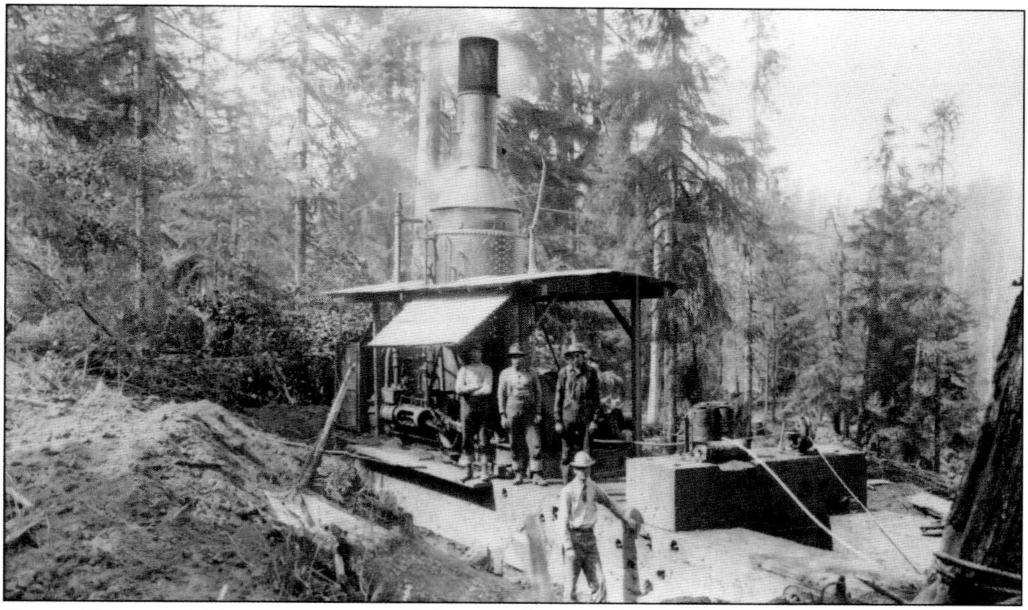

Steam Donkey. When steam entered the woods around 1900, operations reached an almost frenzied pace. Logging became even more dangerous. Donkey engines, like the one pictured here, were used to drag logs out of the woods and load them on railcars, which were waiting to run to the dumpsite. Railroads were cut right into the forests, and no tree could escape the loggers' cut. By mid-20th century, ideas about replanting the forests began to take root and ideas of forest management came into vogue. (CRMM No. 262-5440.)

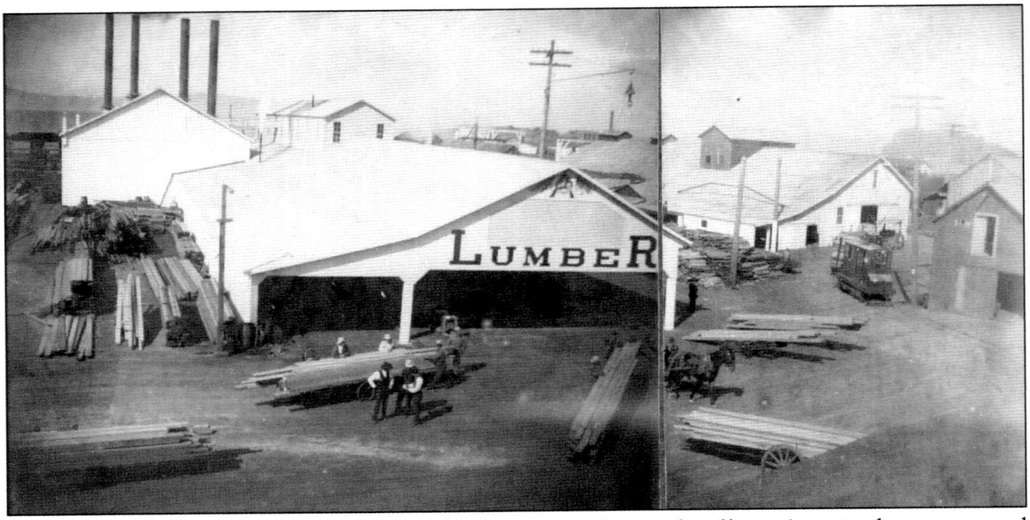

ASTORIA BOX COMPANY. This photograph shows one of several mills in Astoria that consumed the logs coming out of the woods. The Astoria Box Mill did what the name implies. Their boxes were used to pack fish for processing and ship canned product afterwards. (CRMM-262-5528.)

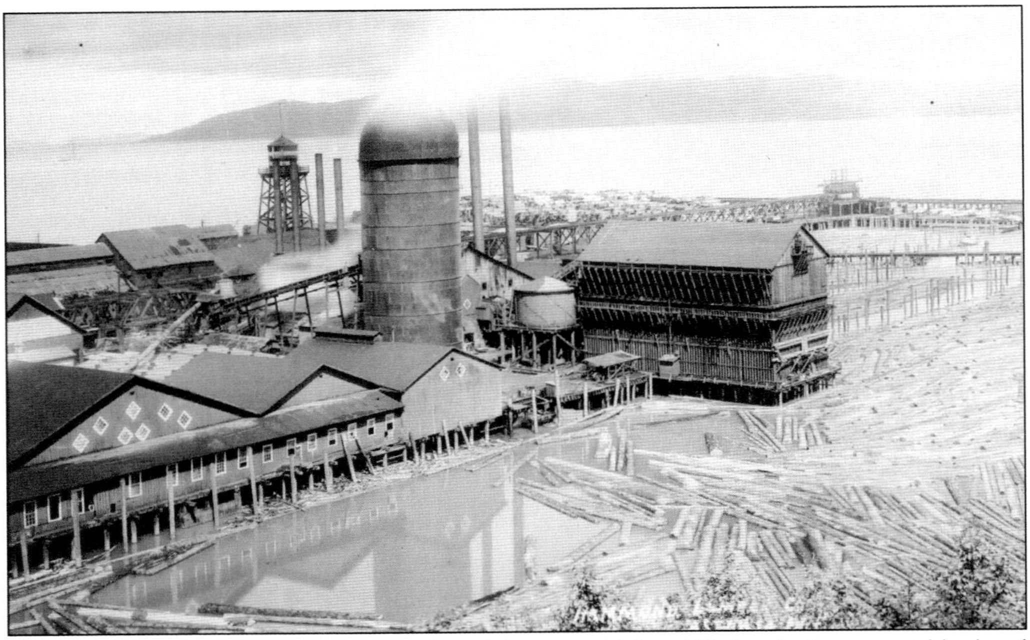

HAMMOND LUMBER COMPANY. This view shows Hammond Mill in Alderbrook, the east neighborhood of town. When this mill burned in 1922 (before the fire that burned most of downtown later that year), it put many Greeks, Eastern Europeans, and East Asian Indians out of work. The workforce included Sikhs who lived along a small street in worker housing referred to as "Hindu Alley." Children from the time remember the men with turbans walking to and from the mill. Although the mill is gone, vestiges of Hindu Alley still exist. (Clemson collection No. 2011.1.)

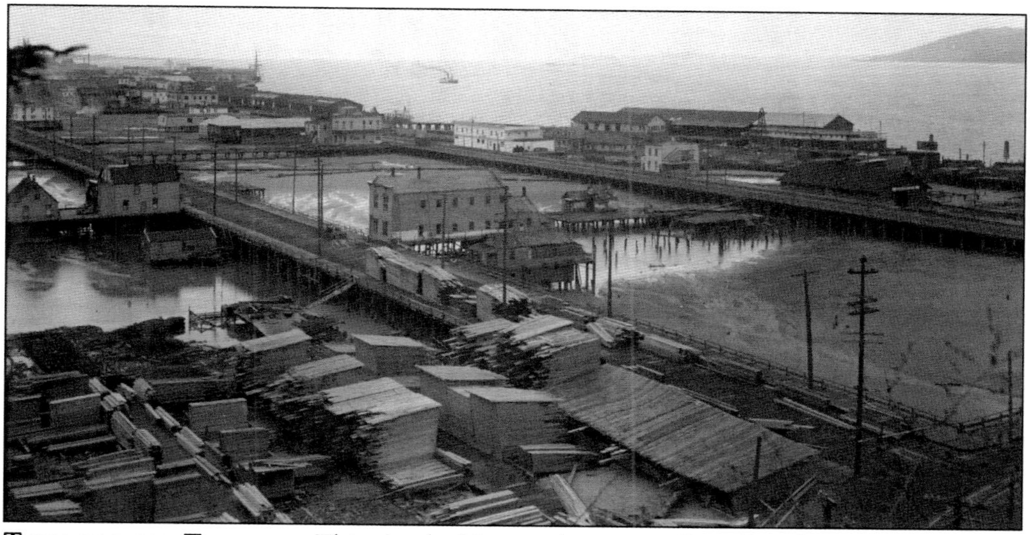

Town over the Tidelands. This view looking northwest over Scow Bay shows a portion of the Clatsop Mill in the foreground. The way the streets are built-out over the tideland is shown here, and the practice of setting buildings over pilings is revealed as well. One can understand how fire could be a concern. (CRMM No. 262-19541.)

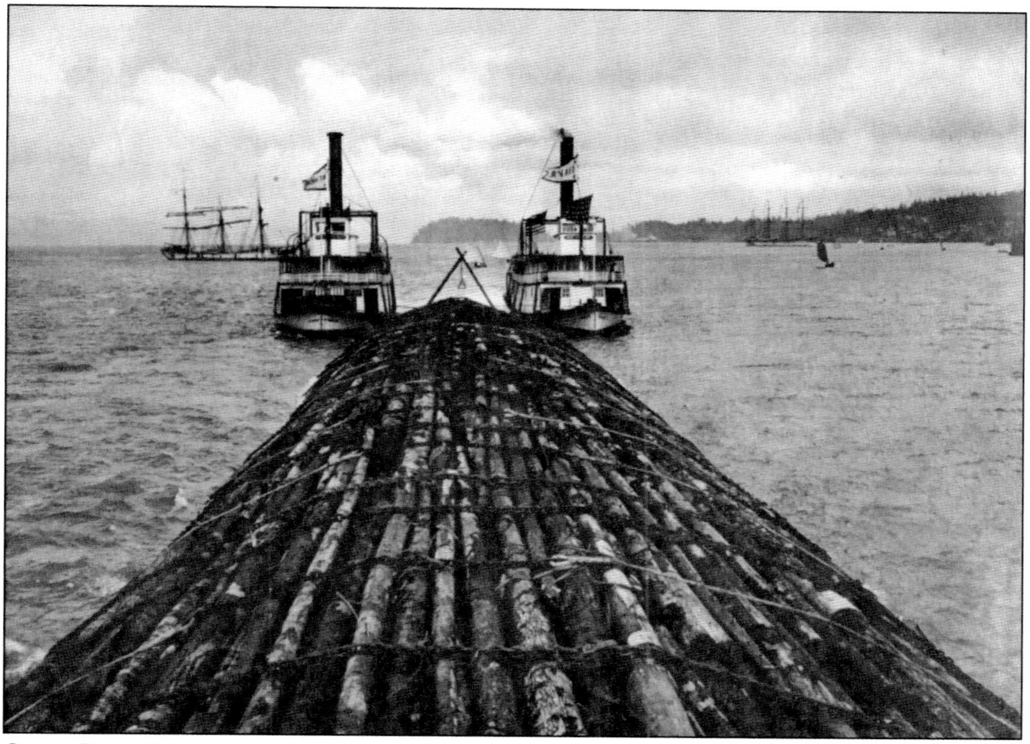

Cigar Raft. Massive rafts of logs were chained together into "cigar rafts," so called because of their shape, and towed to California. Two sternwheelers would escort the raft on either side, which is shown here, in order to get the raft over the bar. Once there, the sternwheelers would cut loose from the raft and allow the ocean-going tug to proceed. Two cradles used to assemble the rafts were in operation on the Columbia River during the 1930s. The rafts consisted of millions of board feet of logs. (Woodfield collection.)

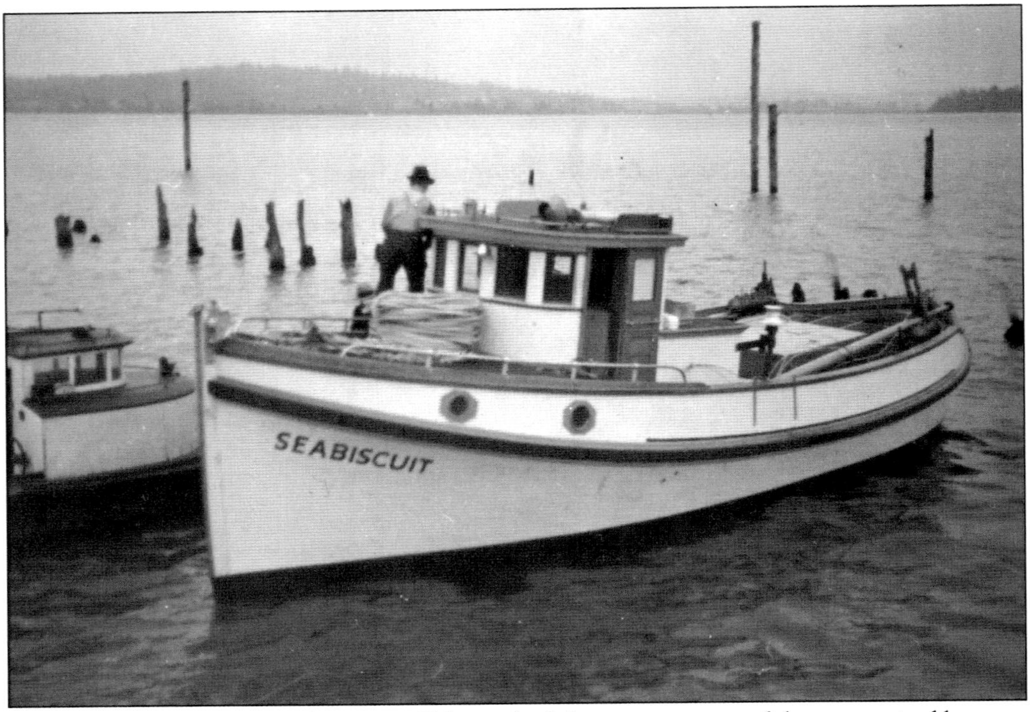

COLUMBIA BOAT BUILDING COMPANY. Tolonen-built boats were some of the most prized because of their lines and craftsmanship. This nice little troller *Seabiscuit* is shown just launched from Columbia Boat Building Company at 600 Taylor Avenue on Young's Bay in Astoria, around 1940. (CRMM No. 541-11148.)

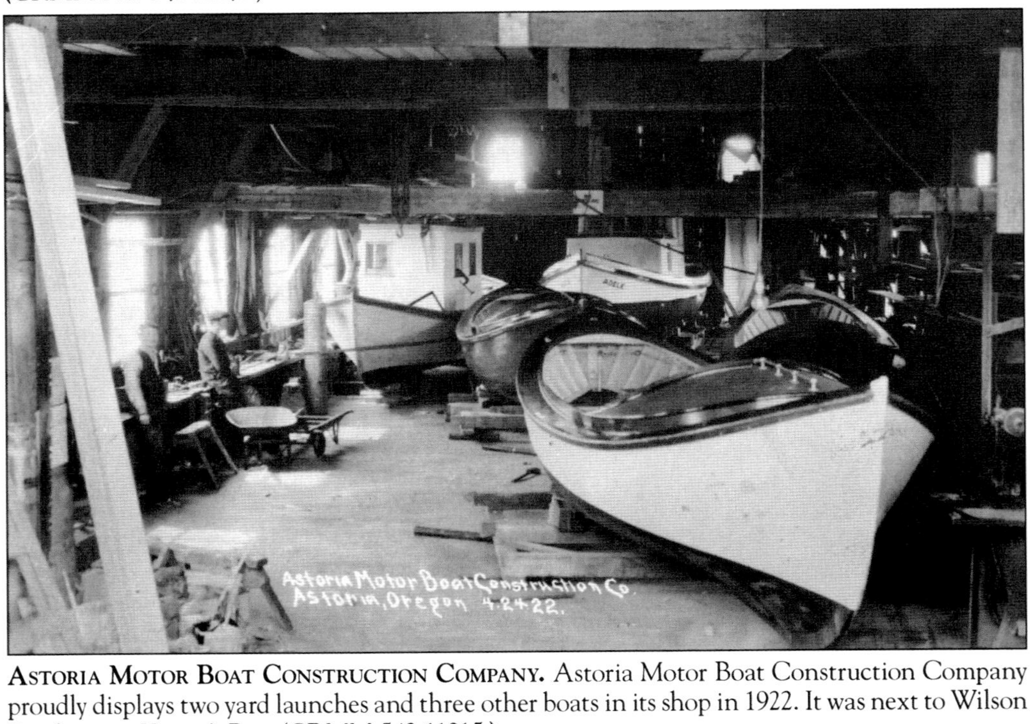

ASTORIA MOTOR BOAT CONSTRUCTION COMPANY. Astoria Motor Boat Construction Company proudly displays two yard launches and three other boats in its shop in 1922. It was next to Wilson Brothers on Young's Bay. (CRMM 542-11015.)

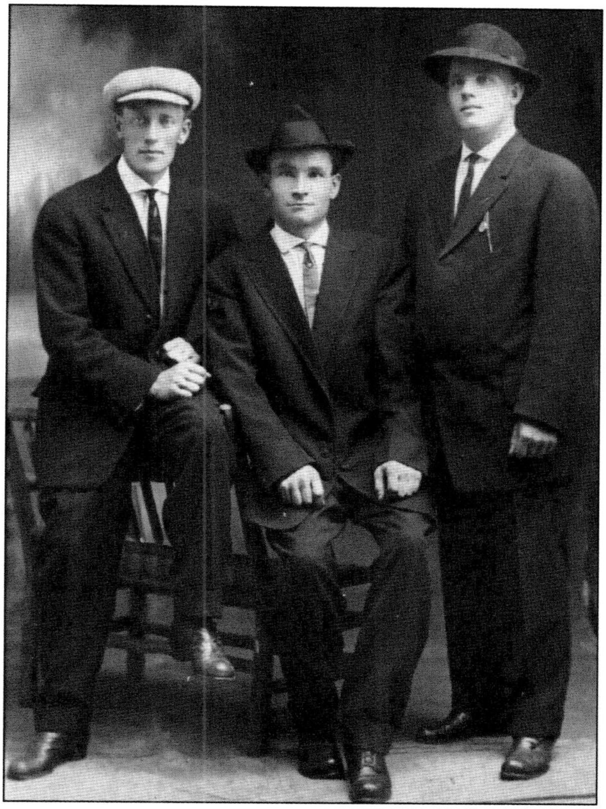

Astoria Boat Builders. This photograph shows the partners of Wickstrom and Nyman boat builders. Pictured from left to right are unidentified, Axel Wikstrom, and John Nyman. (CRMM No. 542-11059.)

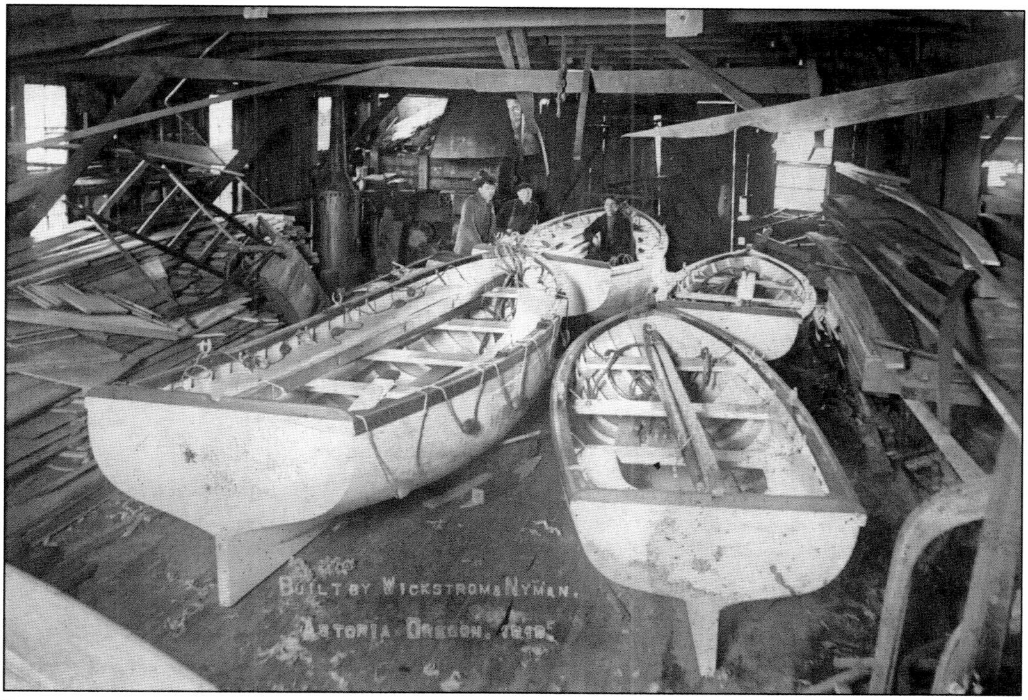

Boats by Wickstrom and Nyman, 1916. This 1916 photograph shows the interior of the boat shop of Wickstrom and Nyman. (CRMM No. 542-11019.)

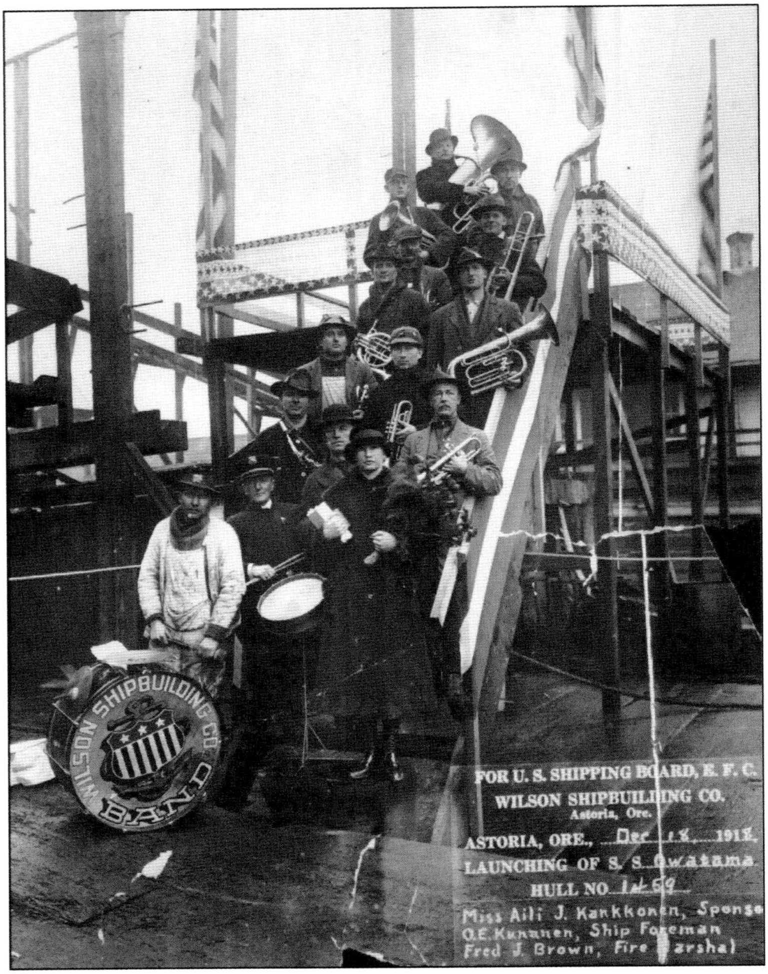

WILSON SHIPBUILDING COMPANY BAND. Aili Kankkonen is shown here with the Wilson Shipbuilding Band ready to christen the *Owatama* on December 18, 1918. At the height of the US Shipping Board's effort to build wooden freighters during World War I, Wilson Shipbuilding employed almost a thousand workers. (CRMM No. 542-11070.)

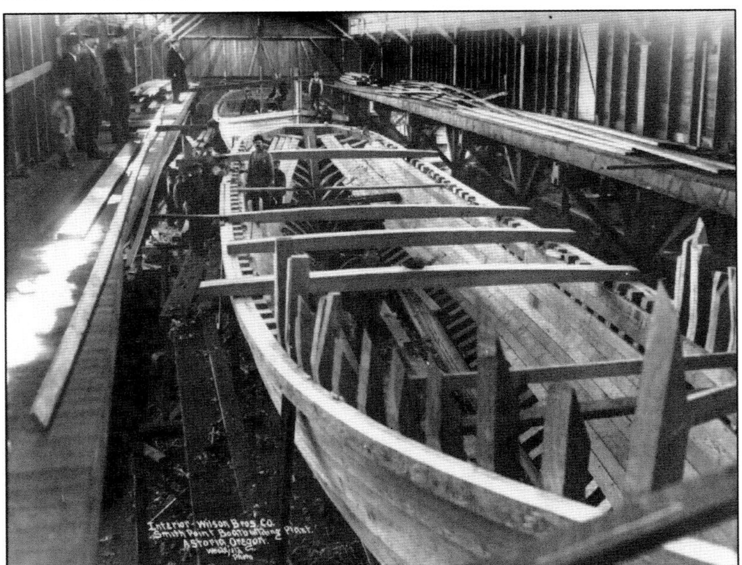

INTERIOR OF WILSON BROTHERS BOAT SHOP. Before it became Wilson Shipbuilding in 1917, it was known as Wilson Brothers Company. They specialized in building cannery tenders for the Columbia River and Alaska canneries. (CRMM No. 542-10997.)

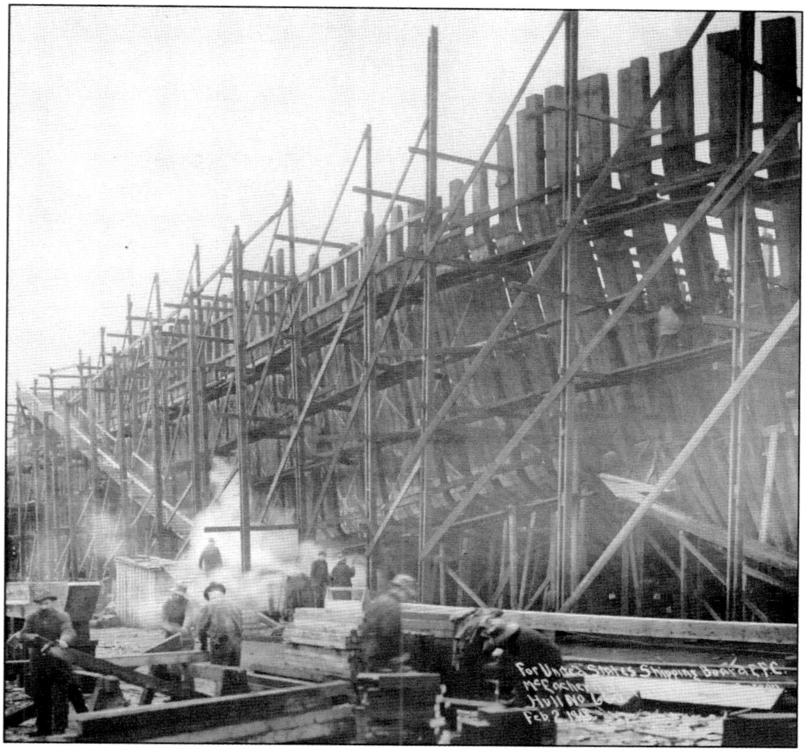

A Forest to Build One Ship. McEachern Shipbuilding was just east of Wilson Shipbuilding on Young's Bay. McEachern had contracts with the US Shipping Board to build the Ferris-type freighters during World War I. This photograph shows just how much timber went into constructing these wooden freighters that were 325 feet long. (CRMM No. 542-11051.)

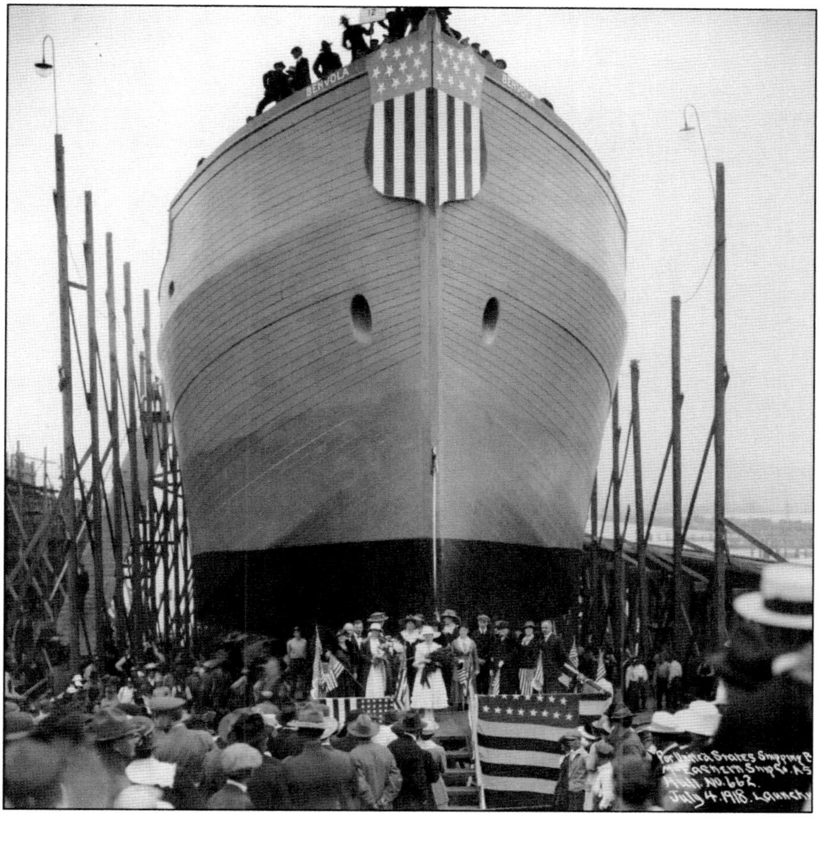

Launching Day for Hull No. 662, Benvola. Hull No. 662 launched out of McEachern on July 4, 1918. By the time many of these hulls were completed, they were no longer needed because the war had ended. The ones that were finished and put into service proved to be too slow to be effective, and many were abandoned or turned into scows or barges. (CRMM No. 542-11125.)

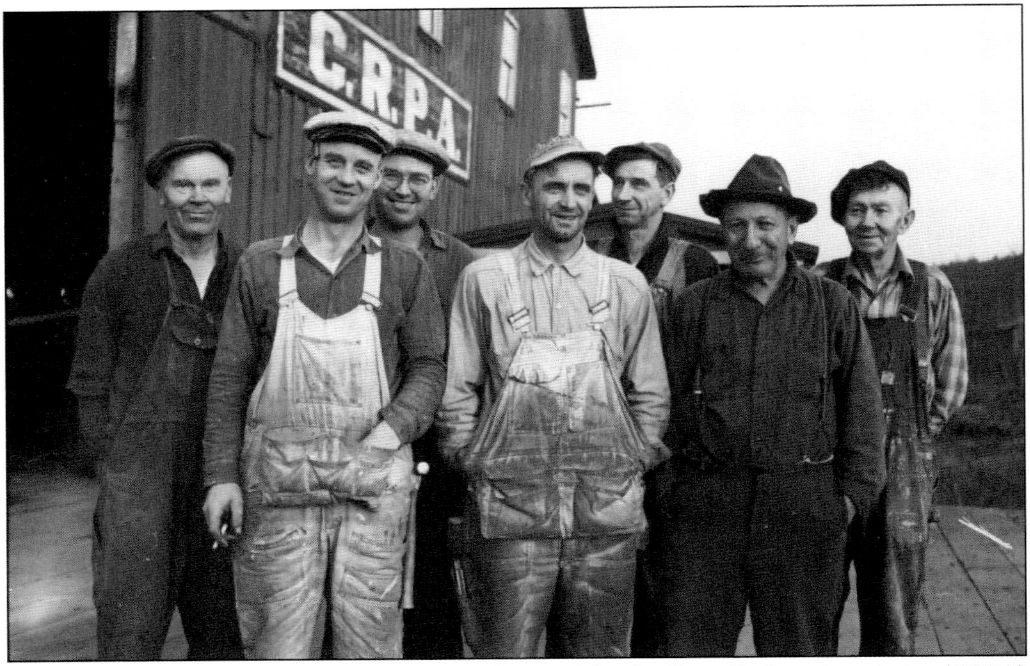

George and Barker Station, Boatbuilding Crew. Columbia River Packers Association (CRPA) had a small boat shop at the site of the old George and Barker cannery, which was located at the east end of town. It also operated a larger shipyard on Young's Bay where McEachern had been. This image shows the crew out in front of the shop in 1946. (CRMM 072-1809.)

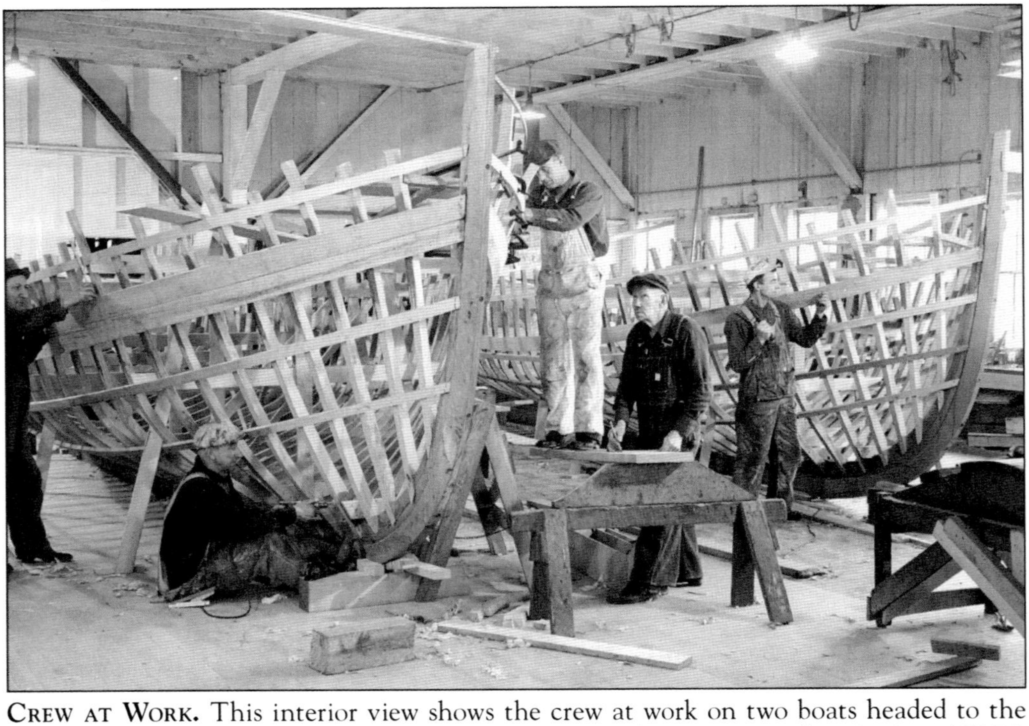

Crew at Work. This interior view shows the crew at work on two boats headed to the Alaska fishery. This Ned Thorndike photograph was taken on December 6, 1944. (CRPA collection No. 0071a.)

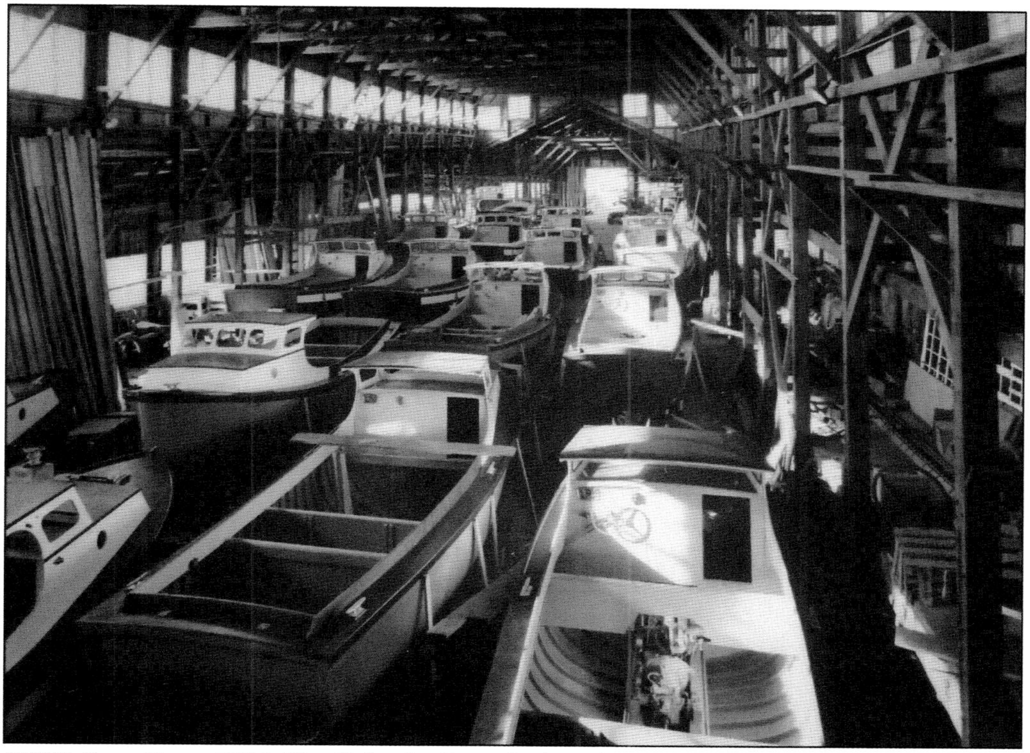

CRPA Boat Shop, 1956. The Columbia River Packers Association (later Bumble Bee) Shipyard is shown in this 1956 photograph full of stern-pickers intended for the Bristol Bay Alaska fishery. (CRMM No. 542-16014.)

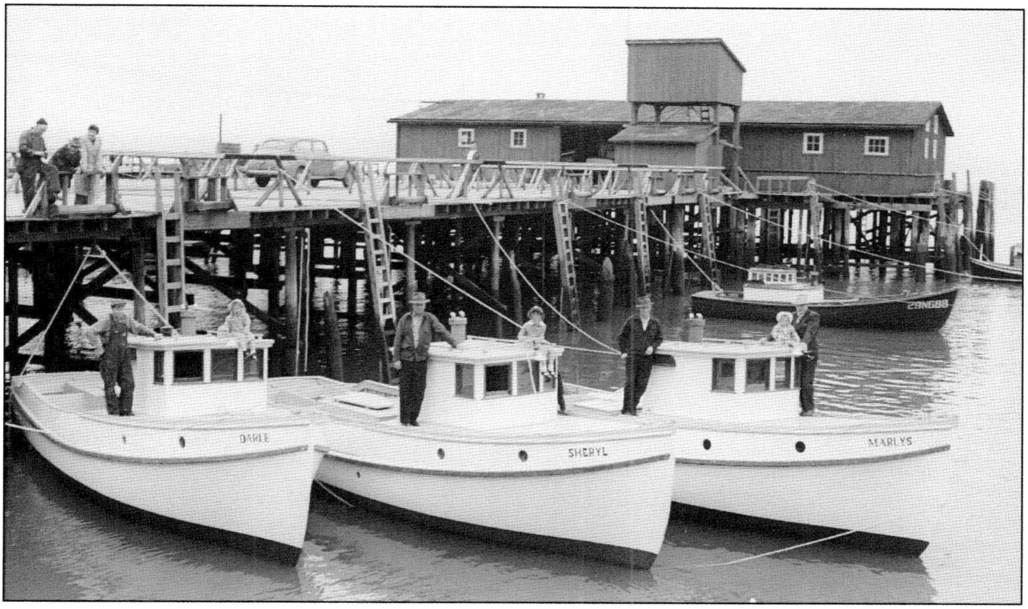

Three Sisters, Three Boats. These three identical trollers were built at CRPA and were named after three of the Hoaglund children, Darle, Sheryl, and Marlys, who can be seen seated on top of their respective boats. The *Darle* is on display in the collection of the museum. (CRPA collection No. 184f.)

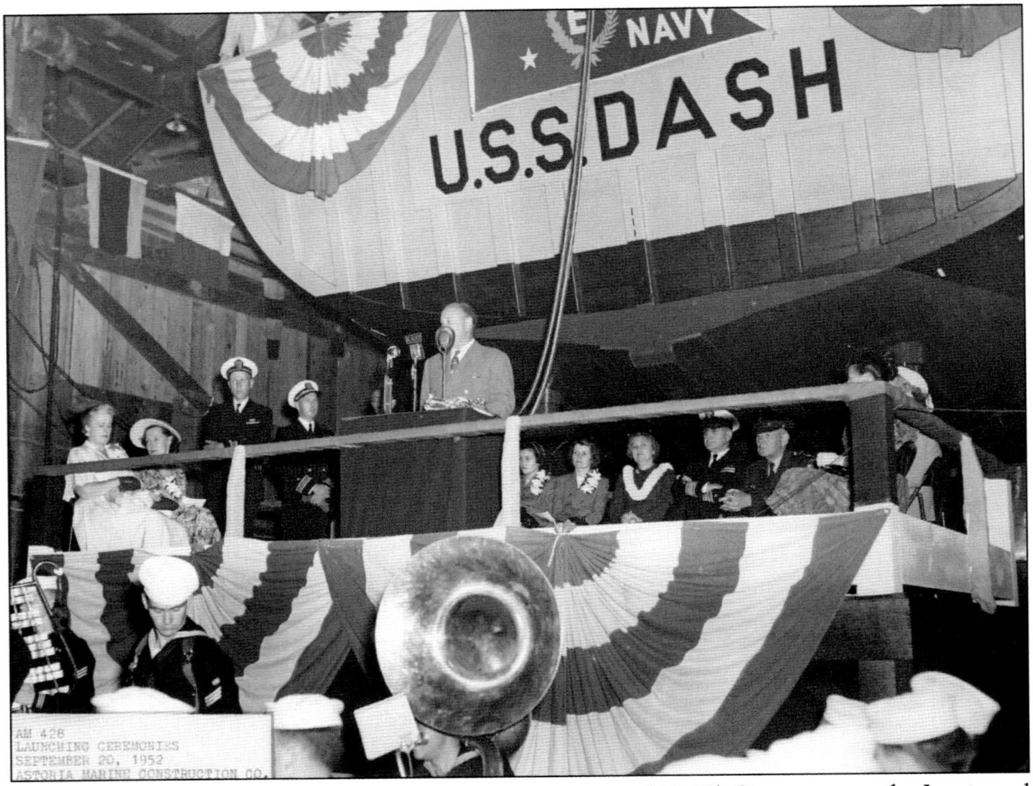

BIG DAY FOR AMC CO. The Astoria Marine Construction (AMC) Company, on the Lewis and Clark River south of Young's Bay, got the contract to build nonmagnetic minesweepers for the Navy during the Korean conflict. These specialized craft had to be built without any iron to avoid falling victim to the magnetic mines then in use. This required special construction methods using bronze fittings instead of steel. This photograph shows owner Joe Dyer addressing the crowd on the launching day for the first of the vessels, the USS *Dash*, on September 20, 1952. These contracts kept many skilled workers employed during the post–World War II economic slump. (CRMM No. 542-16415.)

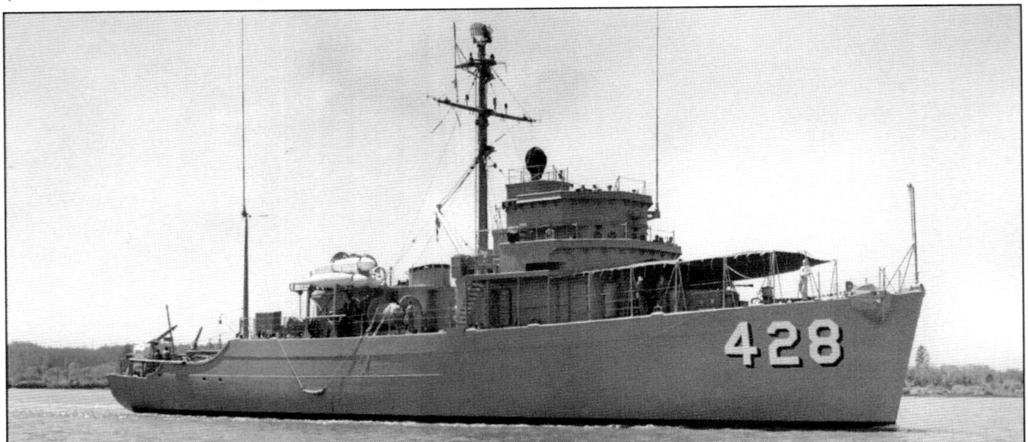

USS *DASH* (AM 428). Eight months later, the vessel had undergone trials in Young's Bay, making it ready for service. These vessels saw active duty in Vietnam as well; a testament to their being well-constructed. (CRMM No. 542-16451.)

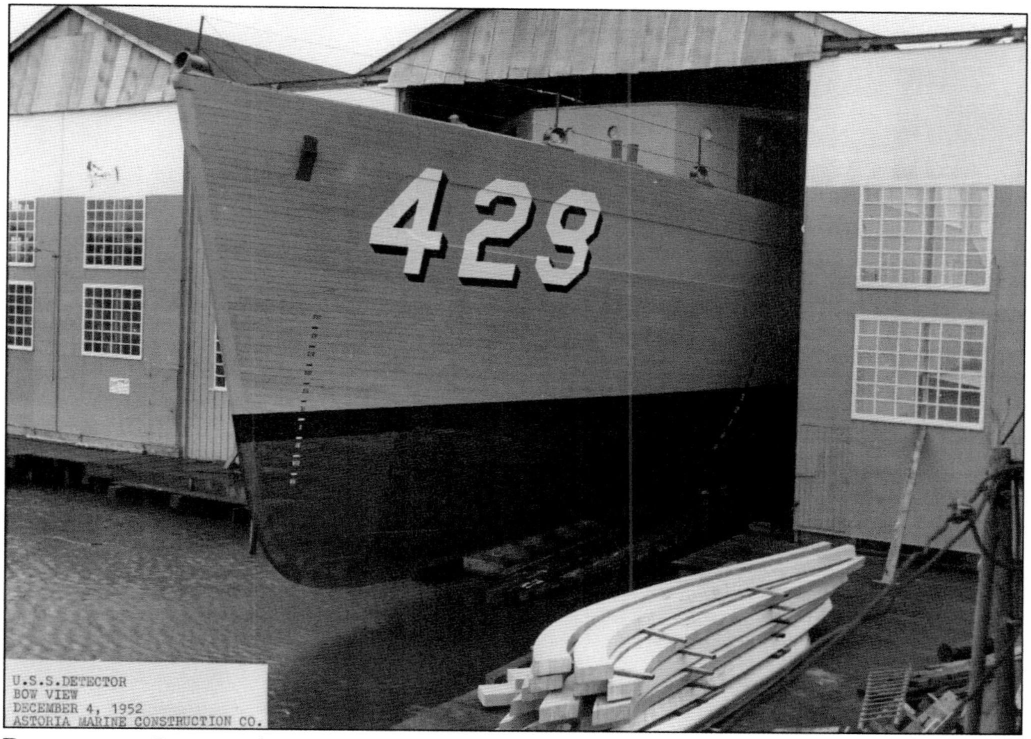

PUSHING THE LIMITS. The minesweepers were some of the largest vessels AMCCO had ever attempted to build. In fact, when this one was launched, it hung up on the corrugated metal at the top of the doorway and knocked it out of square as it went. (CRMM No. 542-18545.)

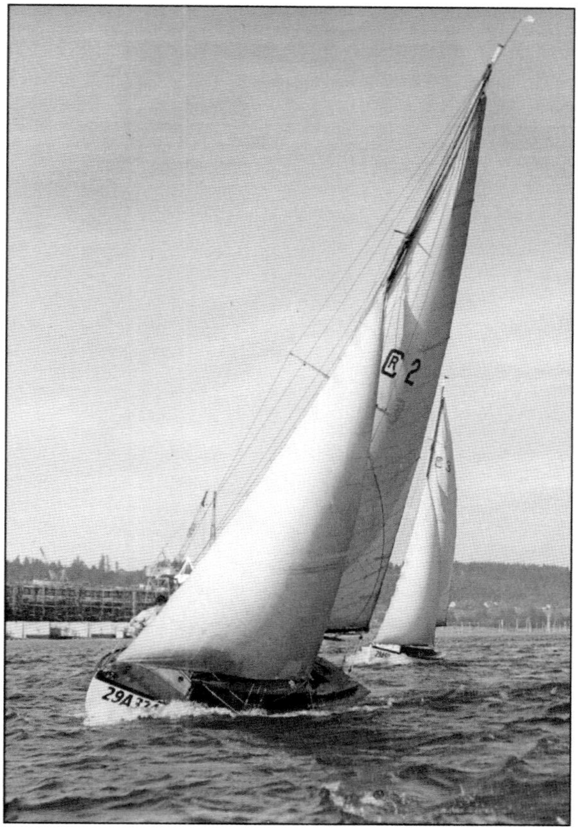

PEACETIME PURSUITS. Dyer's company also designed and built fishing boats and workboats of various types in addition to recreational boats. This sailing sloop was designed and built by AMCCo for the Columbia River Yachting Association, whose members were looking for a uniform design suited to the conditions on the lower Columbia River. It needed to be stable, have a shallow draft to accommodate the many sand bars, and sail well in all wind conditions. The answer was the Columbia River One Design (CROD). The one in this image is now in the collection of the museum. (CRMM No. 055-13834.)

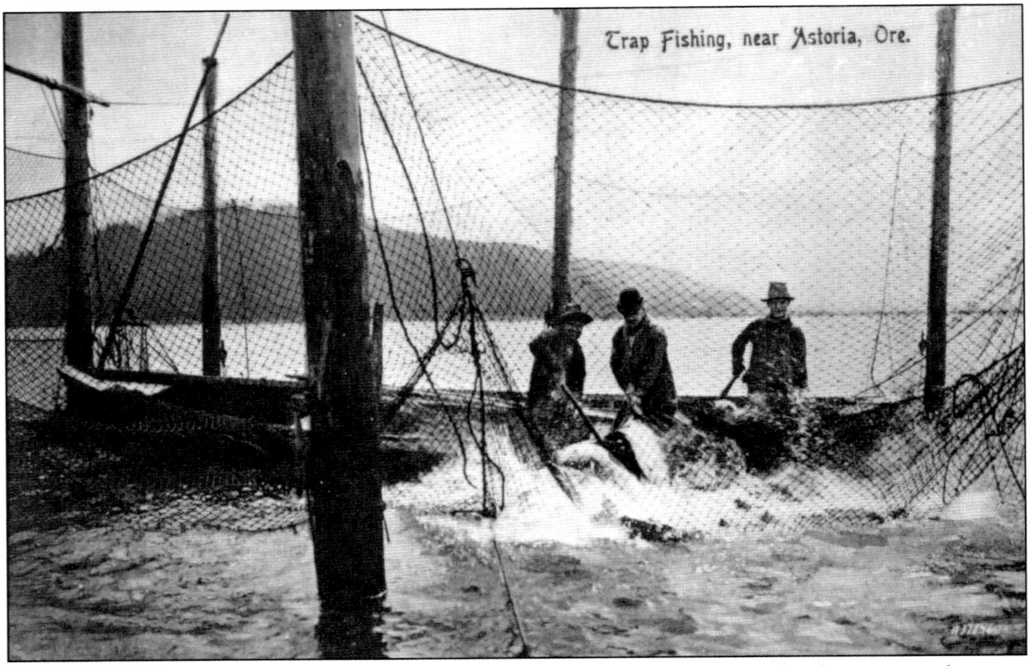

Fish Traps. Fish traps were stationary shallow-water nets anchored to piles driven into the river bottom. Fish would swim into the long lead of the trap. The fish traps were quite effective at catching fish, but they were not as selective as other methods. Because it was a passive system, the traps had to be monitored and any fish caught removed promptly. These factors affected the freshness of the catch. Fish traps were later outlawed in Oregon in 1926. (CRMM No. 165-2870.)

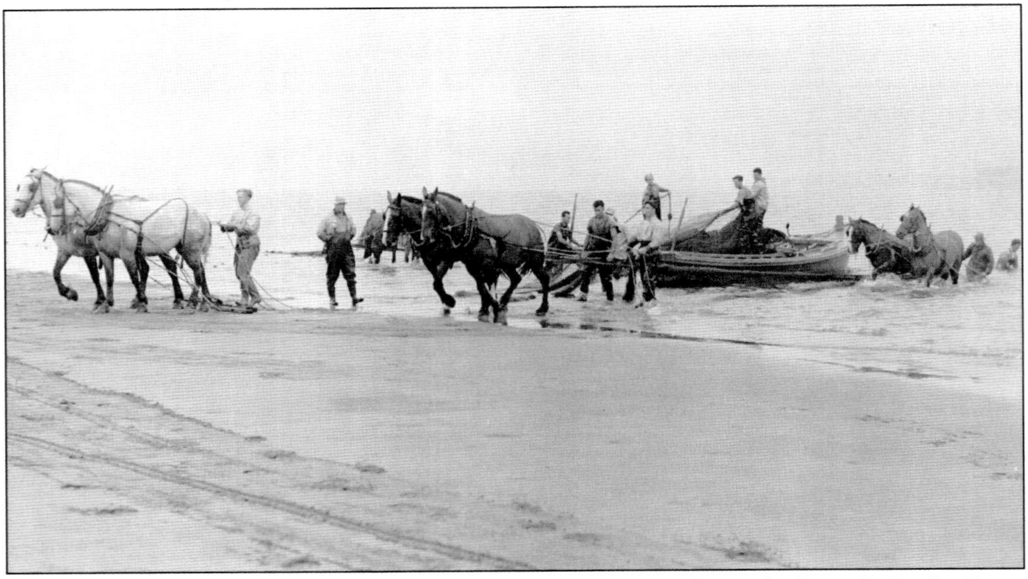

Horses Pulling in Seine, Sand Island. This was a common sight on the lower Columbia River until Oregon outlawed the practice in 1948. The seine was let out from a skiff, and the ends were attached to horse teams that pulled the net onto the beach or shallows. The crew loaded the fish on to waiting wagons or trucks, transferred to the tender, and then delivered them to the cannery. The canneries owned the rights to the seining grounds, and the work was good employment for students during the summer season. (CRMM No. 170-3104.)

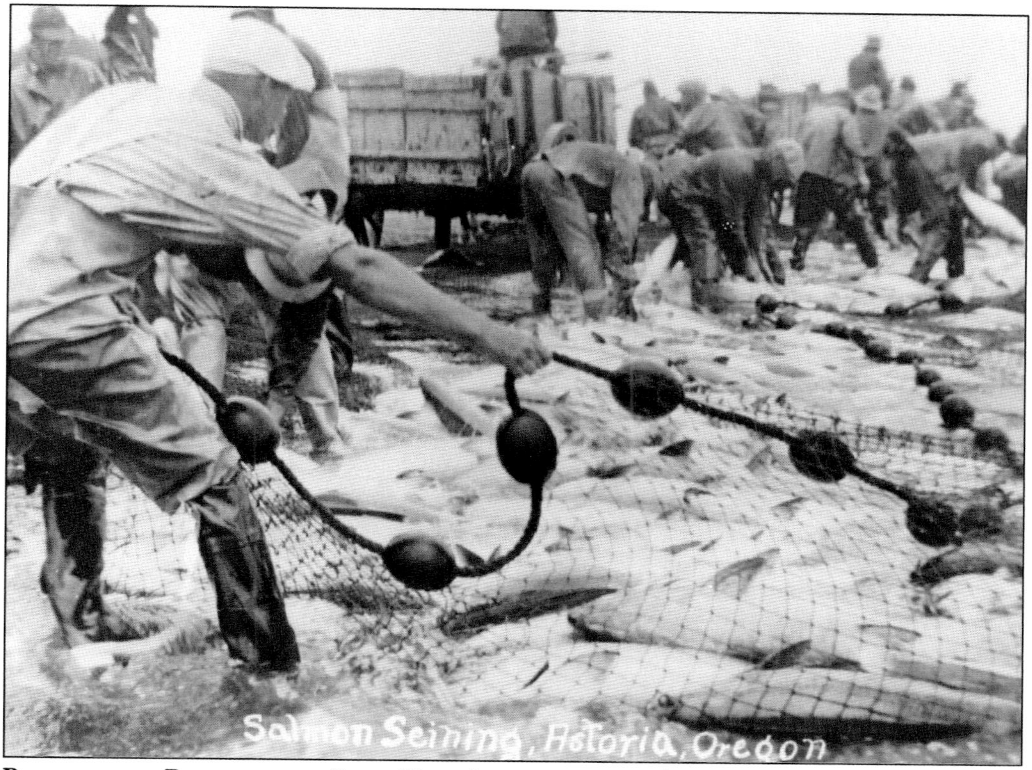

BEACHCOMBERS PULLING IN THE BUNT. Here, the seine is near to shore, and some of the crewmembers hold the cork line up to keep the fish from escaping. The "beachcombers" pick the fish out of the bunt of the net and then put them into the wagons. When the seine is in the water, the cork line is buoyant and holds the top part of the net near the surface. The lead line is weighted and keeps the bottom of the net near the bottom of the river. (CRMM No. 170-3291.)

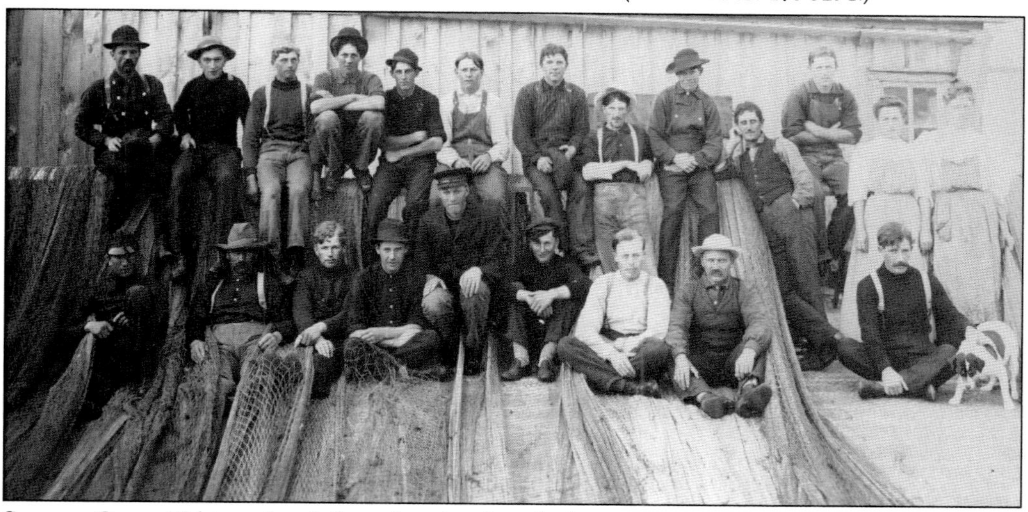

SEINING CREW. Taking a break from their hard work, this crew poses for the camera. The working day went from sunrise to sunset. The most productive time was in the early morning. Crews on remote seining grounds could be put up in barracks built by the canneries. They worked, ate, and slept on the seining grounds as long as the fish could be caught. Horses were often kept in barns out on the river during the season. (CRMM No. 175-3448.)

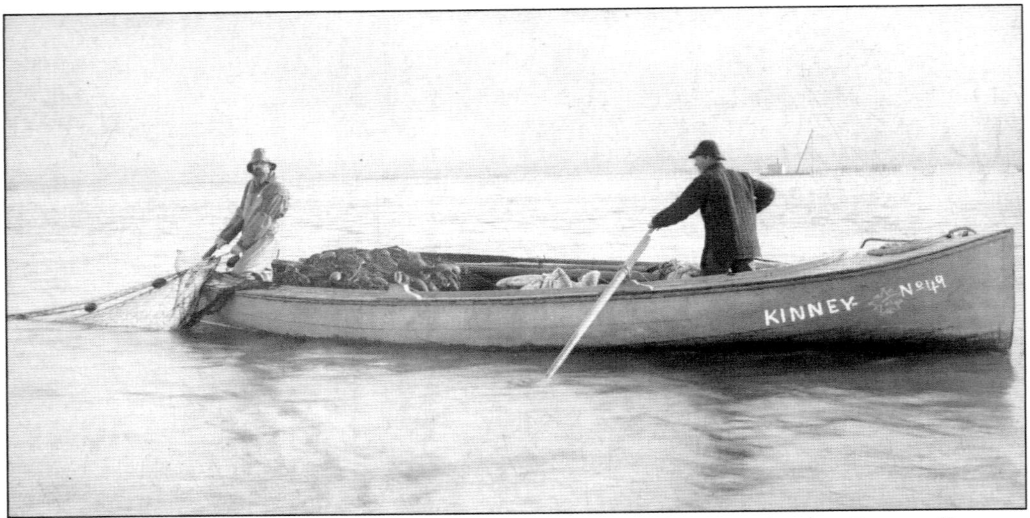

Gillnetting, Two-Man Crew. This type of boat is the classic Columbia River gillnetter. Thousands of these were used in the 1880s and 1890s. Fishermen sailed to the area, let out the gillnet, drifted, and then pulled in the net with the fish caught by the gills in the mesh of the net. By varying the size of the mesh, the method could be selective with regard to the size of fish caught, with larger mesh only catching the larger fish. (CRMM No. 166-2924.)

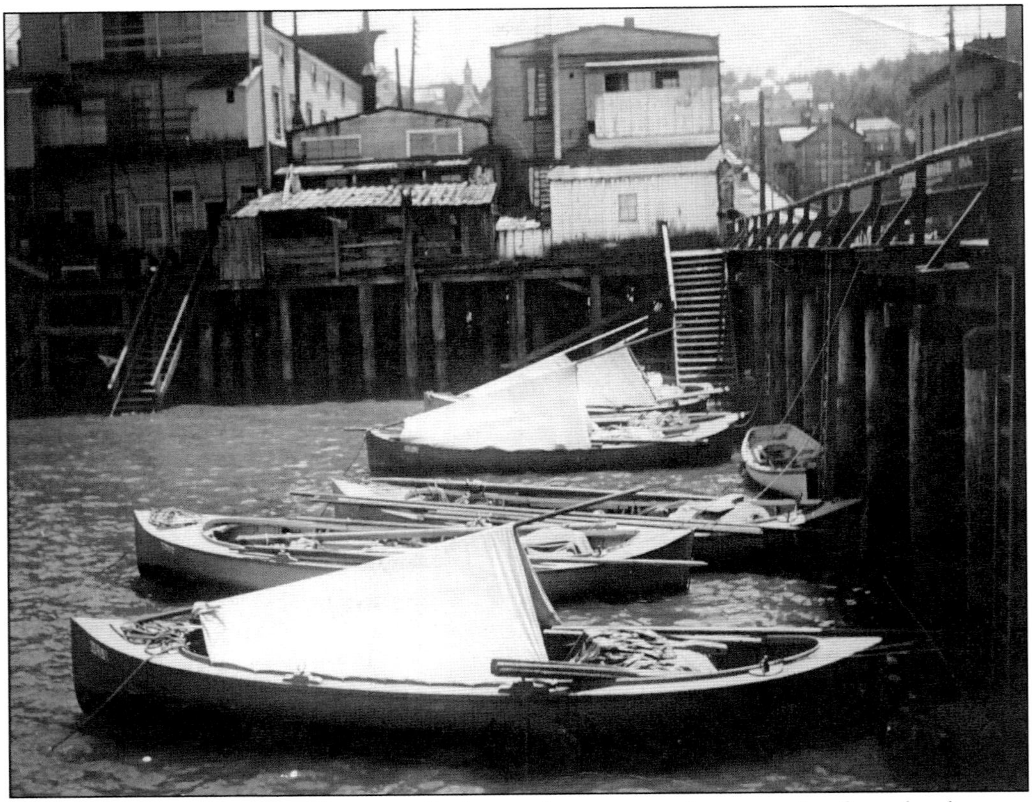

Gillnetters at the Dock. This specially designed tent was used as protection from the elements by the gillnet fishermen. When boats were out fishing at night and lanterns were hung from the poles, it was said they looked like a city out on the water. (CRMM No. 167-3009.)

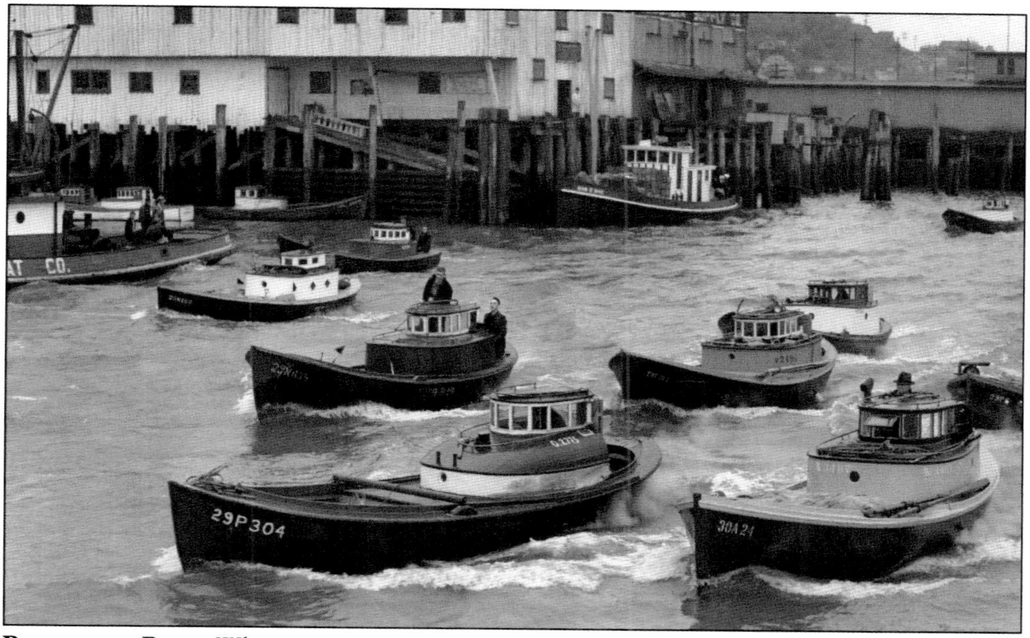

Bowpickers Race. When engines started going into gillnet boats around 1900, the design of the boat was modified to adapt to the change. The handling of the nets was done at the bow, away from the engine and propeller. The boats of this type were given the nickname "bowpicker." Every year at regatta, the fishing boats engaged in friendly competition to see who had the fastest boat. (CRMM No. 167-3007.)

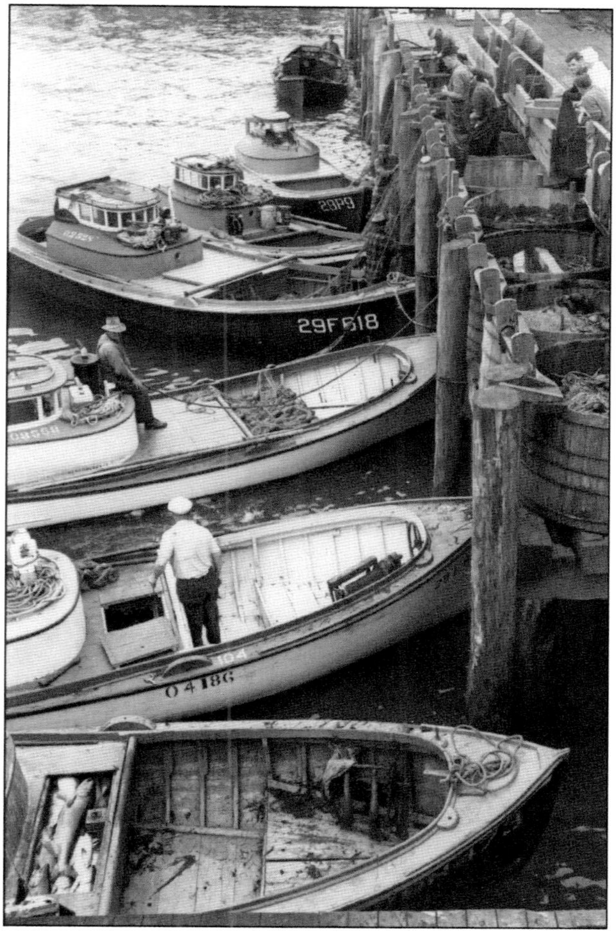

Bluestoning Nets. In order to preserve the linen nets, they were hauled out, mended, and dried on net-drying racks after use. To further preserve the natural fiber and to make it less visible to the fish, the nets were dipped in a barrel of copper-sulfate solution, which dyed the fiber a darker bluish tint, making it less noticeable in the water. This "bluestoning" treatment also fended off rot and mildew. (CRMM No. 167-5220.)

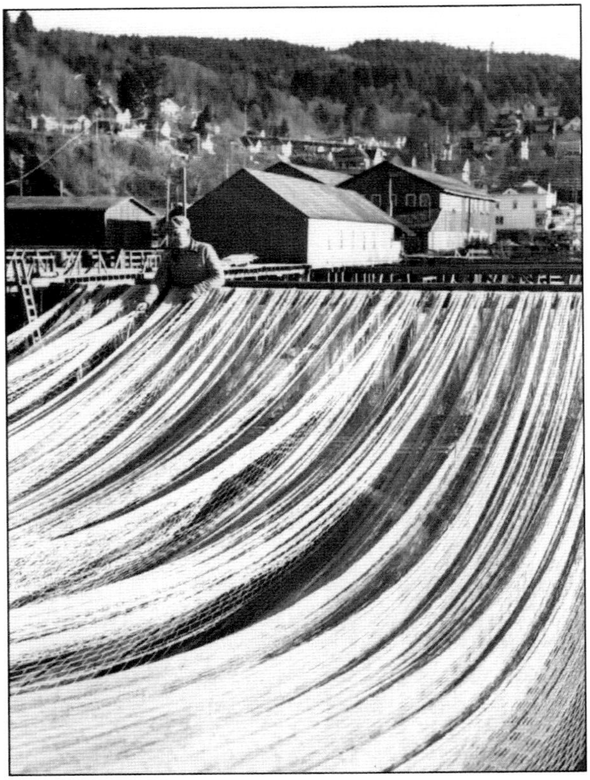

NET-DRYING RACKS. This photograph shows Trygve Johansen laying out a net for drying at the George and Barker Station on March 18, 1946. (CRMM No. 167-2964.)

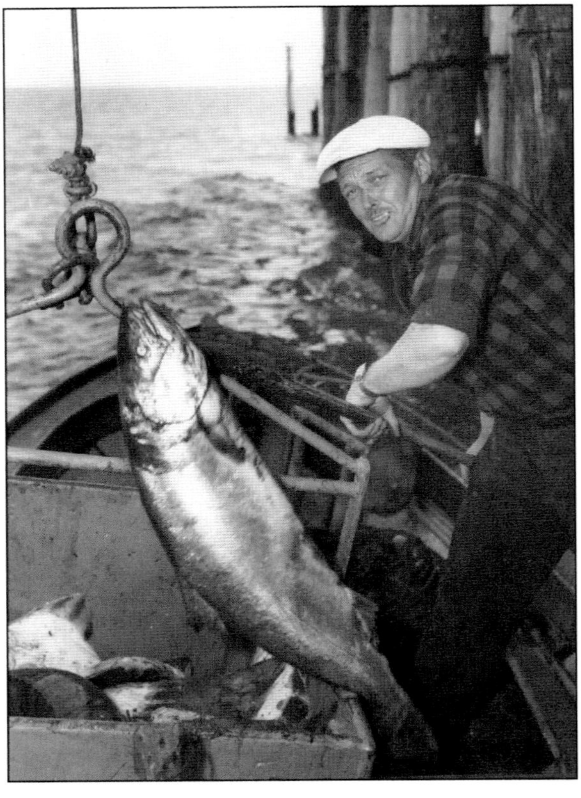

GILLNETTER UNLOADING SALMON. Demonstrating proper technique, this fisherman is gaffing the salmon by the head so as not to damage the saleable meat of the fish. These fish were landed at Occident Station, one of the CRPA properties, on May 13, 1949. (CRMM No. 167-2959.)

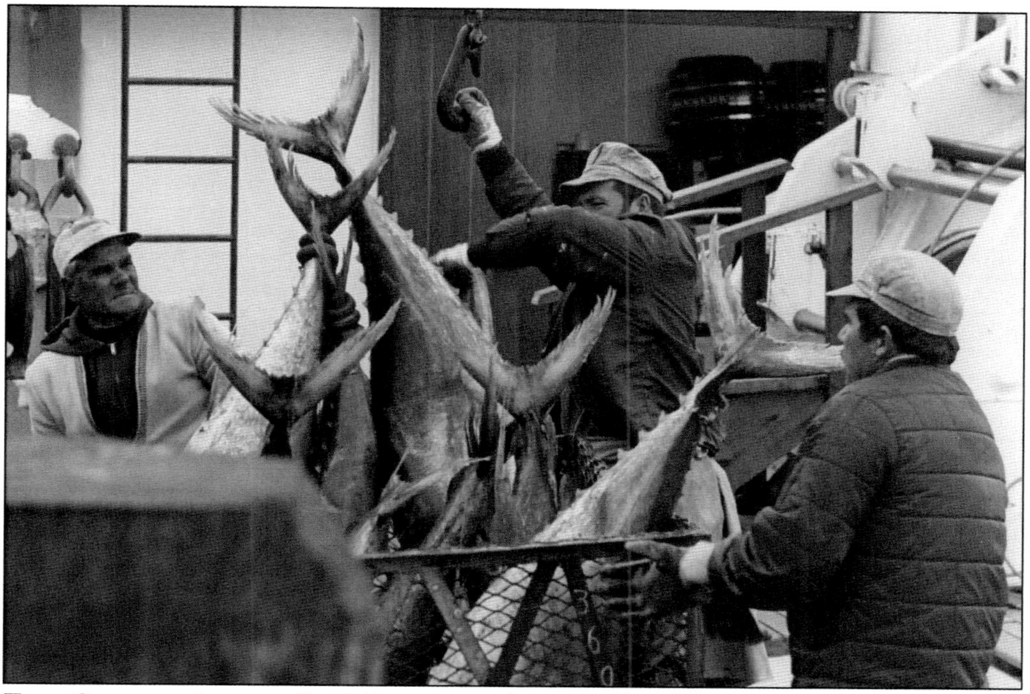

Tuna Comes to Astoria. By 1940, tuna were being caught off the Oregon coast in noticeable numbers. Albacore proved to be a very durable fish that was readily frozen and able to maintain freshness. This allowed canneries to operate on a regular schedule rather than being at the mercy of having to process the catch as soon as possible. By 1950, tuna packing had out-produced salmon. (CRMM No. 181-3698.)

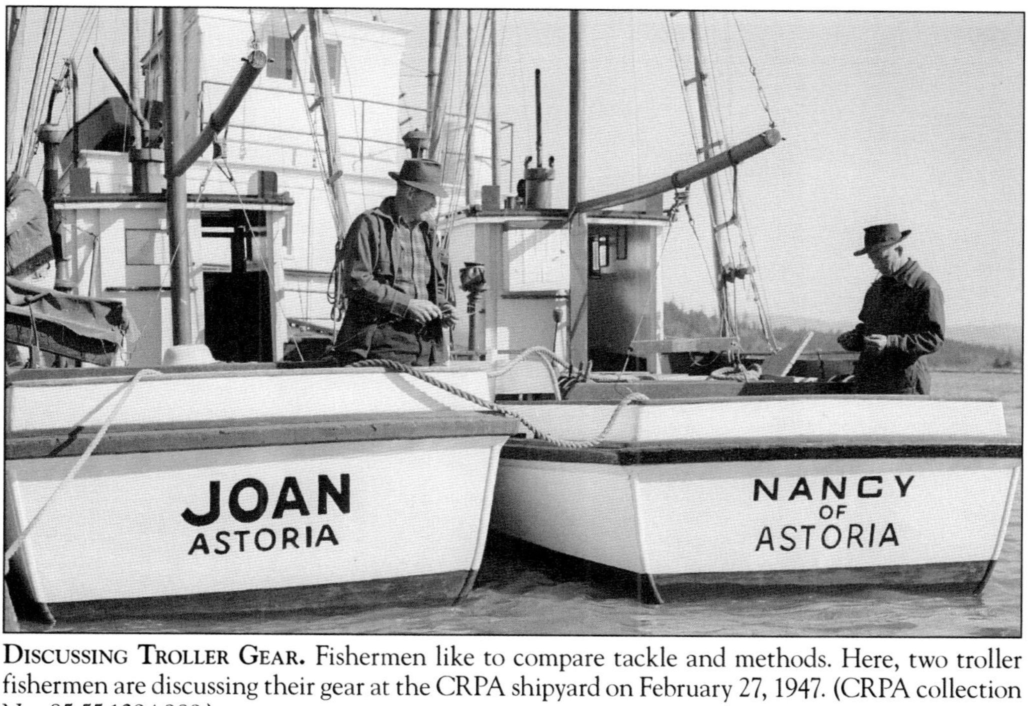

Discussing Troller Gear. Fishermen like to compare tackle and methods. Here, two troller fishermen are discussing their gear at the CRPA shipyard on February 27, 1947. (CRPA collection No. 85.55.1394.989.)

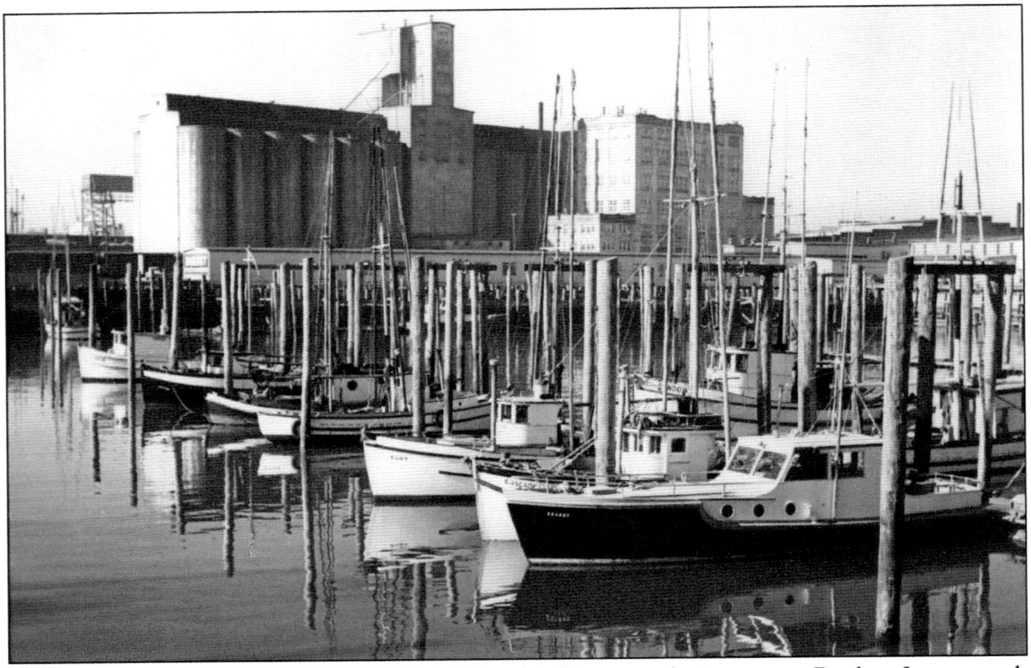

Fishing Fleet at West Mooring Basin, c. 1970. Photography instructor Reuben Jensen took this photograph of a calm west end mooring basin full of fishing boats. In the background looming above the basin are the flourmill and storage silos at the Port. The Barbey Packing Company is just visible behind the pilings. (CRMM No. 180-3628.)

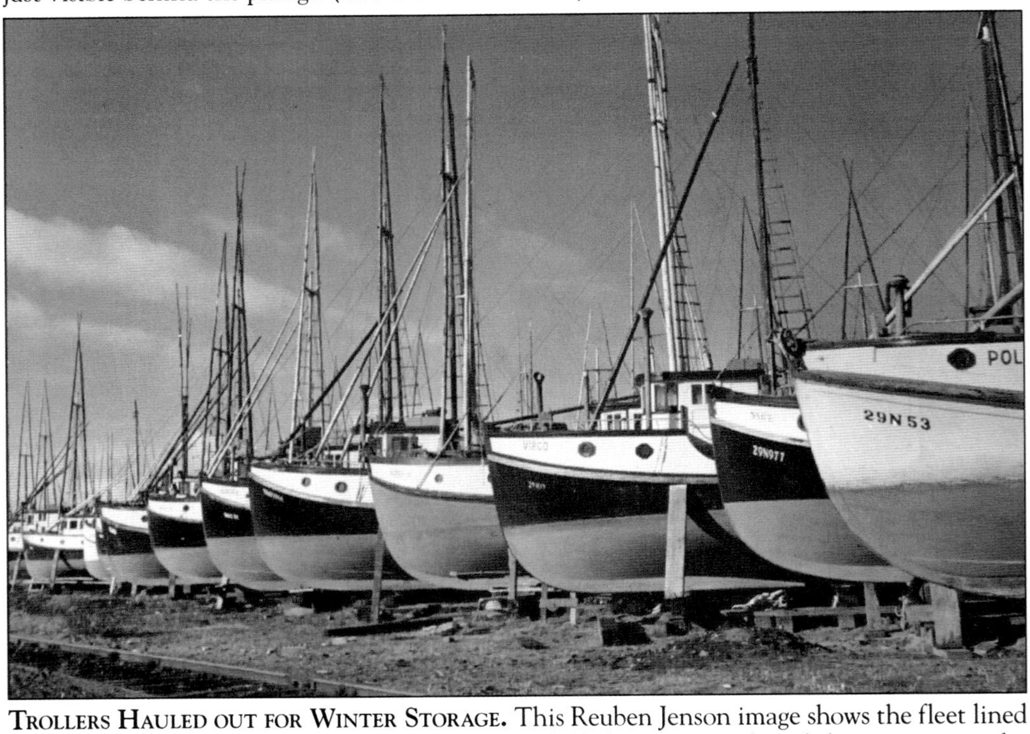

Trollers Hauled out for Winter Storage. This Reuben Jenson image shows the fleet lined up out of the water for maintenance and repair. A skilled eye can see the subtle variations in the design of these craft and distinguish one builder from another. (CRMM No. 180-9502.)

Eight

THE SMELL OF MONEY

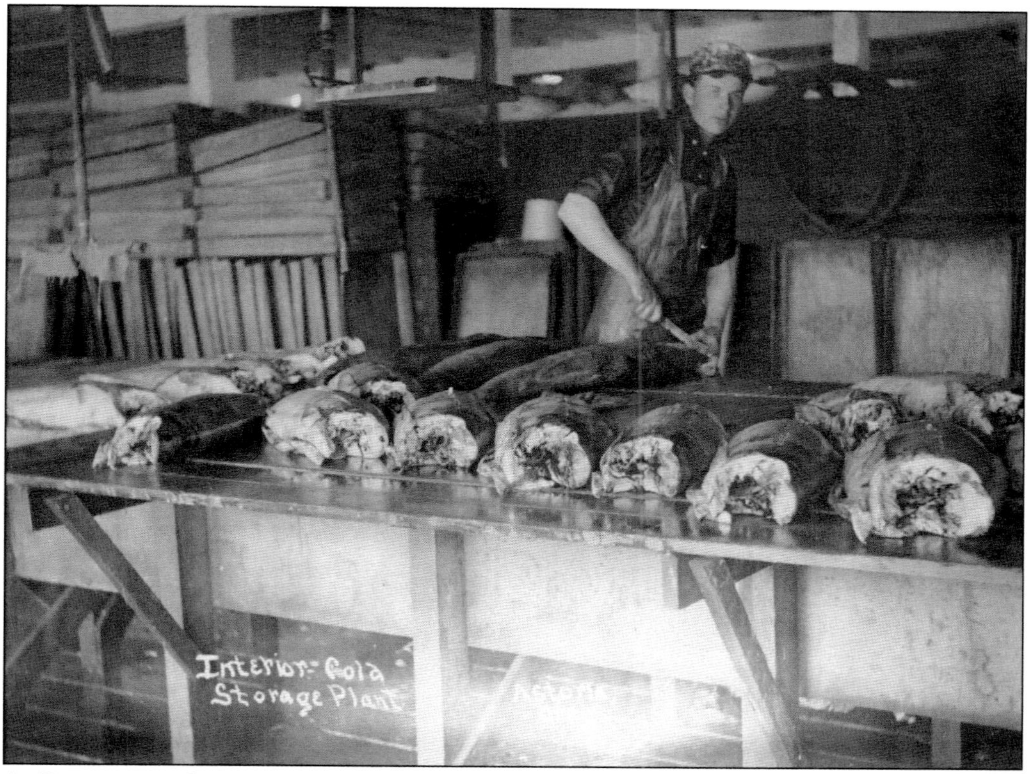

A. BOOTH AND COMPANY. August Booth opened his cannery in 1874. The photograph above shows the interior of the Cold Storage Plant in 1907. (CRMM No. 074-1634.)

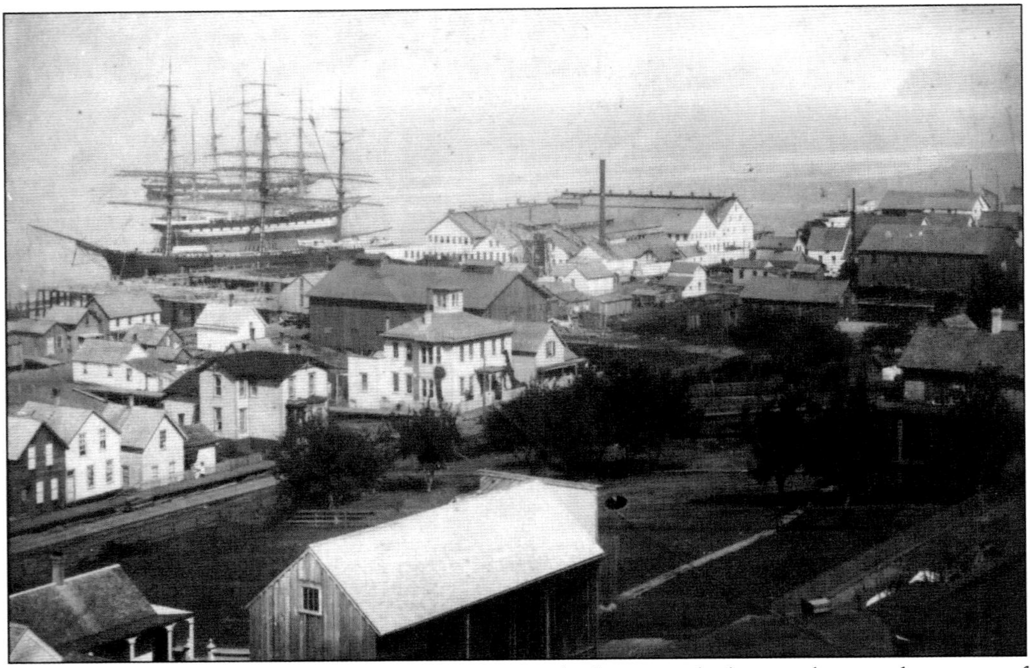

Tallant House and Kinney Cannery, c. 1886. The house with the cupola near the center of this photograph belonged to E.W. Tallant. He was a prominent business owner and operated the Tallant-Grant Packing Company in 1908. Beyond is the Kinney Cannery, which burned to its pilings in 1894 and was completely rebuilt. It later became part of the CRPA. (CRMM No. 072-1804.)

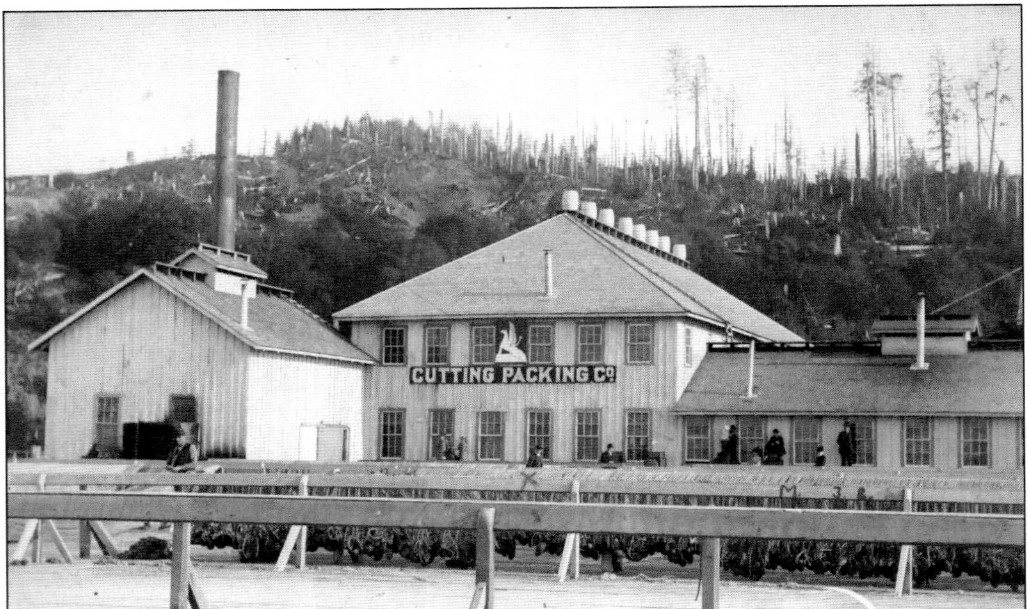

Cutting Packing Company. The Cutting Packing Company started operations in 1875 at the west end of Astoria. This area would come to be known as Uniontown, so named for Union Packing Company, which incorporated in 1881 just to the west. As more canneries were built in the area, Finns from Upper Astoria and elsewhere moved into the neighborhood. Eventually, Uniontown was also referred to as Finntown. (CRMM No. 030-17597.)

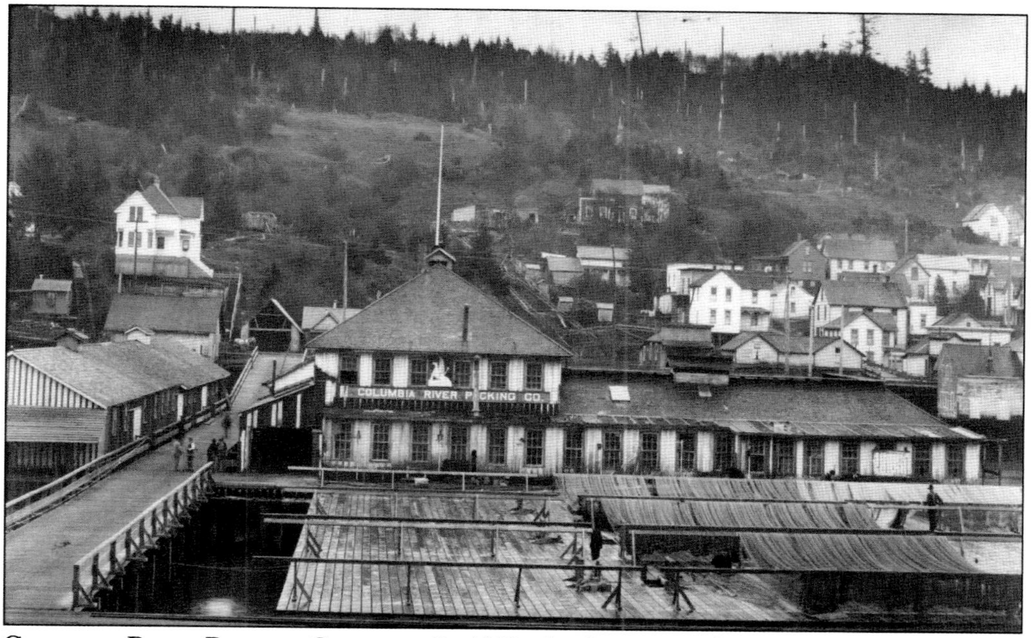

COLUMBIA RIVER PACKING COMPANY. By 1892, the Cutting Packing Company had become the Columbia River Packing Company. It still had the characteristic emblem of the previous owner. On the right half of the photograph, one can see a considerable amount of development as the forested hillside has been cleared. This dense housing was a neighborhood referred to as Uniontown. (CRMM No. 072-1740.)

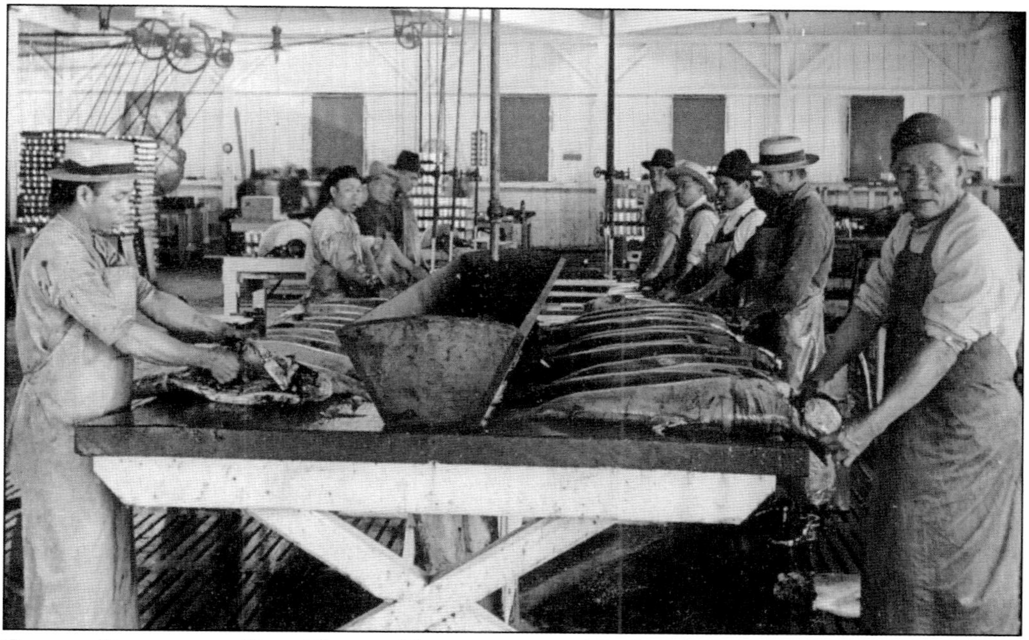

CHINESE BUTCHERING FISH. Chinese laborers were employed in the canneries as early as 1871 and quickly established a reputation as capable, reliable workers. By the 1880s, Astoria had over 2,000 Chinese people, most of them men, living and working in town. Many became butchers in the cannery, deftly wielding a knife to gut and clean up to 15 tons of fish a day. Later, this work was done by machine, and these highly skilled workers were displaced. (CRMM No. 074-1638.)

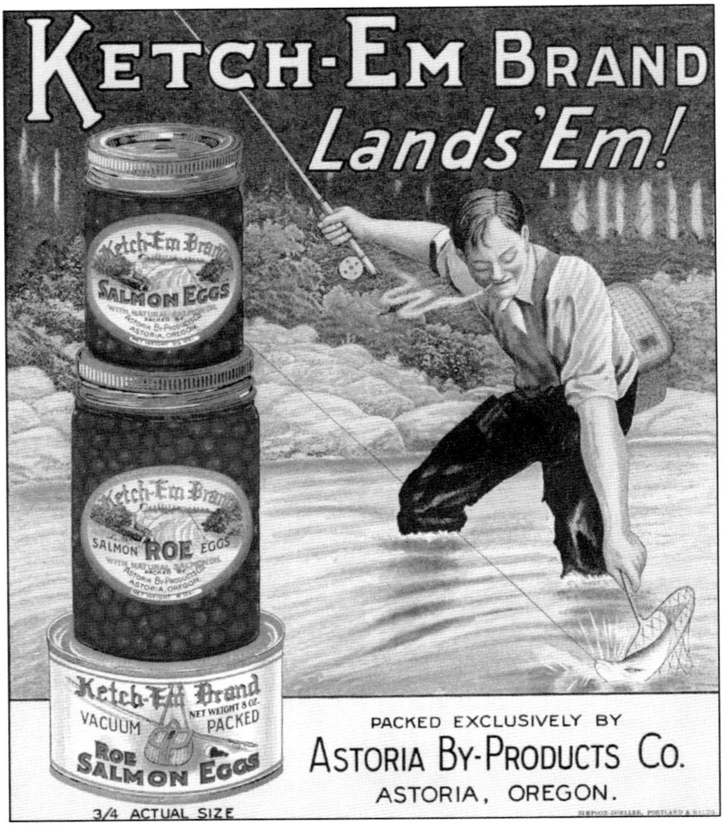

KETCH-EM ROE. Tallant-Grant Packing Company was established in 1908 just west of Elmore (Union) Cannery and took advantage of some of the byproducts of salmon canning by packaging the eggs that previously had been thrown out. This was the box label designed to market this reputedly effective fish bait. (CRMM collection.)

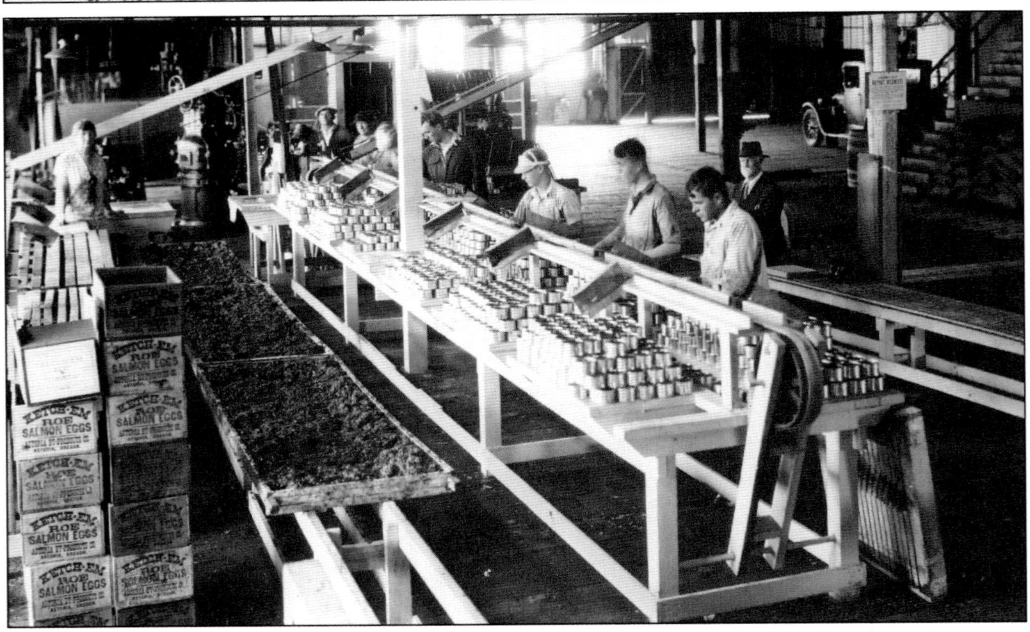

TALLANT-GRANT PACKING COMPANY. An interior view of the Tallant-Grant Packing Company shows the tables loaded with fish roe and cans ready to receive them. E.W. Tallant is wearing a dark hat and has a white beard. He is keeping a watchful eye on the process from the far right. (CRMM No. 074-1552.)

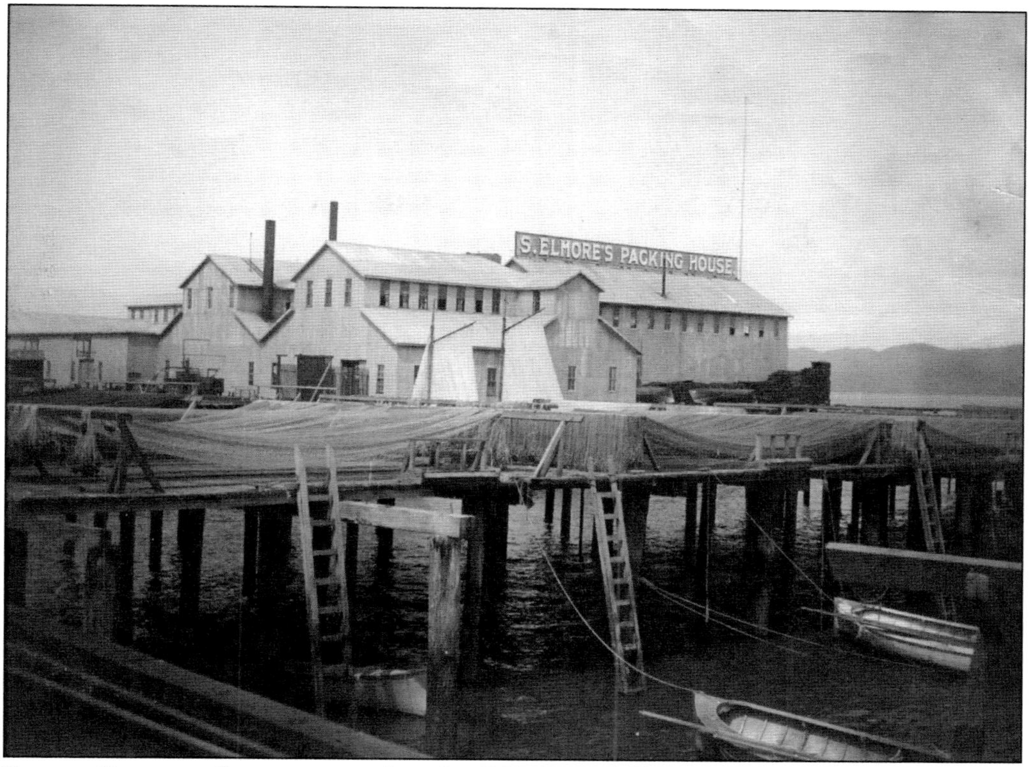

ELMORE CANNERY, STATE OF THE ART. In 1898, Samuel Elmore's Packing House had all the best equipment and the highest standards of sanitation. His operation had absorbed the earlier Union Packing site and, in 1899, became the main cannery for the newly formed "Combine," the Columbia River Packers Association, a group of cannery owners that consolidated operations to keep profits up despite declining salmon runs. (CRMM No. 072-5197.)

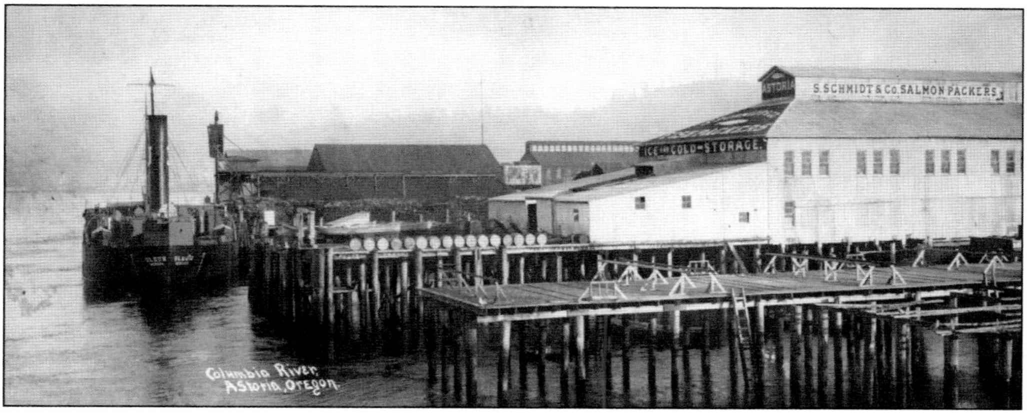

SCHMIDT AND COMPANY SALMON PACKERS. S. Schmidt Cold Storage appeared on the waterfront between the Astoria Electric Company Power Plant and Astoria Wharf and Warehouse in 1908. By 1948, it was bought out by Van Camp Sea Foods. By this time, many of the local canning operations had been purchased by national processing or distribution firms. (CRMM No. 072-1814.)

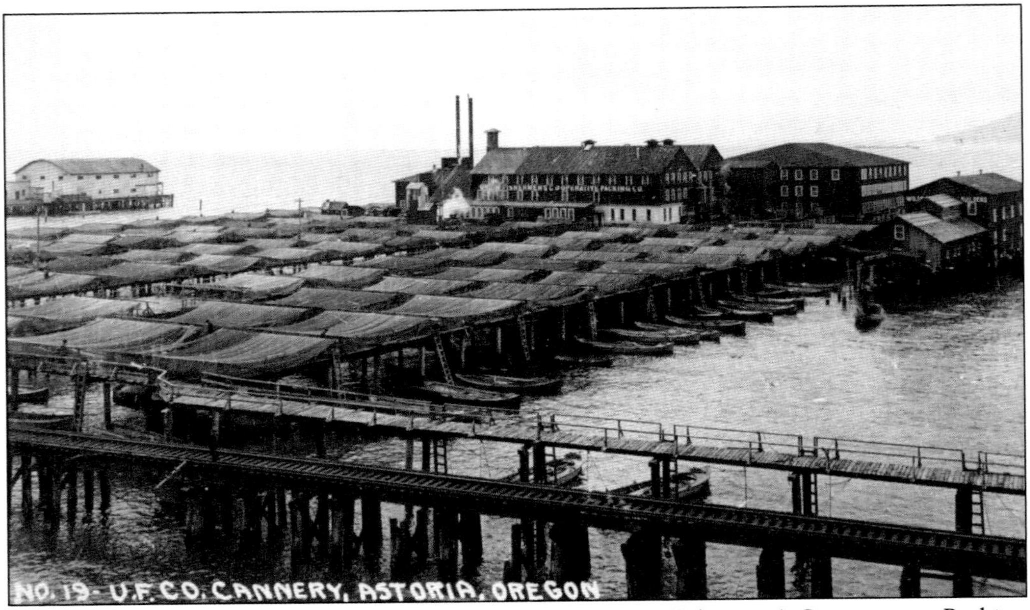

Union Fishermen's Cooperative Packing Company. Union Fishermen's Co-operative Packing Company, or Union Fish, was established by fishermen seeking a fair price for their catch at the cannery. In 1896, following the fishermen's strike, 200 mostly Finnish fishermen pooled their resources and created the cooperative. By 1904, it was the largest cannery in Astoria. Today, a luxury hotel resembling the cannery building is located on the company's old site. (Clemson collection No. 2011.1.)

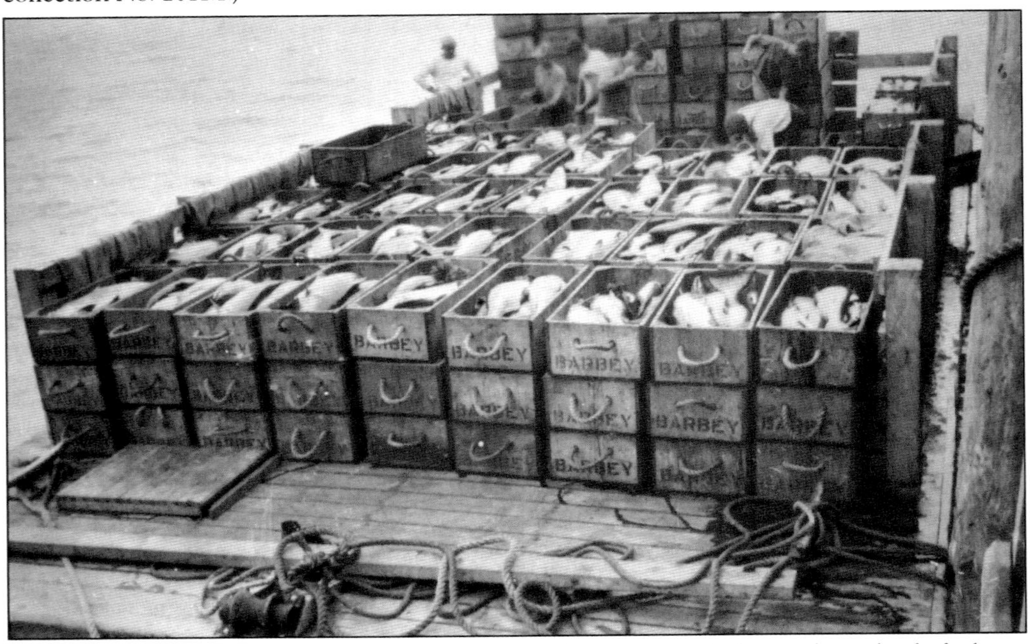

Barge of Salmon for Barbey Packing Company. This photograph shows a barge load of salmon being brought to the Barbey Packing Company at the Port of Astoria on August 22, 1950. The boxes of fish were likely loaded from receiving and transfer stations along the river. These stations were where gillnetters could unload their catch and then have them delivered to the cannery by the barge. (CRMM No. 072-1817.)

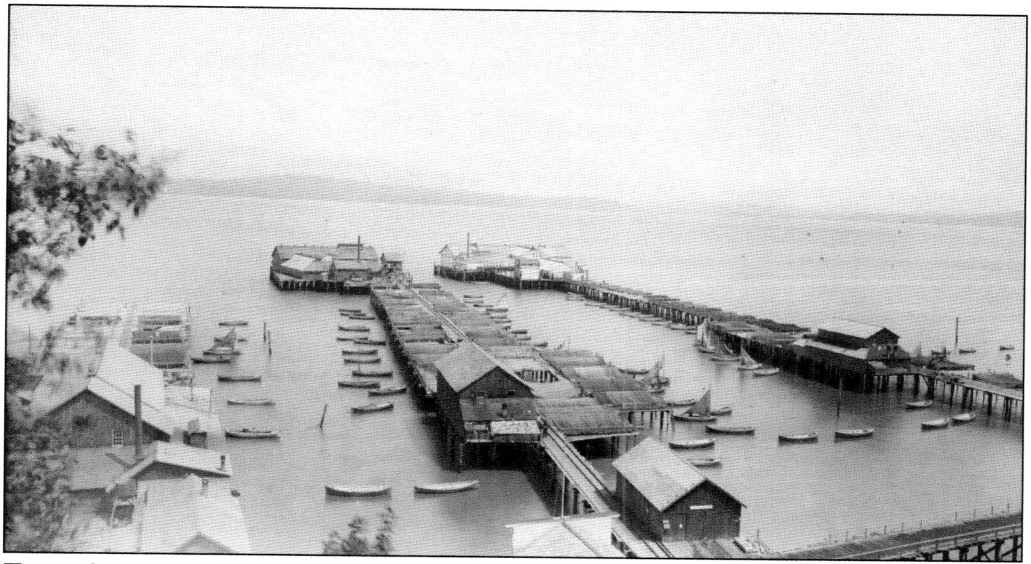

Three Canneries. This c. 1898 photograph shows, from left to right, the George and Barker Cannery, White Star Cannery, and J.O. Hanthorn Cannery. The fishing boats appear to all be sailing gill-netters. Gas-powered engines arrived in this year, and by 1906 half of the fishing boats were using them. Of the three cannery buildings pictured, only Hanthorn Cannery remains today. It now is part of Pier 39, a business and office complex with a museum devoted to the canneries and their workers. (CRMM No. 072-1767.)

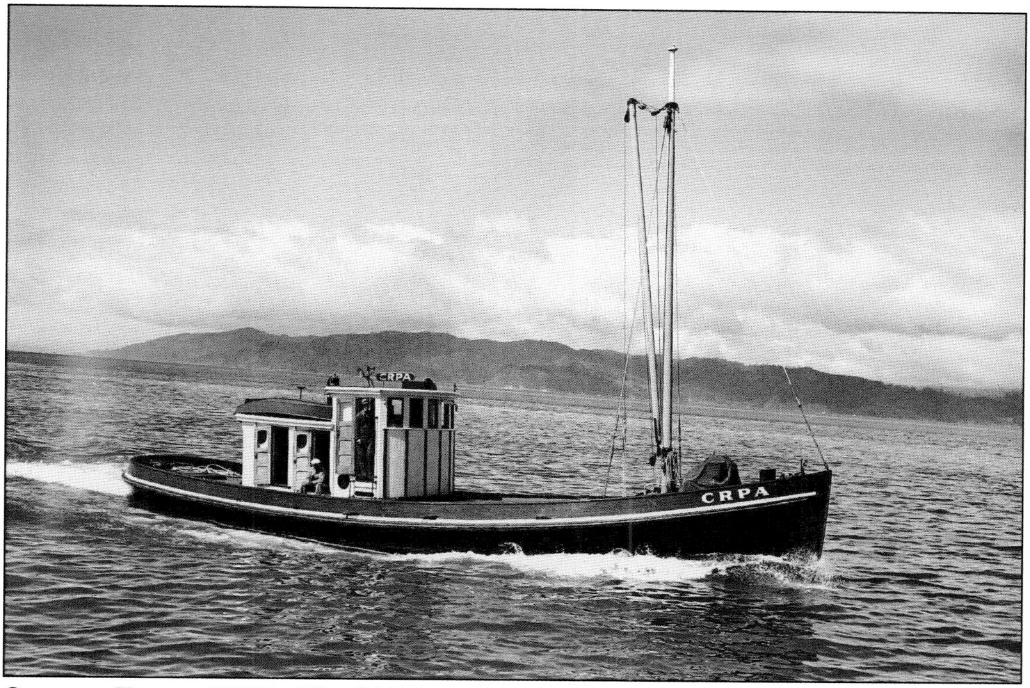

Cannery Tender CRPA. The *CRPA* was launched on September 6, 1945, by the Columbia River Packers Association and serviced the receiving stations up and down the river. This and other cannery tenders were a familiar sight on the river, and they were examples of excellent boatbuilding skills. The boat ended her days in Alaskan waters and was eventually chopped up and burned in 2004. (CRPA collection No. 0359a.)

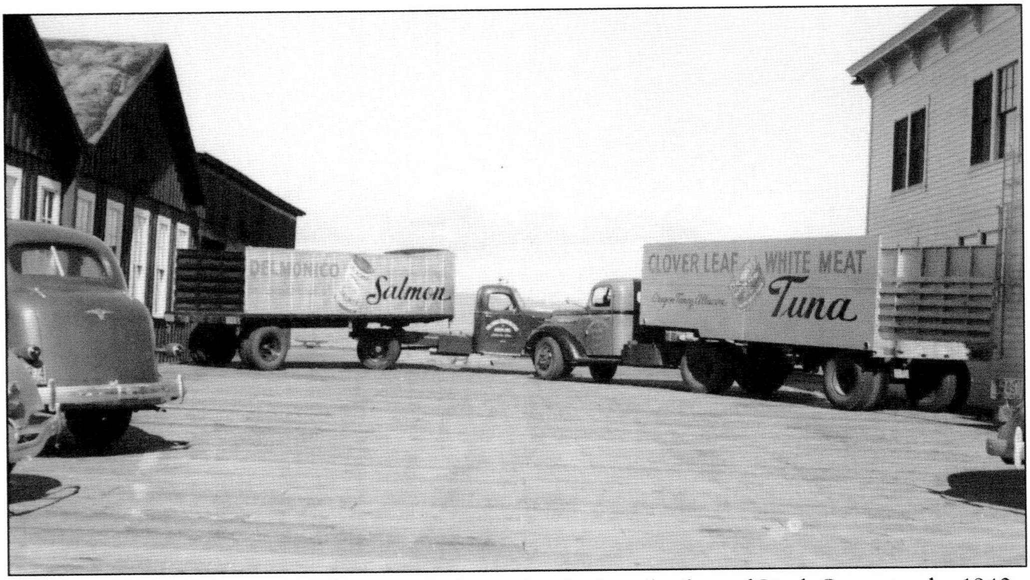

Foot of Sixth Street. This photograph shows the dock at the foot of Sixth Street in the 1940s. On the left is warehousing for CRPA (remnants of the former Kinney cannery), and on the right is the building that served as the corporate office for CRPA. The office later became Bumble Bee Seafoods, Inc. At the time this photograph was taken, tuna had been discovered off the Oregon coast. Catches of tuna were quickly exceeding those of salmon. This dock and these buildings were gutted by fire on December 16, 2010. (CRMM No. 072-1792.)

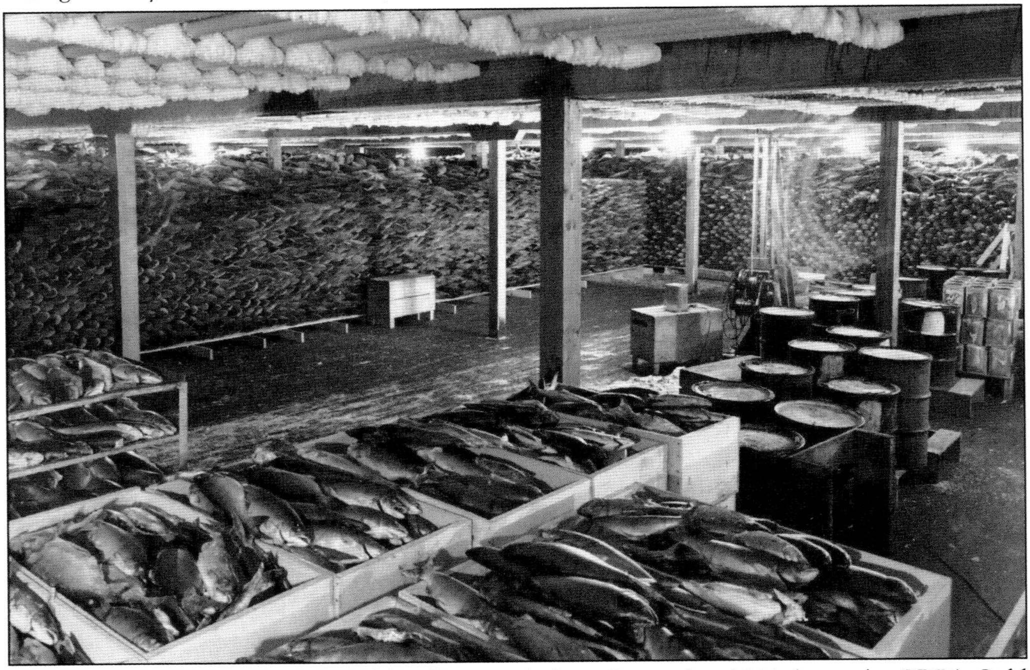

Cold Storage. This Ned Thorndike photograph from September 1944 shows the CRPA Cold Storage Plant with 1,500 tons of frozen fish. Tuna is in the background and troll salmon are in the foreground. Tuna had the advantage over salmon because it held up to freezing better and maintainined its quality. Because of this, tuna could be packed year-round, providing steady work for the canneries. (CRMM 074-13859.)

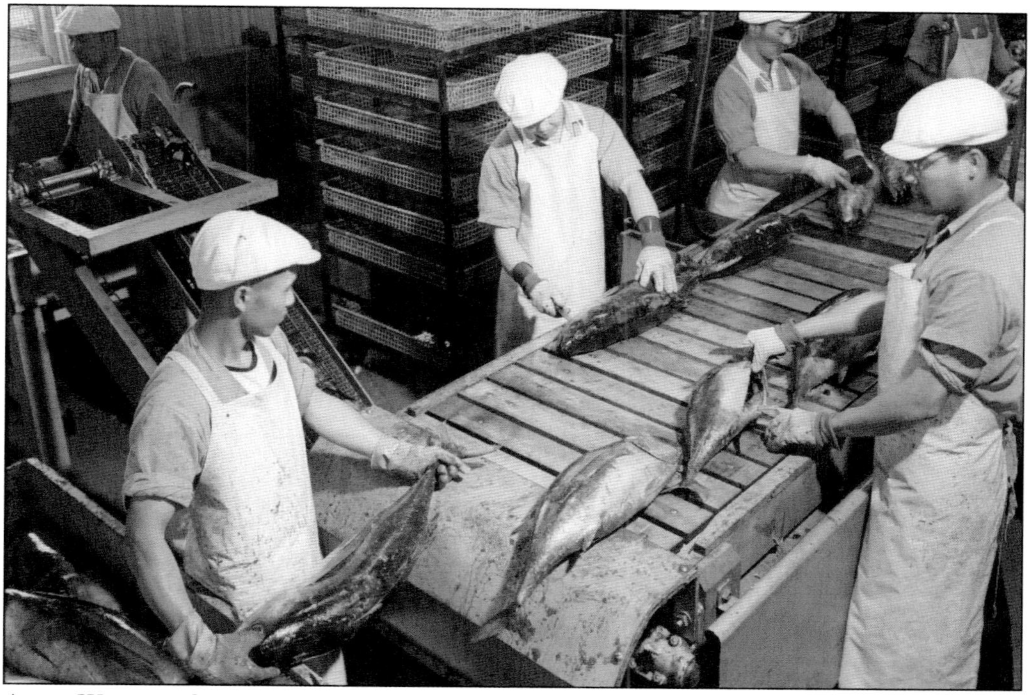

ASIAN WORKERS GUTTING TUNA. This photograph shows long-fin tuna being gutted and cleaned by a group of Asian workers at the tuna plant of Bumble Bee Seafoods. (CRMM No. 074-1623.)

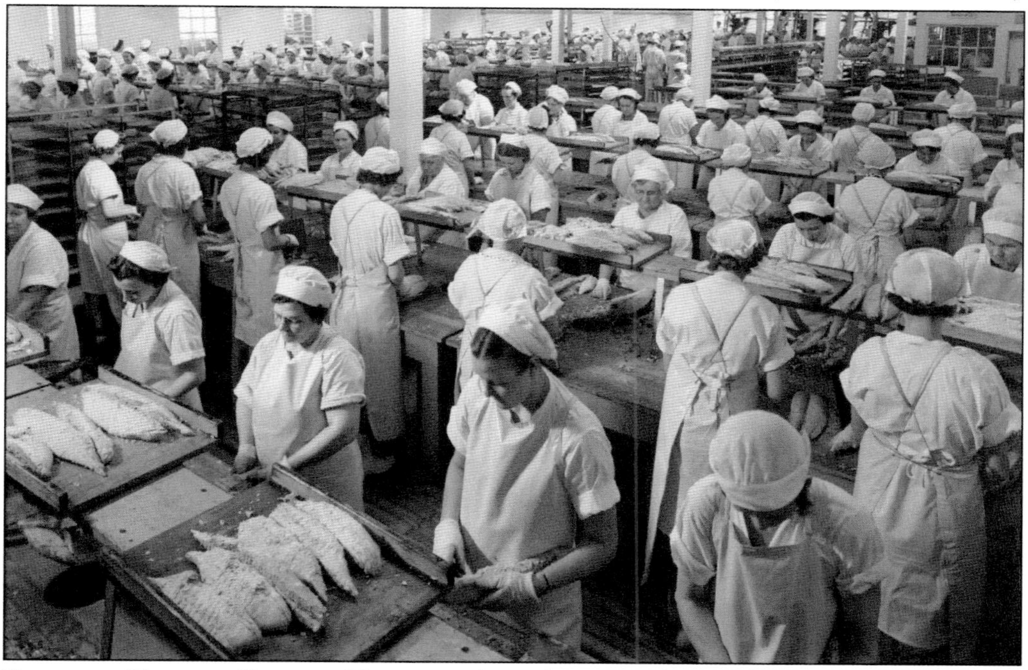

PREPARING TUNA FOR PACKING. This image shows the tremendous workforce required to operate a cannery. These women are packing tuna at the Elmore Plant for the Columbia River Packers Association. The clothing they are wearing was provided and laundered by the cannery laundry service. The ability to spend hours standing in noisy, odorous conditions was required to work these lines. (CRMM No. 074-13858.)

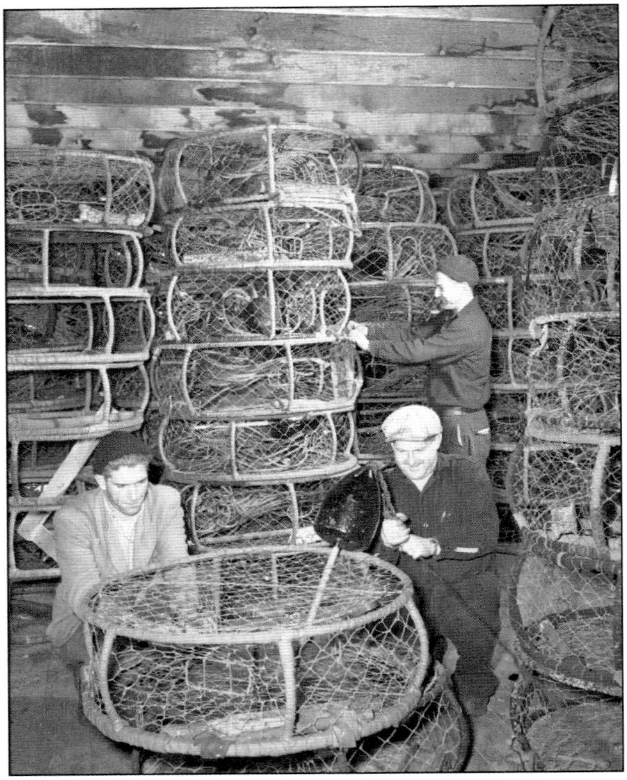

Workers Readying Crab Pots. In addition to tuna and salmon, CRPA also packaged crab meat and other seafood. This photograph shows a crew readying the crab pots for the next season of crabbing. (CRPA collection No. 521b.)

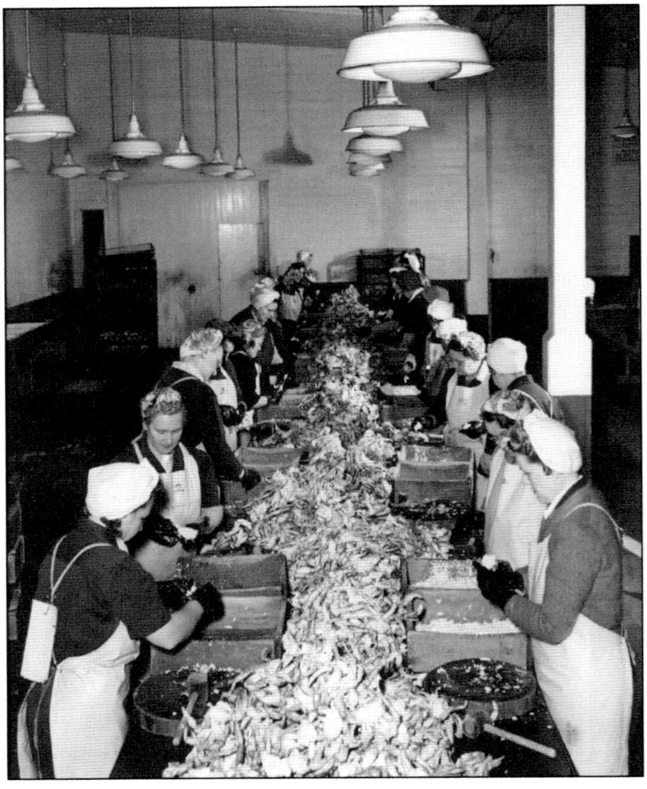

Crab Picker Line. These women are cracking the crabs and picking the meat out by hand, separating the shell and the cartilage from the meat, which was a labor-intensive process. In the foreground at the left and right, one can see the mallets used to crack the crab shell. Hanging on the backs of the workers' aprons are their timecards. Supervisors walked down the line and checked the shifts and time of their workers without disrupting them. It also kept the cards from getting soiled or lost. (CRMM No. 074-19554.)

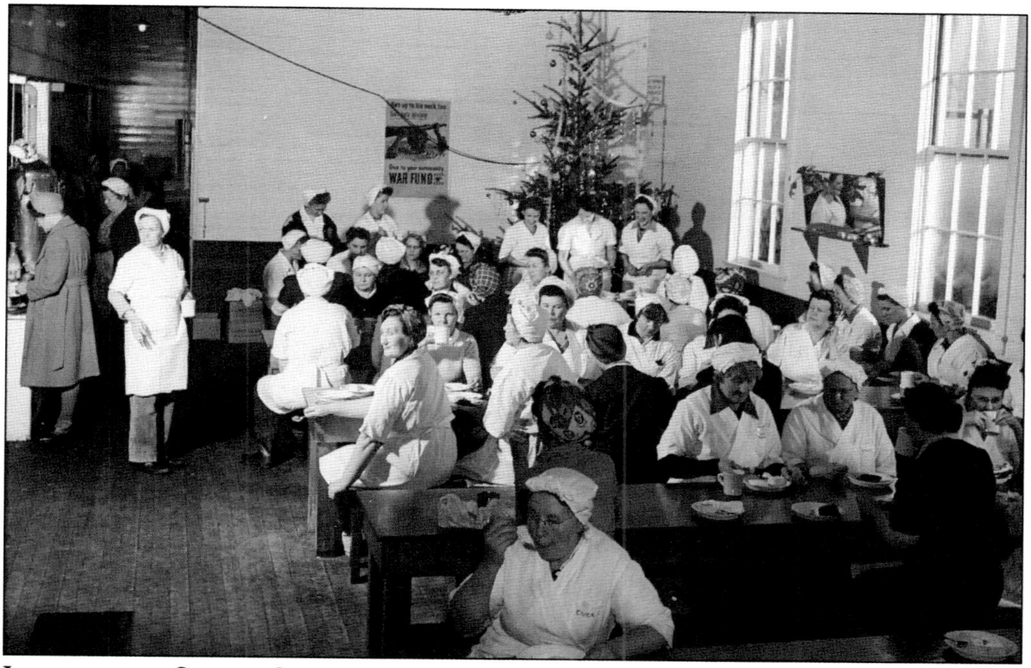

Ice cream and Cake at Christmas, 1944. During a break in their shift, workers at CRPA were treated to cake and ice cream during the Christmas season on December 20, 1944. The war-fund poster on the back wall is evidence of the home-front attitudes of workers during the war. (CRPA collection No. 0084b.)

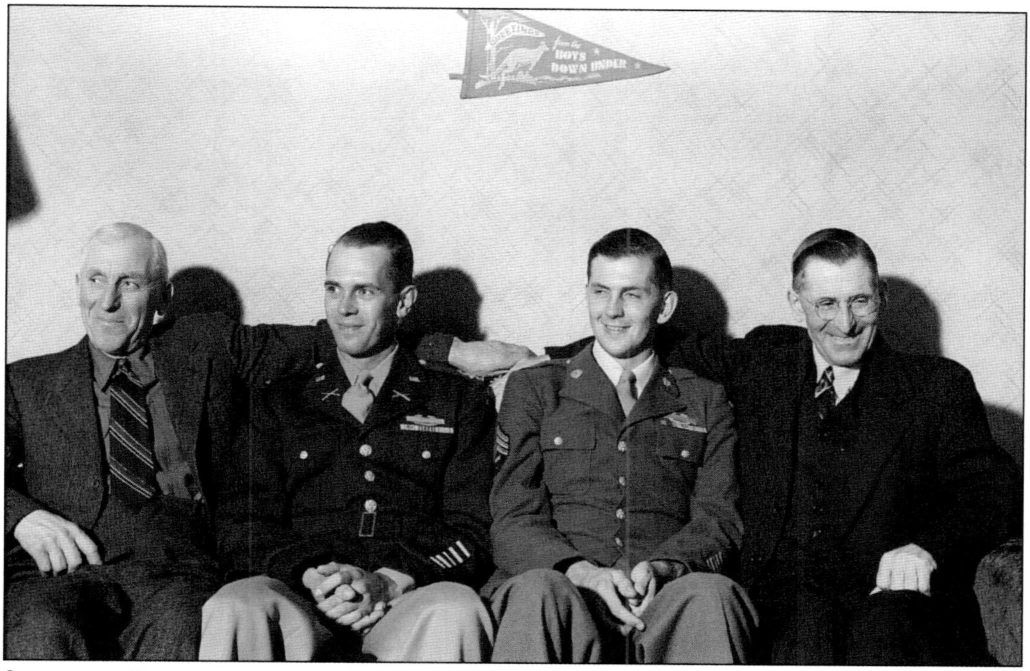

Soderberg Sons in uniform. This Ned Thorndike photograph was taken on January 19, 1945. The two younger Soderbergs in the middle were on leave from the war in the Pacific. Pictured from left to right are Fred Soderberg, Lt. Richard C. Soderberg, Sgt. Walter Soderberg, and Charles Soderberg. (CRPA collection No. 120a.)

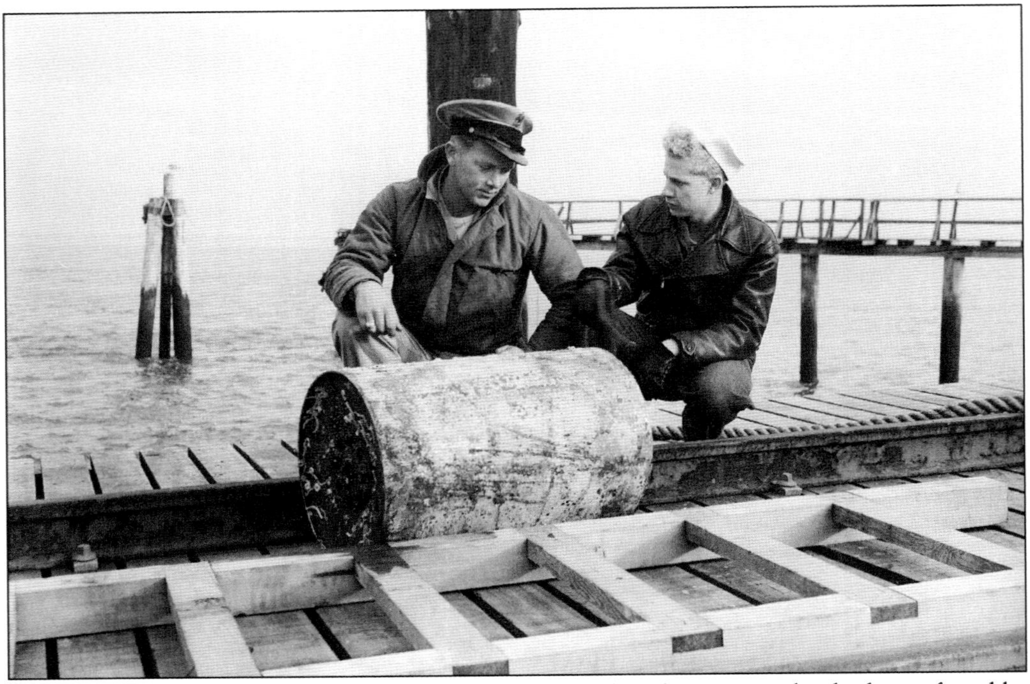

Reminders of War. Chief Bosun's Mate Jensen and Ashcraft inspect a depth charge found by a fishing boat in 1947. Mines, depth charges, and other war paraphernalia were discovered by trawlers for many years after the war. (CRPA collection No. 1168b.)

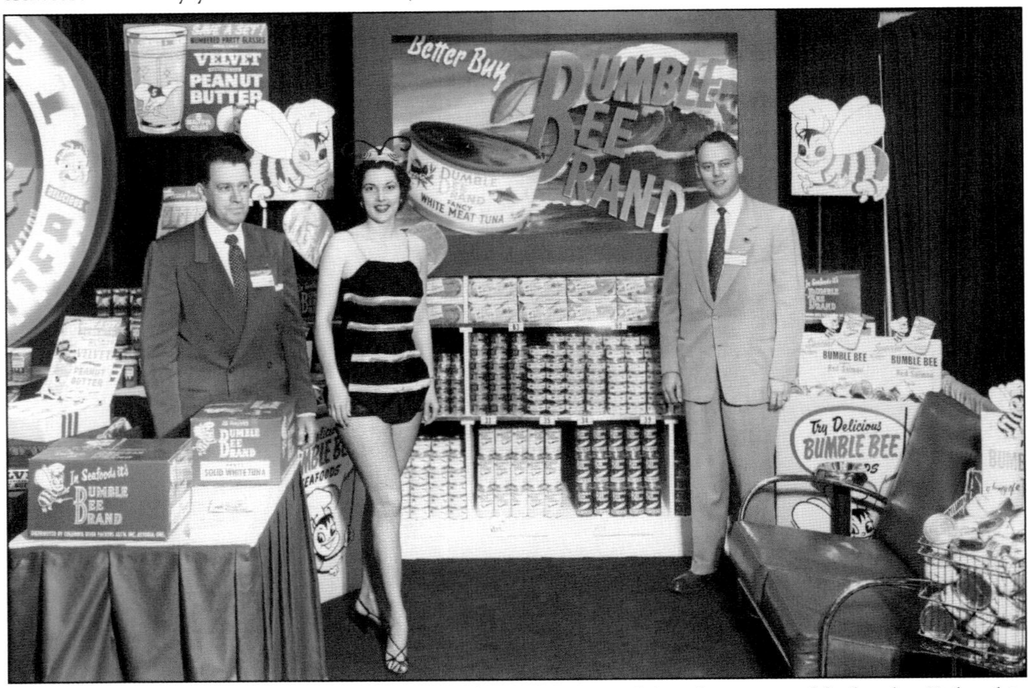

Bumble Bee Brand. The Bumble Bee Brand was so successful and recognizable for the Columbia River Packers Association that, when Castle and Cooke in Hawaii bought out the company, they renamed it Bumble Bee Seafoods, Inc., preserving the brand recognition and consumer loyalty. This photograph is of the Super Market Institute Exhibition in the 1950s. (CRMM No. 076-1714.)

Nine

FEDERAL AFFAIRS

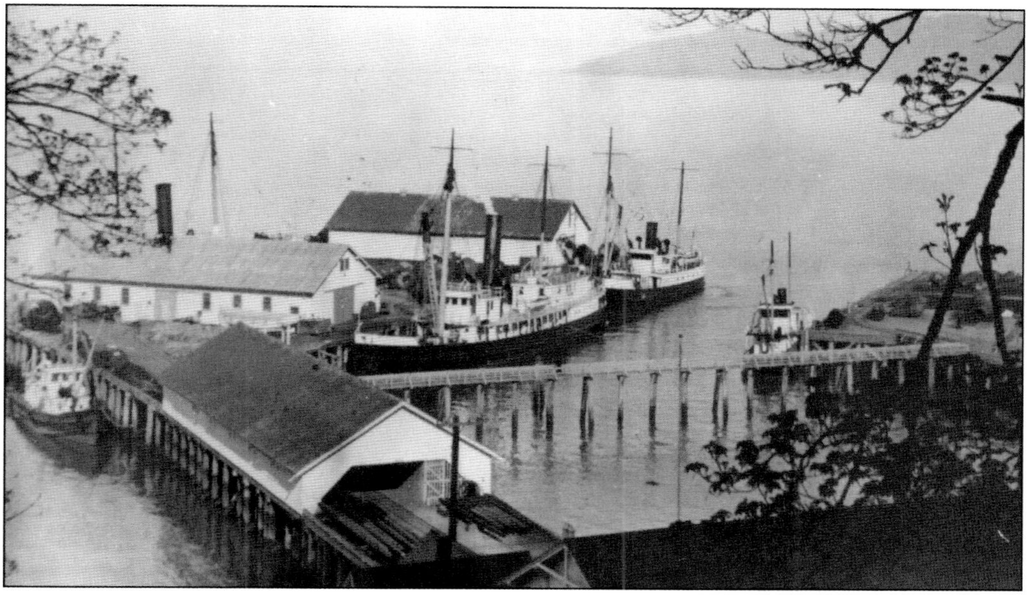

BUOY DEPOT AT TONGUE POINT. The US Lighthouse tenders used Tongue Point Buoy Depot as a supply station and repair facility. This c. 1937 photograph shows, from left to right, the *Larch*, *Manzanita*, *Heather*, *Rose*, and *Rhododendron*. The masts of the *Manzanita* can just be seen behind the building on the left. (CRMM No. 010-7.)

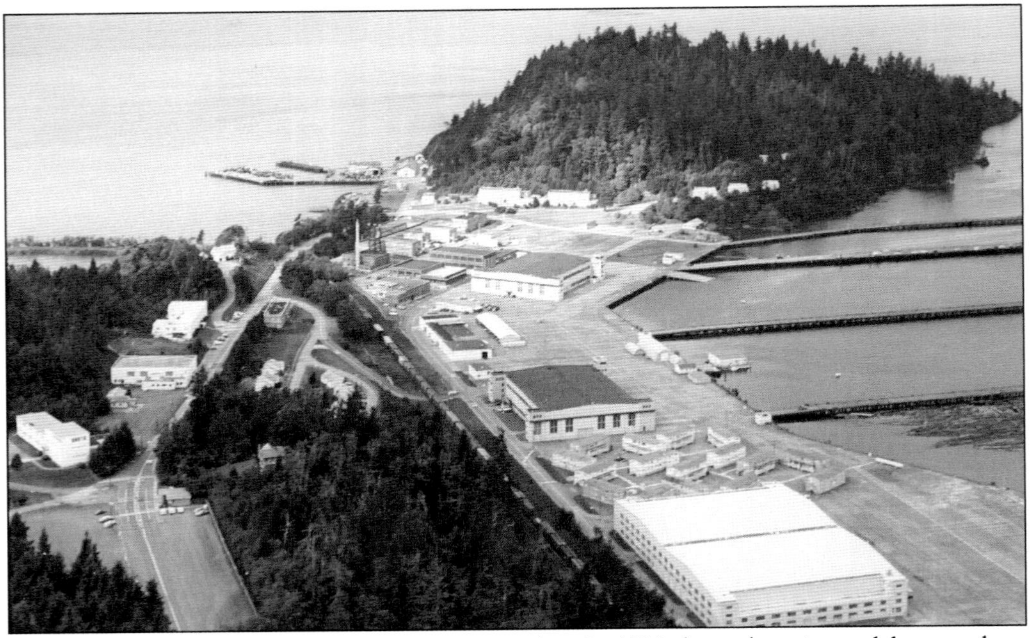

Tongue Point Naval Station, Astoria. Surveyed in the 1920s for a submarine and destroyer base that never materialized, Tongue Point became a Naval Air Station when the United States entered World War II. Flying Boats (PBYs) were used to patrol the river and coast for enemy forces. When one of the planes struck a submerged log during landing and killed members of the crew, the practice was abandoned and patrols were taken up by airships out of Tillamook. (CRMM No. 037-846.)

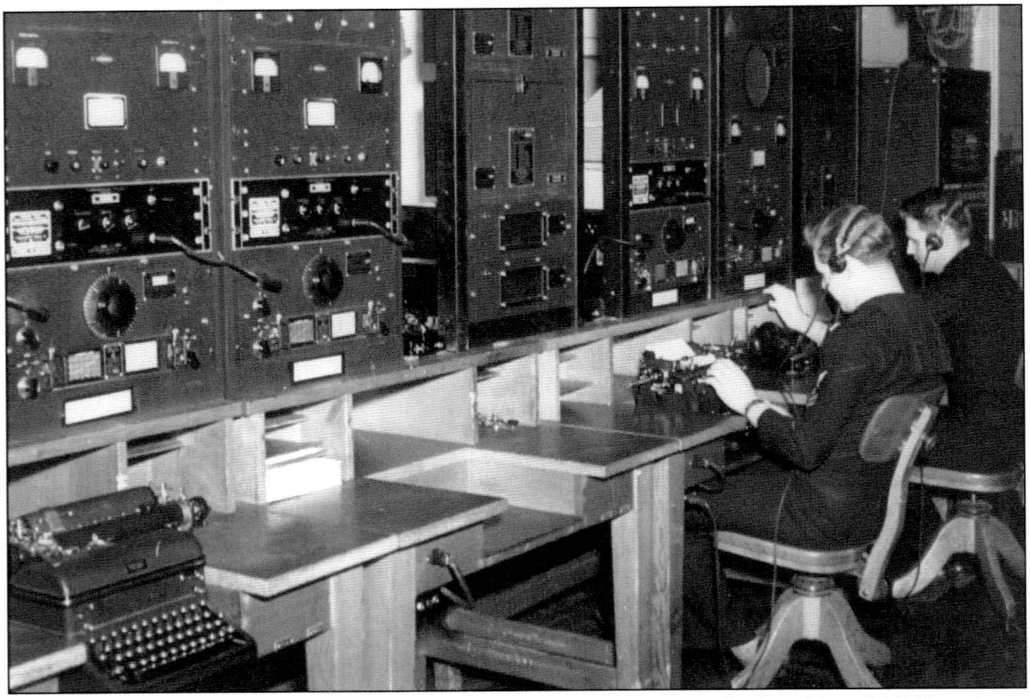

Communications Center. Pictured here are Francis "Cliff" Crawford (left) and Wilbur Gates (right). Both were radiomen second-class and were working in the communications center at the Tongue Point Naval Air Station, Astoria, on February 28, 1945. (CRMM No. 037-849.)

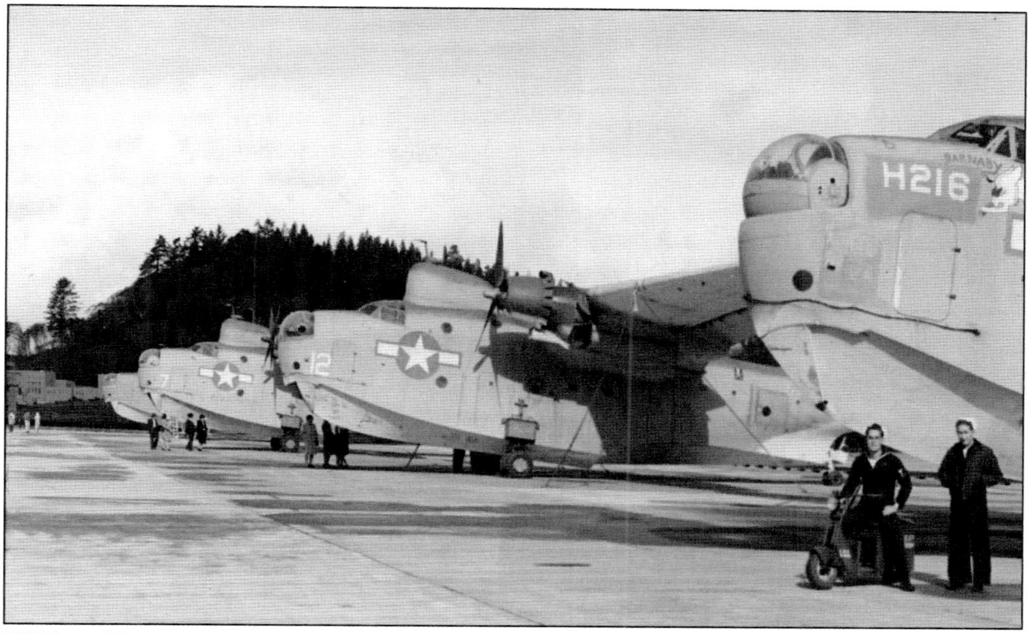

PBMs at Tongue Point. On Navy Day, October 27, 1945, people are viewing the Martin Mariner (PBM) aircraft at Tongue Point Naval Air Station. Over 1,000 of these Martin Mariner patrol bombers were supplied to the Navy and became the mainstay of their patrol aircraft during and after World War II. (CRMM No. 037-934.)

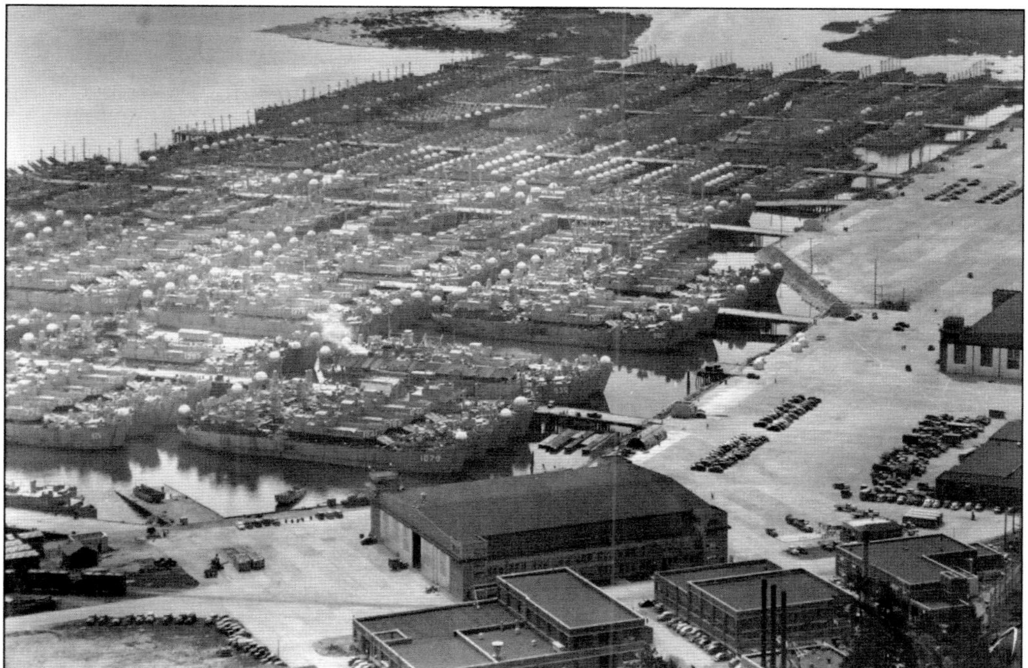

Ready Reserve Fleet. After World War II, Tongue Point became the home of the Pacific Reserve Fleet, mothballing landing craft of all types as shown in this photograph. Many were eventually towed upriver to Portland and scrapped. (CRMM No. 037-842.)

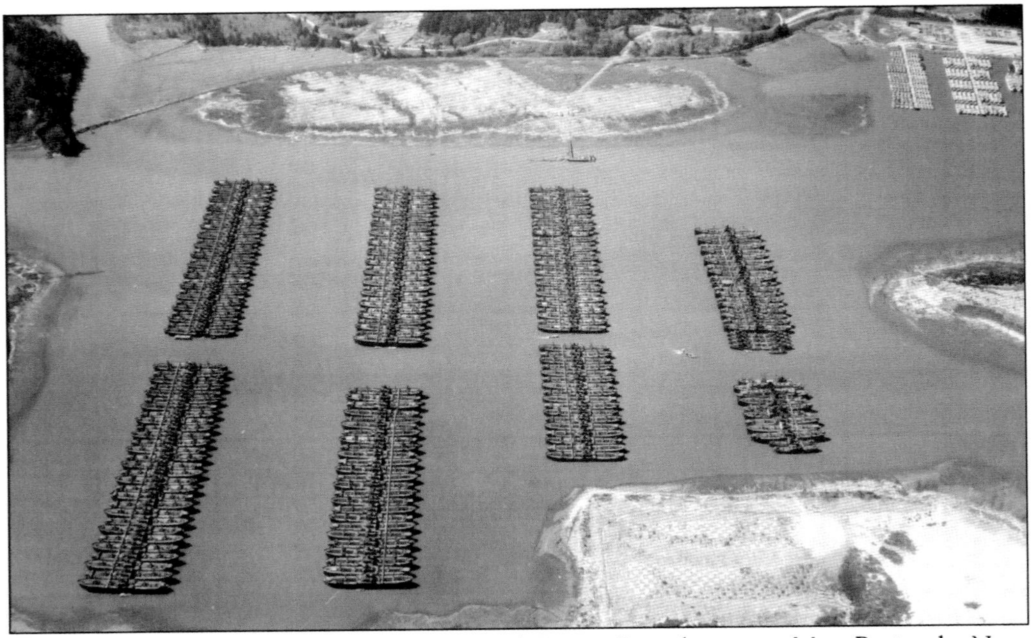

Mothballed Liberty Ships. In an area east of Tongue Point known as Mott Basin, the Navy mothballed an additional fleet of cargo and transport ships, with as many as 500 lying at anchor. These were sold off to other countries or hauled away and scrapped. During the Korean War, some were put back into service. By the mid-1960s, the Navy had abandoned Tongue Point and the facility became a Job-Corps Training Center, as it is today. (CRMM No. 037-844.)

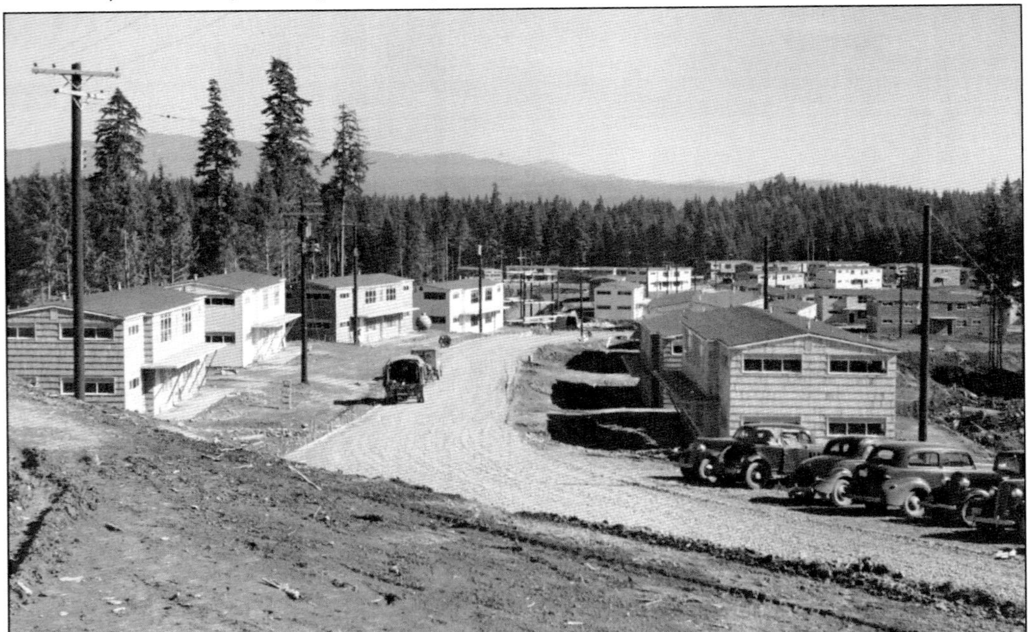

Military Housing Extended at Tongue Point. Additional housing was required after the war, and areas to the south of Tongue Point were developed to fulfill that need. The units shown here were built in 1947 and today are rental apartments in an area known as Emerald Heights, just east of Astoria. (CRMM 037-969.)

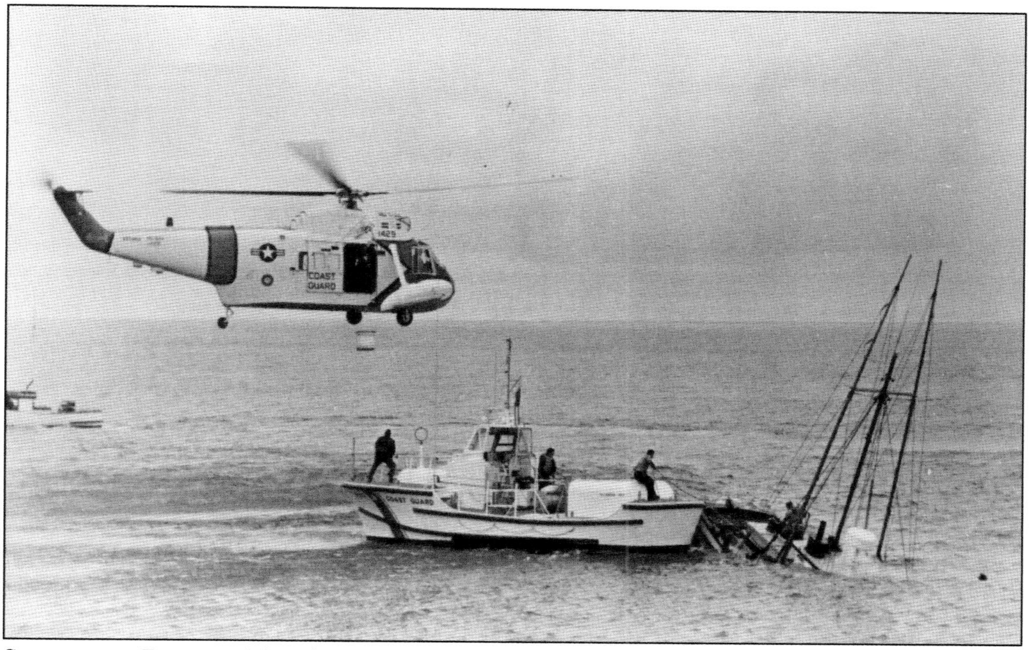

Search and Rescue. After the Navy left Tongue Point, the Coast Guard established Air Station Tongue Point and was supplied with Sikorsky HH-52a helicopters to aid in search-and-rescue missions in the Columbia River and offshore. Here, one is lowering a pump to a waiting 44-foot Coast Guard motor lifeboat assisting a foundering troller. The photograph was taken off the mouth of the Columbia River in the 1960s. (CRMM No. 250-3829.)

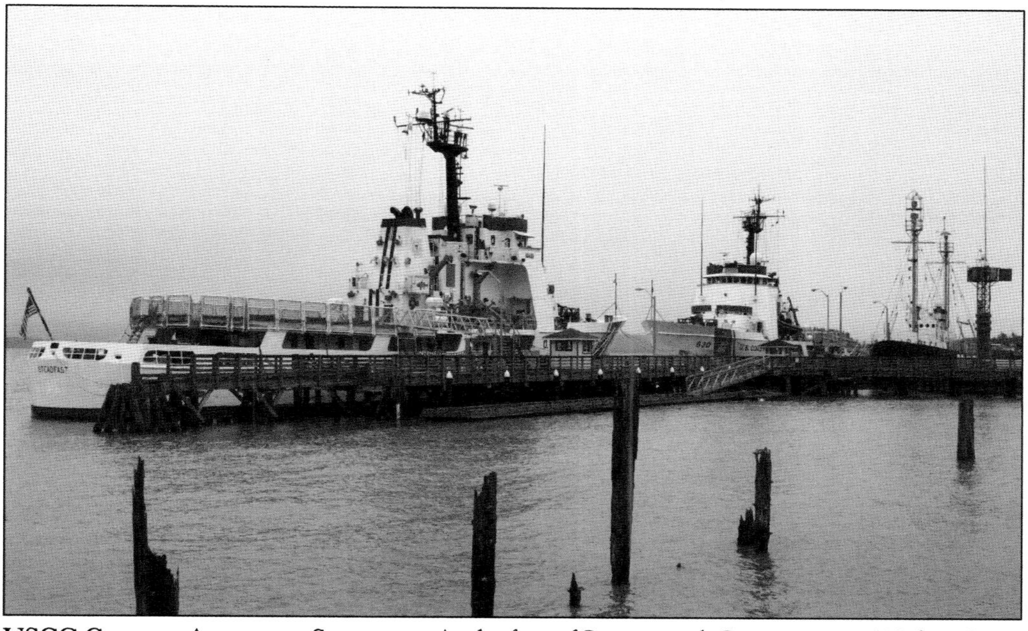

USCG Cutters *Alert* and *Steadfast*. At the foot of Seventeenth Street are two 210-foot Coast Guard Medium Endurance Cutters called the *Steadfast* and the *Alert*. Together with the crews of the buoy tender *Fir* at Tongue Point and the personnel at Sector Columbia River at the airport, the Coast Guard is the largest employer in the area. It performs over 400 search-and-rescue missions per year in addition to its enforcement and security missions. (Author's collection.)

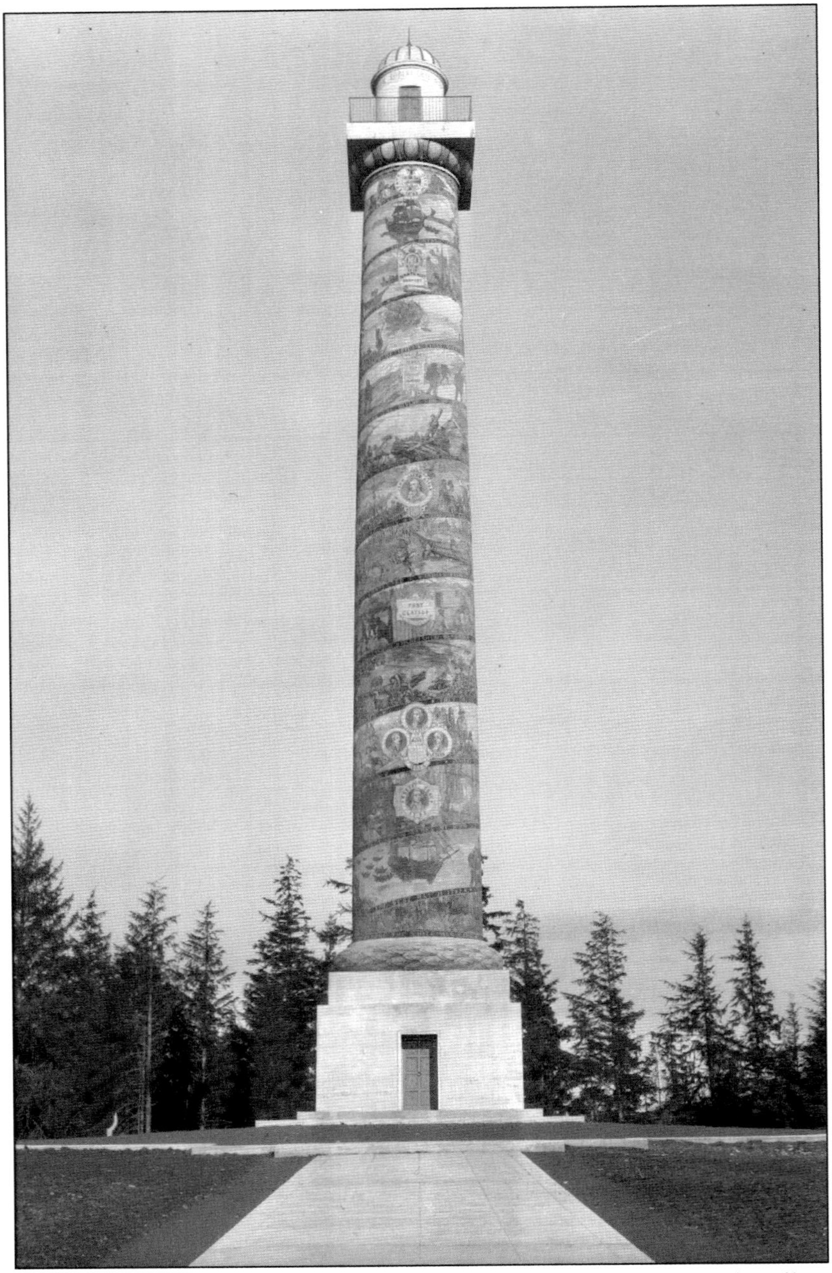

Astoria Column, 1926. This 125-foot monument stands on top of Coxcomb Hill in Astoria. The column was the idea of Ralph Budd, then president of the Great Northern Railroad. He had planned to have 12 such monuments along the route to mark significant events in history. The site in Astoria was chosen to recognize the contribution of explorers and early settlers in the United States expansion to the Pacific. The column was modeled after Trajan's column in Rome. Italian artist Attilo Pusterla was commissioned to etch the images in plaster onto the surface of the concrete column. Spiraling up the length of the column, the illustrations tell the story of first contact, discovery, exploration, settlement, and the arrival of the railroad. Climbing inside up the 164 steps, one has a commanding view of the surrounding area and can appreciate the panorama of history below. (Woodfield collection.)

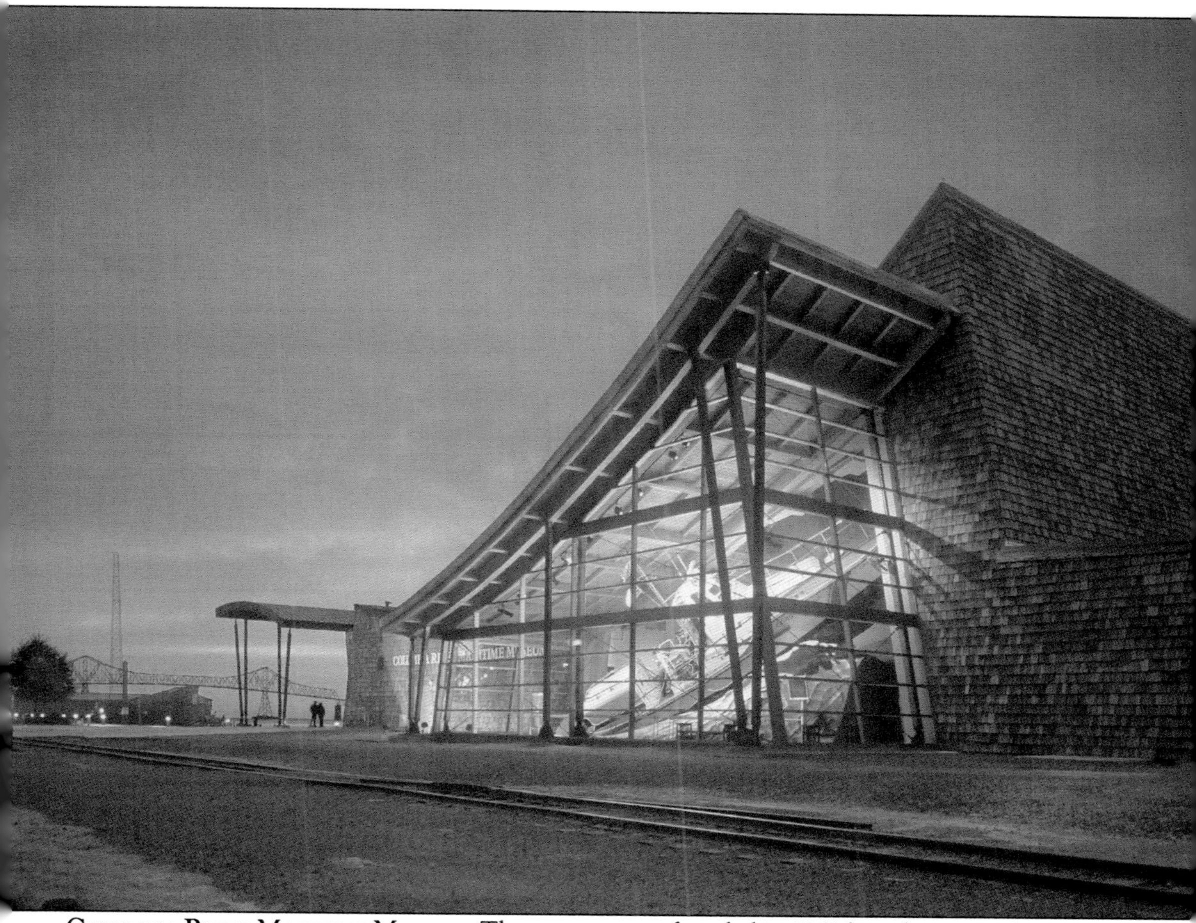

Columbia River Maritime Museum. The museum was founded in 1962 by a determined group of Astorians led by Rolf Klep, who believed this community deserved a world-class maritime museum. Rolf had a career in the US Navy during World War II and had been a successful graphic artist on the East Coast before returning to his native Astoria to retire. His dream of creating a museum to recognize the incredibly rich maritime history of the region occupied the last 20 years of his life. Even as objects were moved into the old city hall building and exhibits were being created, Rolf was busy making plans for a newer, bigger facility. The new building opened in 1982 and was remodeled and expanded in 2002. The museum has indeed grown to be considered "world-class." Rolf would have been proud. We continue to collect and preserve historical and cultural maritime material relevant to the Columbia River and present it for the enrichment and enjoyment of our members and visitors. Join us! For more information visit www.crmm.org. (Photograph by Michael Mathers.)

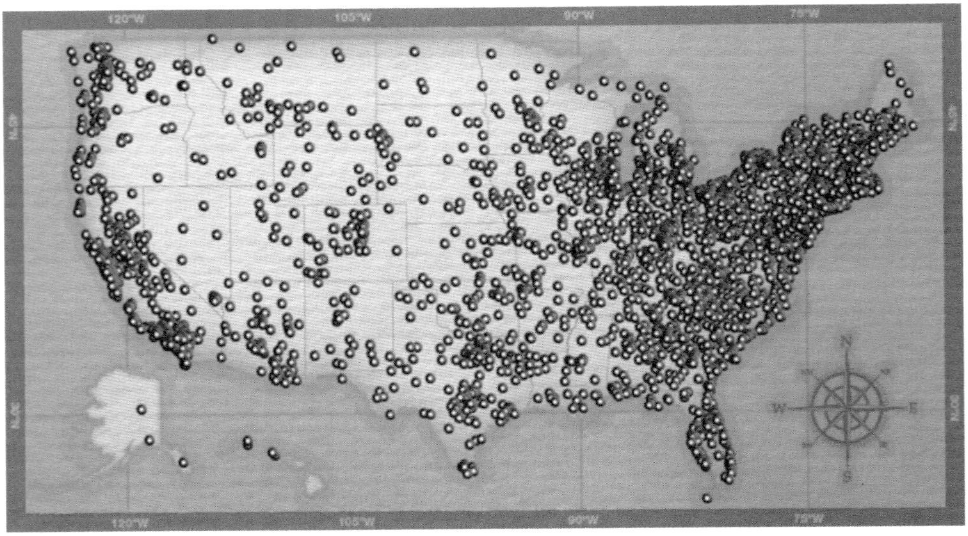

Consistent with our mission to preserve history on a local level, this book was printed in South Carolina on American-made paper and manufactured entirely in the United States. Products carrying the accredited Forest Stewardship Council (FSC) label are printed on 100 percent FSC-certified paper.

MADE IN THE USA